From Out of the Blue

From Out of the Blue

Frank Broad
Tony Gladwin
Bob Marvin

2000

First published in 1996 by Management Books 2000 Ltd
Cowcombe House,
Cowcombe Hill,
Chalford,
Gloucestershire GL6 8HP
(Tel. 01285-760722 Fax.01285-760708)

Printed and bound in Great Britain by The Orbital Press, Letchworth

British Library Cataloguing in Publication Data is available

ISBN 1-85252-207-0 (paperback)

Acknowledgements

First of all, we would especially like to thank all those people who have helped us in compiling this book. In particular Patrick, Paul and Brian for their time devoted to proof-reading and offering many constructive comments and suggestions.

Secondly, we acknowledge the following sources of material:

Richard Thomas De Lemarter, *Big Blue, IBM's Use and Abuse of Power* (Macmillan)
Robert Heller, *The Fate of IBM,* (Little, Brown)
Thomas J Watson, *My Life at IBM and Beyond*, (Bantam)
Buck Rodgers, *The IBM Way...*, (Harper & Row)
Jacques Maisonrouge, *Manager International, Inside IBM*, (Collins)
David Mercer, *IBM: How the World's Most Successful Corporation is Managed* (Kogan Page)
James Chposky, *Blue Magic*, (Collins)

Thirdly, registered names and trademarks. This work is not a technical one. However, it does make reference to certain companies and their products. Annotations of registrations and trademarks are listed on page 255, rather than throughout the book.

And finally, but not least...IBM was an enjoyable company to work for, populated by a wide spectrum of people, both male and female, from many different backgrounds.

Until there is a natural noun implying either sex, you will excuse our use of traditional words such as "salesman", when what is meant is either "salesman" or "saleswoman". Likewise, where we often use a general "he", we usually mean "she" as well. We trust readers will accept this for the sake of readability.

RM AJG FMB

Contents

Contents

Disclaimer

Anybody familiar with IBM's ways of working – customers and employees, past and present – will expect to see some version of a "Disclaimer". You could not work for IBM for as many years as the authors of this work without some of its philosophies being absorbed into the blood.

We cannot repeat the exact words of the IBM Disclaimer which preceded all IBM written proposals; these were standard clauses specifically crafted for such proposals relating to IBM's products and services. So we have constructed some phrases of our own:

"The material, views, comments and observations contained within this book are based upon the collective recollections of the authors. While we believe those recollections to be sound, the degree of accuracy may have been affected by many factors, not all of which are under our control. Therefore any expectation as to benefits to be obtained from reading this book cannot be supported by the authors."

Preface

"There are no problems in the computer industry that would not be solved by the disappearance of IBM." So said the Chief Executive of ICL in the early 1970's.

To some people, IBM appeared to be almost the devil incarnate, the unacceptable face of predatory US capitalism. To others, IBM represented the ultimate business ideal, well-managed, well-motivated, forceful yet forbearing – and highly profitable.

The company began in 1911 as the Computing-Tabulating-Recording Company through a merger of three smaller companies. After absorbing the International Business Machines Corporation in 1924, it adopted that company's name. Thomas Watson came to build IBM into the USA's largest manufacturer of time clocks, and then marketed the first electric typewriter. In 1951 the company entered the computer field, largely funded by contracts with the US government's Atomic Energy Commission. It entered the commercial marketplace soon afterwards.

From the 1960's, IBM's growth was rapid and relentless, with no slackening of its grip on profitability. Projections of future annual revenues seemed rival the theatre of the absurd: $100 billion – $200 billion; would it ever stop? Why should it ever stop? IBM would soon become the world's largest company, with revenues exceeding the GNP of all but a handful of countries.

But stop it did, and by the end of the 1980's corrective actions, unthinkable but a few years before, concerning organisation, structure, marketplace engagement and even IBM's business goals were being taken. Who would have thought that IBM's shareholders, Watson's shareholders, would oust the Chairman, and bring in someone from outside?

The 30 year period of 1960-1990 saw massive changes in what has become known as the information technology industry. Where the IBM corporation once enjoyed 60 per cent of the world computing business in the 60's, this eroded to less than 20 per cent by the 90's. It grew rapidly to a $60 billion+ revenue company operating in over 100 countries, and stayed pretty much at that level for the very first part of the 90's. Encouragingly, it enjoyed a good year in 1995 – a portent for the future?

IBM employed almost 400,000 people world-wide by the 80's; today it is down nearer to 220,000. Likewise, IBM UK went from some 18,000 to nearer 12,500 "on-the-books" employees. Today this is complemented by some 4-5,000 permanent contractors and many more non-permanents, as the changing business needs dictate.

IBM's core business has also changed dramatically in the last five years. This book addresses the era when the revenue topics were hardware, operating systems and application packages. Branches staffed by sales people and systems engineers, owned customers, or they owned "third parties" who owned customers. Today the business is more about out-sourcing, consultancy, open systems, and long-term contracts – even risk-sharing!

Where yesterday it was about branches selling products to customers, today it is very much a case of managing a geographic network of resources to meet clients' needs.

Your perceptions

Coming to this book, you will have your own perceptions of this great company. You may indeed have worked for, or be currently employed by, IBM. You may have been, or are, a customer; a competitor, or a business partner.

Phrases such as "outstanding marketing company", "high quality", "world leader", "most successful company in the world", "ahead of everyone in everything", "awesome" – have all been used when describing IBM. On the other hand, your own view may include other perceptions such as arrogant, inflexible, American, expensive, mainframe-oriented...

Whatever your views, in our experience IBM, for the most part, did things very carefully and deliberately. Where it could, it would do them for the mutual benefit of its customers and itself, but sometimes because of factors and constraints outside its own control, policies and practices were not always easy to understand or accept. Very often the causal factors in these circumstances were not of IBM's own making, and consequently were not immediately visible or obvious to its customers.

Subjects covered in this book

The principal themes of this work are three:

- IBM, for all its external image of being "a great marketing company", was definitely a "great selling company".
- The company developed many internal practices and formal procedures so that it might function more effectively. Yet it was the "People" who really made IBM as successful as it was.
- Just as the IT industry changed dramatically over the 60's to the 90's, so IBM's increasing bureaucracy and slowness to respond to marketplace requirements caused much of its demise.

Addressing these themes, the issues discussed in this book are:

- What was the driving force behind IBM's relentless growth – excellent marketing, superb products, or what?
- Was its success based on visionary pioneering product strategies, or was it more opportunistic?
- What was the image of IBM people – was this due to nature or nurture? Were branch people all the same? How was this prime resource managed? How were "wild ducks" kept in formation?
- What motivated sales people and their colleagues to jump over the ever higher sales targets?
- Did IBM lead the marketplace in everything it wanted to? Or could it not hold a tight enough rein to maintain its high marketshare?

    and

- How did IBM view its customers?

In this book...

This book does not intend to set out "how it should have been done'" or "how it should be done", à la Harvard Business School. You will find a collection of personal observations, recollections, stories and people- and situation-related anecdotes resulting from the authors' three decades with IBM. The contents are not the IBM company's view.

The authors collectively enjoyed almost a century of working for IBM in a variety of field and staff functions. This period was a demanding mixture of hard work, good times, good companionship, spiced naturally with a flavouring of frustrations and disappointments.

You will find that the observations and stories reflect the range of emotions experienced during this "century". Some are humorous; some are complimentary; some critical; and some, indeed, contain what might be construed as just a hint of a cynical ingredient. You may also notice some subtle differences of interpretation from chapter to chapter reflecting the individual experiences of the authors.

To have worked continuously for IBM during that period, as the authors did, was to have witnessed at close hand not only the extraordi- nary all-round capabilities of a unique company, but also some of the signs of its vulnerability.

The Authors

The authors all worked for that part of IBM UK "where the rubber hits the road" – facing the customer – selling, installing and supporting IBM's increasingly complex products in an increasingly complex business environment.

You may be thinking, "30 years is a long time to work for one company". Rest assured that each of the authors was tempted to leave IBM on a number of occasions. Offers of resignation were tendered and refused. In the early days, it was a cataclysmic event for somebody to leave IBM. Management went to extraordinary lengths to retain (good) people. The company itself was proud of its low attrition rate (1 per cent); compare that with today, where it sees a *minimum* target of 4 per cent as desirable.

So what kept us?

High on the list would be the camaraderie and universal team spirit. Next would come the job itself, which was always demanding and kept "you on your toes". Then, there would always be changes, either at a personal level, or because of the very frequent company reorganisations, or in one's role or location. IBM was definitely a moving feast enjoyed by, dare we say it, intelligent people doing an interesting job.

After leaving the cloisters of IBM, the authors still met the company in a number of ways from the "other side", through employment by an IBM customer, consultancy with an associated industry, or indeed endeavouring to help IBM improve its own internal business processes; thus providing a further external view of this intriguing company.

We hope that when you turn the last page you feel as we do: we were privileged to have had the opportunity of being employed by IBM, working with our colleagues there and, most of all, meeting and supporting its customers.

Perhaps you will be thinking by that last page... it would be good to have been there as well!

RM, AJG, FMB

The Prologue

In the Beginning...

It was July 1960. O-levels had been completed but the results were not yet known.

Tom Greaves, the lad's English master, a man whom he respected totally, discussed with him the possibility of staying on at school for A-levels and maybe, ultimately university. The lad was School Captain at both football and cricket, and Head Boy too. He enjoyed the academic side of school life, though his ambition was to play football or cricket professionally. He had recently had an interview with a local building company and had been offered a job at £3 per week.

Tom said, "The School has received a letter from a company in Birmingham asking whether we had a pupil with particular attributes. I have put your name forward. The company is called IBM."

It was a horrendous morning, high winds and torrential rain. The lad in his best school blazer and grey trousers, clutched a silver sixpence, his bus fare to Birmingham.

He arrived outside the IBM office. He stood in front of the huge plate-glass windows, behind which were large grey machines, the like of which he had not seen before. People were bustling around carrying metal trays containing rectangular pieces of cardboard with holes in them.

What was this IBM? What was going on behind those windows?

At the appointed hour, a soaking, bedraggled young lad entered the building. A very pleasant, pretty receptionist welcomed him warmly. She knew he was self-conscious about his appearance and pointed to the toilets. "I will let Mrs Slann know you are here."

He emerged, feeling a little smarter, and was introduced to Mrs Slann, the Office Manager. She was a most pleasant lady with an air of confidence and calmness that was reassuring to his nerves. He felt comfortable... there was something about this place that exuded a presence and a feeling he had not encountered before.

An interview with Mrs Slann concluded with the words, "I would like you to take our aptitude test next, it will only take 45 minutes." That sinking feeling came over him. An aptitude test... what is an aptitude test?

He sat in the office. The test was to be in three parts. A small alarm clock was set for the first 15 minutes and Mrs Slann left the office with a warm smile that said, "You can do it."

The clock rang out, startling the lad. Fifteen minutes had come and gone but he was quietly pleased. The questions, logical sequences, had seemed easy. Parts 2 and 3 came and went; the 3rd part all mental arithmetic. It had not been as bad as O-levels by far.

It seemed an age waiting for Mrs Slann as he sat back in reception. He could not get over those grey machines, the young people, the pieces of cardboard... It was a world he had not known existed.

"You did an excellent score in the test." It was Mrs Slann. "Come this way, we'll meet Mr Hooten, the Service Bureau Manager."

He was ushered into his office and introduced to him. The mood changed dramatically. A stern-looking, fair-haired man, smoking Nelson cigarettes, fired questions rapidly. The interview probably lasted 15 minutes, but it was a blur, and afterwards he could not remember the questions, let alone the answers he had given.

The friendly face of Mrs Slann again – what a relief. "I would like you to meet Mr McMorrow next."

Mr McMorrow was the Branch Manager. When being introduced to him, it crossed the lad's mind that he had not seen anyone so immaculately dressed before. He was a round-faced Irishman, possessed of a gentle and disarming presence – easy to talk to and someone who gained your immediate respect.

On the bus returning home, the lad was elated, yet confused, excited yet concerned as to how he had done. He knew one thing for sure, he had been somewhere very special, had met people the like of whom he had not been with before. He wanted to go again.

Success

The letter arrived. £4 per week, Office Junior. He had got the job; start 8th August 1960.

It was late July. Speech Night at the school, the leaving ceremony, the presentations. The O-level results were not through yet, but his proudest moment to date came as he was summoned to the stage by his headmaster, Mr Collins.

After receiving awards for being School Football captain, Cricket Captain and Head Boy, he was about to leave the stage when Mr Collins stopped him with... "In addition, I have a telegram for you."

He was dumbstruck; a telegram; from whom?

Mr Collins read it out. "Congratulations on your achievements and our warmest wishes for a great night." It was signed Mr McMorrow and Mrs Slann.

He had not even begun to work for IBM but he already felt very much part of it.

Clocking on

It was 8th August 1960, 8.50 am, as he entered the IBM offices. Little did he know that his time with this company would last for more than 31 years.

The grey machines were still there, the smiling receptionist, and, "Hello we have so been looking forward to seeing you again." It was Mrs Slann. In the background Mr Hooten was berating a young blond man. Mr McMorrow entered. "Hello, young man, welcome," he said smilingly. It had been the right decision, surely.

"Let's meet a few people, shall we?" Mrs Slann took him by the arm and led him amongst those grey machines. "This is John, Janet, Bob, Marion" – all were not much older than he.

In the basement where the salesmen worked – "This is Doug." A tall broad man with wavy blond hair, a flattened nose. A boxer, rugby player?

"This is Stan." He stood up, a giant, yet with a soft lyrical voice, a cheeky chuckle.

"And this is your desk," pointed Mrs Slann. He had his own desk!

Mrs Slann continued the tour and introduced him to some of his duties. The "CopyCat" copier. "Change the fluid twice a day when the copies start to go brownish. Take care, the fluid is acid-based." "The franking machine, for the letters to be posted. Weigh them on these scales, and set the value accordingly." "The Gestetner..."

Mr Hooten appeared. "So these are the most important jobs. Here are the train times for both collection and despatch throughout the day each day of the week."

Carrying 10,000-card boxes was not something he had expected, but the Service Bureau, he learned, processed these punched cards for its customers. Many of these cards were sent by rail. Fortunately the station was under a mile away.

His predecessor had moved upstairs to work with those grey machines, visible through those large plate-glass windows. This was to be his next career move, he hoped.

Day 2

"Mr McMorrow wants to see you," said Margaret his secretary. It was day 2 as the Office Junior. Blimey, second day, the Branch Manager wants to see him. What major disaster had he already perpetrated?

Mr McMorrow was his usual friendly self, and any doubts disappeared. "Can you give me 45 minutes of your time," he said, in such a way as to make the lad feel important.

They left the office together and walked briskly across the city centre. It was easy to feel at ease with this "Senior Manager". He talked about the business, the customers, how the Electric Typewriter Division was doing, and about the imminent visit of Mr Hudson, the IBM UK General Manager. They turned into the Burlington Arcade and entered a tailor's.

"Good morning, Mr McMorrow." He was obviously well known and respected. He handed over the suit he had carried with him. "Usual steam and press. My colleague will collect at 4.00 pm." Day 2 and he was already the Branch Manager's "colleague".

Each day in his role as Office Junior, he walked to the tailor's to arrive at 10.00 am and hand over a suit of Mr McMorrow's and then again to collect it at 4.00pm.

Mr McMorrow was always immaculate, and it was not long before the lad realised that the dress code in IBM was a fundamental part of its culture.

Promotion

The CopyCat, the franking machine, the Gestetner and the box-humping to and from the railway station were history. He was with Bob,

John, and Janet amongst those grey machines, wired panels, punched cards. The basement was behind him.

Mrs Slann had wished him well and now his new manager was Mr Hooten. His reputation was frightening to the young people – the sergeant major. He barked out orders, he ranted, he raved, he wrote letters to personnel files.

As the lad learned how to use the grey machines, he was constantly aware of how people passing the large plate-glass windows would stop and stare. He could tell that they were curious, even bemused by what they were watching. It reminded him of that day of his interview, how he had stared too.

During the months of operating those machines, he learnt that Service Bureau work demanded concentration, organisation, commitment and discipline. One small mistake could take a lot of time to correct.

As the lad became more experienced and adept, Mr Hooten seemed to mellow. He now bellowed at the new operators. It dawned upon this recent employee that Mr McMorrow, Mr Hooten, and the other senior people he had now worked with, were in practice setting the standard for which IBM's reputation would become recognised: "Excellence".

Passers-by continued to stare through those plate-glass windows, little realising that they were watching the birth of data processing, the beginning of new techniques and processes that would become an integral part of their everyday lives. They were also watching the birth of IBM in the UK, a name that was to become both famous and household.

He knew his employer selection had been the right decision; he was on the ground floor of a career of challenge, change and considerable excitement. So many other IBM'ers started their careers in the early sixties. They would become the people who would form the IBM company in the UK to become as respected as it did.

Thirty Years On...

The end and the beginning....

As he left the "celebration" party, he shook hands with another of his colleagues who had completed his last day with IBM. Strange really, he mused, some would call it "last day with IBM", some "in IBM". (A little like we used to say "Which bank do you belong to?" as opposed to nowadays "Who do you bank with?". Perhaps the first is more apt.)

The "package", as it had become to be known, had released another talented professional who had given years of his life to the great corporation. He wished his colleague well, for he knew that his friend was worried, uncertain, and even depressed as to what the future held for him. A "job for life"; that was the IBM commitment when he had joined, but that was now completely overturned by the relentless process of "downsizing".

The package was the "golden handshake". For most, financially a good farewell, and with it came the offer of help and counselling towards a future new career. IBM had put together an "offer" that was better than most other companies going through the same process.

So many had already left, and there were so many more who knew that they were "targeted". There was endless speculation as to who would be next, and what would be the terms and conditions of the next package. There were also many who wanted it, but who would be anguished when they realised they had missed the "cut".

There were endless rumours: "This is the last optional package, the next one will be obligatory and targeted" – even, "There will not be another package. It will be more a case of redundancy." It was a very unsettling period for long-serving IBM'ers in their late 40's and early 50's.

The young lad who had stared at those grey machines in 1960 knew that he was near to the day when he would "qualify". Endless discussions with his peers about their packages meant he understood the ramifications of the deal. He was briefed and ready.

When the envelope arrived, it was still a shock. He was 47 years old, a pension at 50, a lump sum, but the reality was clear. He would need to work with someone other than IBM.

So many who had already left were struggling. They had been protected and secure in IBM, insulated from the outside world. When they had joined IBM, they had been promised such security and till this point IBM had been as good as its word. Now they were faced with a dilemma that, but a few years earlier, was not even a consideration.

In retrospection

What was happening to the great company? How had this happened? Where had it all gone wrong? Who should be blamed? What had happened to the Watson "commandments"?

The lad who had joined in 1960 reflected on his career of over 30 years. Office boy to operator, those punched cards, the grey machines, being a programmer, an analyst, the challenge of being a salesman, and years of being an IBM manager. Reorganisations too numerous to catalogue, thousands of people met and worked with, characters, difficult folk, nice people, autocratic people, democratic people. The customers, the wins, the "non-wins". Where had those 30 years disappeared?

What now?

The telephone rang; "I hear you have been offered the package." It was an old pal, an ex-IBM'er. The grapevine still worked. "Do you have any plans for when you leave?" The caller had been one of the lads from 1960 too.

They reminisced for a while. "Do you remember when we worked together at that little company in Shropshire?" He did; they had worked to provide a Service Bureau solution, and then upgraded to a System/3, then a System/34 and then System/38. They were happy memories.

"I was speaking to the Managing Director the other day and he has a need for which you are ideally suited. When I mentioned you may be available, he was excited at renewing his relationship with you."

So a new life was about to start.

He reflected again on what IBM had taught him over those many years. Standards of performance, of conduct, presentation. To strive for excellence and to encourage others to do likewise. Recognition and reward when earned. There had been no short cuts to success and experience. Attention to detail, completed work, a complete demonstration of professionalism. Customer service at the highest level. These were the bedrocks of IBM's reputation.

He was soon to become a "customer" of IBM and learn that things were very different in the 90's compared with his first two decades with the company.

He finished packaging the work he was to leave to others. The terminal on his desk was still active. It did not take long to delete his files, to break the links to information systems. He flicked a switch and the screen went dark. He had severed his intellectual cord with IBM.

Gathering a few mementoes, he saw that his desk and his terminal were now with "vacant possession". He handed his identity badge to Security, left the building, and the "heavy gates closed behind him".

He now possessed a non-company car. Looking down from the car park, his emotions were a mixture of happiness and pride with the lifetime he had spent and enjoyed with IBM, and sadness that what he was leaving was not what he had joined. IBM had changed....

He still held some concern for what the future held for "his IBM". Would it survive, would it rejuvenate? He knew only one thing: he was no longer a part of it. But, he still cared.

The car park barrier went up, as usual, and came down, psychologically and emotionally, not as usual. Shropshire beckoned. A new beginning....

1. Driving the IBM Business

Introduction

When you read all those weighty volumes written by Harvard MBA graduates about IBM, you could be fooled into thinking that here was a remorseless corporate machine, crushing all before it, as it drove ever onward to the rhythms of the corporate plan. No doubt someone has scoured the parchment pages of Nostradamus, looking for the evidence that must surely be there, predicting the arrival of this malevolent corporate juggernaut.

Well, yes, there were corporate plans – probably quite good ones. Any visitor to the IBM corporate offices in the US would have been lucky to escape without at least an overview of both the long-term strategic, and the short-term operating, plans. And any organisation as dependent upon leading-edge, high-cost capital investment in its manufacturing plants, needed to plan ahead pretty thoughtfully. But no brilliant research, no talented development, no innovative engineering, no quality-driven manufacturing was worth a row of beans if the sales force could not, or would not, sell the products.

It was like the Iron Duke is rumoured to have said before Waterloo, pointing to a poor, sodden, British infantryman: "He will decide the day, Gentlemen." Perhaps, in today's terminology, he would have said: "He will do the business." Not that all IBM salespeople were either poor, or, for that matter, regularly sodden; but you get the idea.

This book is based upon the experiences and memories of its three authors. We spent most of our century of toil in IBM at the sharp, selling end of the business. It is only fitting, therefore, that we begin by describing the environment and the mechanisms that IBM created to motivate its field force, whether a newly qualified salesman, or a very experienced large account manager. It was through these "persuasive mechanisms" that IBM endeavoured to direct its business, and to motivate those within IBM directly responsible for securing, retaining and growing the customers, without whom everything would have come off the rails. Indeed, some will argue that when IBM did begin to come off the rails, it was precisely because it ceased to heed the advice of those closest to the customers. Not for nothing has the IBM of today adopted the slogan of Customer Relationship Management (CRM).

Within an organisation as large as IBM, different people have different views on the relative importance of this or that process, this or that function. Most of the autobiographical volumes written by some very senior executives, after long and distinguished careers in IBM, have concentrated upon the IBM Corporation itself. Certainly they will have reported the events they experienced with proper accuracy. But very little of what those learned authors have had to say is actually about the "real" customers of IBM, or about the "real" IBM people who worked with those customers. It is much more about the internal machinations, within the corridors of power of IBM itself.

Fascinating though it may be to contemplate one's corporate navel, one does not need to move far away from the front line in any large organisation to lose touch. In the complex world of information technology, it would be those who dealt directly with the customers on a day-to-day basis who have the best idea of what *they* were thinking.

IBM explicitly accepted this. It required its sales force to understand everything there was to know about its customers and prospects that could influence a sale. Then it all had to be analysed, written down, and presented up the IBM management line. In view of what had begun to happen by the late 80's, one wonders whether IBM did actually bother to read and to understand it.

Who were these sales people then, so important to IBM's success? That is covered in some detail later in this book. Let us just say, for the moment, that they were a wide spread of personality types, commonly well-educated, alert and responsible. However, as with any large group of people, there were extremes – at the margin....

Nick was an interesting fellow. He was still quite young when, after sales training, he qualified to become an IBM salesman, though he had had an interesting, but brief, career following university, selling insurance to Californians. There wasn't much Nick didn't know about selling, and he somewhat resented the, for him, modest earnings to which his newly qualified salesman status entitled him. At any business group gathering where those present were required to introduce themselves, Nick would always do so with the concluding words: "...and I am the lowest-paid person in the room!" He was not without courage, particularly when fortified by copious quantities of ale, which he often was.

There were few customers for whom Nick would have been the natural choice as salesman. But there was one for whom he was ideal. The customer systems director was another "Nick", in almost every respect but name. They got on like a house on fire, though sometimes actually coming to blows when the one overwhelmed the other at snooker.

On one occasion Nick and this customer travelled down to Cardiff Arms Park for a rugby international. IBM regularly took a table for lunch beforehand at the Angel Hotel, alongside the stadium. The table was often hosted by a particular IBM director who would willingly have surrendered everything – career, family, the lot – to have had the chance to play rugby for Wales. This director had a fearsome reputation for drive and determination. Not for nothing was he known as "Black Pete".

On this occasion, unusually, the IBM lunch-table was sparsely populated; only Nick, the customer and the IBM director were present, and they were required to empty a table of wine laid for eight, with beer beforehand – and warming whisky to follow once they reached their seats for the match. During the match, the customer was seated securely between salesman and IBM director... who knows, he might have toppled over, or tried to escape? You could never be sure.

No customer executive, in those circumstances and however inebriated, would turn down an opportunity to "bend the ear", ever receptive, of a captive IBM director. Now this particular IBM director always carried a large supply of blank punched cards on which he would write peremptory, executive messages. Sure enough, within minutes of the start of the game, a copious flow of punched cards began, via customer to salesman, containing written notes, along the lines of Churchill's "Action this day": "I understand your customer has a problem with MVS performance – get a brief to me first thing Monday morning." "What's this about Amdahl claiming they have superior technology?

Get the details to me ASAP, with a copy to...." And so on, all in the same vein.

And then a punched card came back the other way, from Nick, the salesman. The customer got a glimpse of the message, en route to Black Pete. It said: "Stop sending me all these ****ing punched cards!" Black Pete stiffened, and then burst out laughing. No more cards were sent.

At the other end of the personality spectrum you had John. Now John was a steady sort of chap, not given to over-excitement, or anything like that. In the spectrum of personality colours John would have settled comfortably in the grey area. But he did possess a kind of dogged intellectual determination to worry a problem to death whenever appropriate.

One year, the IBM annual sales convention took place in West Berlin, before the Wall came down. Most people took the opportunity to visit East Berlin, by coach, under the supervisory guidance of a lady tour guide no doubt freshly recruited from the Communist Youth. Her comments led one to suppose that East Berlin was, without doubt, the happiest and most prosperous country in the world, and its citizens the best fed and the best housed. John had listened earnestly to all that was said, but something didn't quite "jive", as they say. There was a frown on his face. He was determined to resolve the issue that was clearly "bugging" him.

When the coach returned towards the Brandenburg Gate and Checkpoint Charlie for the crossing back to West Berlin, the guide allowed a brief stop for photographs. John stepped down from the coach, and walked over towards one of the armed border guards who looked as though he had reached this career peak, via the Waffen SS, the Gestapo and half-a-dozen concentration camps.

"Er, excuse me," said John, as the guard released the safety catch on his machine gun. The other coach passengers craned to hear what John was saying. He said the right thing – always.

"Can you, er, tell me whether it is easy to get a mortgage in East Berlin?"

So through all the brainwashing of IBM training, the core personality was preserved. Customers come in different shapes and colours themselves.

Some wanted Technicolor salesmen, and some wanted more modest personalities. IBM had to ensure that it found the right match and could motivate them all to sell more and to install more in order to drive IBM's business.

The Sales Plan – Phase 1

As ever, motivation was a combination of carrot and stick. In the early days of IBM there was not only quite a lot of carrot, there was also quite a lot of stick! The penalties of failure were harsh and unforgiving. Increasingly, though, the carrot remained, while the stick became more gentle. The salesman who lost business was still likely to get a roasting (in the form of the dreaded "lost business review"), but, unlike the old days, he was no longer hit quite so hard in the pocket.

It was quite common, in the 1960's, for a salesman who lost business through no fault of his own to find himself with no option but resignation if he was to feed his family. To remain with IBM on a salary plan comprising 40 per cent basic guarantee, and 60 per cent commission, was no longer viable once all chance of commission had been wiped out, at a stroke, following a lost sale or some equipment discontinuance. The term "taking the debit", meant that the business loss was carried directly by the commission account of the offending salesman. The commission account did not regain equilibrium until compensating sales or installs were made. This was the logic of a time when most equipment was installed on a rental plan. All of this led to some extremely capable sales people resigning from IBM rather than facing impoverishment. But so it was, and so it would be.

Quotas, once set, were rarely modified. This was well understood. The sales force lived with it. It could lead both to occasional injustice, and to occasional massive over-performance. One salesman, in 1963, achieved over 630 per cent of his assigned quota! That suggested either extremely poor quota-setting or extraordinarily brilliant selling, or, most likely, something of both. Whatever the reason, that salesman prospered.

As the 60's came to an end, IBM began to introduce ways of buffering sales people from the slings and arrows of outrageous market fortune, and buffering itself from excessive, fortuitous, commission payments. There were also some sociological forces at work here....

Selling, as a profession, has always had somewhat of a jaundiced reception in the UK. It was not quite the sort of career for a "gentleman". The title "sales rep" conjured up images of the black market "spiv" of the immediate post-war years. Perhaps for that reason, IBM UK sometimes called its salesmen "marketing" representatives – and that was the last thing they were. They were salesmen.

The IBM "marketing representative" of the early 60's needed, therefore, to be someone of "mature" years, with a successful career before joining IBM, well able to withstand the exigencies of this new sales career and with a lifestyle reasonably well-geared to the peaks and troughs of sales earnings. However, during the 60's "selling" began to acquire respectability. IBM began to accept younger applicants for sales positions, even some direct from university on occasions. And it was acknowledged that these newcomers should be afforded better income protection than before.

However, there were some downsides to the new approach. By recruiting staff with little or no previous business experience, IBM had to accept that they would probably have to learn about business the hard way. IBM had taught them all it could about the IBM products, hardware and software, and about selling, but as for business knowledge? Certainly there were a few important business areas where IBM itself could do a little teaching of application skills, but for the most part you learnt from your customers.

This could lead to difficulties....

"Fashion sense... fit and function"

Until the mid-60's, the organisation of IBM UK's sales branches within the Data Processing Division was by geographic territory. The consequence was that a branch might well find itself with a wide mix of industries within its sales territory. Increasingly, it was felt that sales and support skills needed to be developed to match the business bias of customers and prospects. The best way to do this was to create industry-based branches.

This took place in 1965. In the Midlands, for example, there were to be distinct and separate branch offices covering manufacturing, distribution, local government (within which finance, education and medical were also shoe-horned) and an oddball branch called "Special Accounts". This last category comprised accounts which, even in those early years, had developed to a level of size and complexity that required special attention.

It is clear, from this description alone, that much horse-trading took place, and each part of the country had its own little organisational quirks. Indeed one of the wonders of IBM was the way in which any organisation change (and they were both regular and plentiful) was announced as a panacea which would crack all the problems of the previous organisation – until the next reorganisation, that is! To point out potential shortcomings during the announcement euphoria of any reorganisation was to risk severe, negative "brownie points".

Over the following years IBM wriggled, twisted and turned as it attempted to refine its versions of industry versus geographical marketing, in an ever-changing marketplace. No doubt it will continue to do so as it seeks an ultimate Hegelian synthesis. But even if IBM were to know when it reached organisational Nirvana, it could never admit it, because an equally strong corporate belief dictates that "Reorganisation is Good for You".

However, in those early days the new industry-based branch structure promised great things. At last we could now focus the industry application skills needed to enthuse the business management of our customers and prospects.

One such customer, of the "distribution" branch, was a textile company, making high-fashion ladies' jersey knitwear. The company was actually a customer of the IBM Birmingham Service Bureau which was required to process sales order documentation, following the frenzied launch of the new season's range of garments. This data was keyed into punched cards for the production of various order analyses. IBM would also, critically, calculate material requirements so that urgent forward orders could be placed upon suppliers. Everything was always "Urgent, Urgent...".

This application may have had somewhat more in common with the world of manufacturing bills of material than with, say, a mail order company, or a brewer, or a retail butchery chain; but there we were.

When IBM designed the application, the nuances of the world of high fashion were not fully appreciated – for example, that twice a year all that had gone before was abandoned as the customer announced a new range for Spring or Autumn. As luck would have it, the application was successfully first installed for an Autumn range of garments, fairly modest in scope. The range was announced to agents in the Spring, for sale during the following months, and supply to shops in the Autumn. In simple terms, the "range" comprised a number of styles of garment, in various colours and sizes. Each colour of each style had its own material breakdown and carried a number of style/colour-dependent items, such as interlining, buttons, trim, zips, and collars. Also, there was the possibility of second-level material requirements with, say, collars, which might themselves contain trim or other embellishments.

The similarity with a manufacturing bill of material is readily apparent. However, not many manufacturing companies change their complete product range twice a year! To have used a classical bill of material method would have been like attempting to crack a nut with a sledgehammer – both expensive and inflexible.

So the Service Bureau staff set about designing a one-off requirements planning system for the ladies' fashionwear manufacturer. Had it been clear from the outset how radically the ranges might change from season to season, or, indeed (and here was the rub), had IBM's industry skills been as profound as they should have been, then a great deal of pain might have been avoided.

In those far-off days the IBM Birmingham Service Bureau believed it had a pretty powerful commercial computer for any workload. By most of the standards of the time it was quite a juggernaut – a 1401 computer with 16,000 (16K) characters of memory, tapes, disks and the best of IBM's then current array of input/output devices. 16K? What a minnow, by today's standards. Even a modest little personal computer today has at least 2 megabytes of memory – 125 times as much! But that 1401 configuration would have set you back the best part of £750,000 in the days when "the pound in your pocket" was really worth a pound. While 16K may not seem much, programmers had achieved miracles with much less, writing in machine level language or symbolic code. The word used to go round the office about how some genius had programmed the Jaguar payroll (not a simple task, given the endless bonus rates and deductions that typified an automotive company) on a 1401/Model G with 1.4K! Oh, easy for Einstein.

So, to return to our textile customer, IBM was not downcast with a mere 16K. With some adroit programming it was possible to build some simple matrices in memory (even with only 16K), carry out some partial updates and write the results out to disk. By repeating the process a number of times, all the orders could be thus dealt with, and the latest reports produced. The Service Bureau programmers, who were no fools, had even allowed spare capacity should the next range introduce more variations of style and colour.

Well, the next range, the Spring range, did indeed do that – in spades! No doubt the fashion editor of *Vogue* or someone similar would have known that. But this was not a world familiar to the IBM Birmingham Service Bureau in 1966. Our textile manufacturer, for whom everything was "Urgent, Urgent...", brought in the specifications of the new (Spring) range, with the first batch of orders, and the request: "Can I wait while you produce the reports for me?"

The new range had about twice as many styles, at least twice as many colour-way variations, and a much more complex material break-down. Well, these styles were for the Spring season, weren't they, where colour was all-important – wouldn't any fool know that?

There followed a frenzied re-programming, fortunately hidden from the customer, who decided after all not to wait, and by the skin of its teeth IBM cracked it. However, though all the IBM players were in a state of advanced nervous exhaustion by this time, we could see light at the end of the tunnel. As if 16K wasn't big enough, the decision had been taken to replace the 1401 with the recently announced /360 range. The new machine was to be an absolute monster – a 64K 360 Model 30. 64K of memory? Don't be ridiculous. Who could ever want 64K? Anyway it was to be installed in time for the next Autumn range announcement, so we were home and dry.

The whole matrix, covering all styles, colour-ways and sizes, could now be contained in memory where it would rattle about like peas in a can, with all that memory. So what could go wrong? Well, to start with the customer delayed giving approval for a program re-write. This customer ran a "tight shop", and expenditure of any kind (even though IBM, in the interests of the nerves of its staff, had agreed to share the cost of the re-write) was frowned upon. The consequence of the late go-ahead was that final systems test ran alarmingly close to the expected first live run.

We then allowed ourselves to be stampeded by the "Urgent, Urgent, can I wait while you produce the reports?" entreaties. Inevitably, the reports thus produced in the heat of the moment, and eagerly taken away, contained an error.

A torrid series of meetings with the customer ensued. IBM was blamed for just about everything, short of the outbreak of World War II. One particular customer director had a nice line in hyperbole, accusing a surgical IBM of gloating over the patient whose life blood was ebbing away on the operating table! It was conceded, however, that IBM had worked all hours to be ready on time, given the delays mainly caused by the customer's financial indecision.

That error was put right fortunately, and all returned to sweetness and light. There was no more talk of operating theatres. That is, until about a month later, when one particularly acute customer director noticed an apparent discrepancy in the requirements for a certain material. Upon examination, it was discovered that there had been a minor mis-load of some of the master specification data, and, sure enough, IBM had caused the customer to over-order the offending material.

So the final chapter of this learning experience was one of IBM agreeing to pay the customer for the material over-ordered, the customer offering to give the same material to IBM, but IBM turning down the offer on the grounds that it had no immediate use for several hundred yards of double-knit jersey!

A further consequence was that IBM perceived the need for a swift modification to the terms and conditions of its Service Bureau contract: namely, that where, through a fault on IBM's part, a customer suffered consequential loss, IBM should not be liable for more than the value of the contract itself. "'Tis an ill wind...."

Where had we gone wrong, and what had we learnt through all this?

First, we weren't as industry-smart as we ought to have been. You gain that accolade mainly in the school of hard knocks, not by reading books or merely calling yourself an industry branch. We had taken on a job without truly understanding the business requirements of the world of high fashion.

Secondly, we were trapped into releasing systems test output as though it were "real" output. A systems test is a systems test – better to be safe than sorry.

Thirdly, we did not set the customer's expectations right at the outset. It's not easy to do it later, and in the heat of battle.

The trouble was, having gathered all this invaluable experience, we couldn't find any other worthwhile high-fashion prospects to impress with our knowledge – not in the Midlands anyway!

Not all new application areas were as fraught as this, however. Sometimes you gathered knowledge about new business areas, and their finer points, in more restful ways....

"A matter of taste...."

It was usually the lot of the newly-qualified IBM salesman in the 1960's to be given a general territory to work. If he (and the term is used advisedly here since there were very, very few IBM saleswomen then) was particularly lucky then he might take over one or two existing accounts, but that was not the norm. However, life could be quite interesting on a general territory....

Northampton was the headquarters office of what was then probably the third largest retail butchery chain in the UK. (The Co-op and Dewhursts were Nos. 1 and 2.) This group had some 450 retail butchery shops, mainly in the South, plus abattoirs, factories (where sausages, pork pies and similar products were made), and warehouses/cold stores for holding fresh and frozen meat and meat products. By the mid-60's, when our enthusiastic newly-qualified IBM salesman first made contact, this company was starting to show interest in using computers for stock control in their warehouses and cold stores. As any salesman knows, some companies are pleasant to deal with, some are the opposite. This company was very much in the former category. While always business-like in their dealings with IBM and other potential suppliers, the directors and senior management were also direct, honest and, an added bonus, fun to work with.

This story begins when, after a morning with the chief accountant, our IBM salesman is invited to join him at his club in Northampton, for lunch. Since the company supplied this club with its meat, most of the senior management made sure they were members.

On this particular day, the chief accountant and his IBM guest, having "supped" a few beers in the bar, went into the restaurant to find the company chairman talking animatedly to an extremely large, florid gentleman. The chairman immediately spotted the chief accountant, and invited both, including the IBM guest, to join them since they were also about to start lunch. The large, florid gentleman turned out to be some sort of consultant, advising on the in's and out's of setting up an animal by-products company.

Now, while animal by-products (skins, bones, hooves,etc.) are often viewed with distaste (who hasn't at some stage got stuck behind a lorry carrying a fly-blown load of the same?), they are highly profitable to a meat processing company owning its own abattoirs. It is ironic that these smelly products are the source of so much that flavours and adorns the gentler sex – such as soaps, leather fashionware.

Anyway, to return to our story... everybody ordered steak. What else could they do when the chairman of the company that supplied the meat was sitting at the same table?

The large florid gentleman was clearly more than satisfied with his morning's work. He noisily scoffed his starter, washing it down with healthy gulps of wine. However, since the initial conversation took the form of updating the chairman on the progress made regarding computerised stock control, the chairman's guest could not contribute much. He began to fidget. Clearly he wanted to make his contribution to the business and social chit-chat.

He picked his moment during a temporary lull in the discussions. "Yerse," he said, as the steaks arrived. He had the attention of the audience, and intended to make the most of it. He leaned back, thumb in waistcoat, choosing his words with care. "Course, yer animal boi-products, now thaat's a wunnerful business to be in, but oi'll give yer this 'ere bit of advoice". We all leaned forward to hear these pearls of wisdom. A blunt forefinger jabbed the air vigorously, for added emphasis. "If yer wants yer good boi-products yer've gotta keep yer 'oles out – yer nose 'oles, yer ear 'oles and yer arse 'oles!"

Somehow the steak didn't quite taste the same!

Such were the experiences that forged the character of IBM salesmen in the 60's! And it has to be said that our salesman came away from lunch enriched with a little more "industry knowledge", even though he was not entirely sure how he could use it.

Thus did the shy and retiring emergent IBM salesman of the 1960's gather the business experience to face the challenges of subsequent decades. And there stood IBM, ever-concerned to ensure that this new breed of salesman should receive proper compensation for his endeavours.

So, by the end of the 60's, we began to see a gradual increase in the basic (non-recoverable) component of total earnings, and a balancing reduction in the scope for over-performance.

The Sales Plan – Phase 2

With the increase in the basic salary component of a salesman's expected earnings, IBM had to manipulate carefully the commission budget. IBM didn't necessarily want to end up paying its salesmen a great deal more. Much thought, therefore, was focused on deciding how, by flexing the commission budget, the sales force would deliver the corporate product objectives. This became ever more complex.

By 1989 there were 21 possible payment plans for an IBM salesperson, plus a few more unpublished variations for special needs. On top of this was a whole raft of management compensation plans.

The main driver for the business, though, was the sales payment plan. In this there was a clear division between an elite of "prime" quota salespersons, and "overlay" quota "specialists". Those carrying prime quotas were directly responsible for the customer accounts, usually taking credit for all business generated within those accounts. Those on overlay quotas would cover a mix of prime sales territories and receive duplicate credit for sales of their designated products. Over time, more and more of these overlay territories were created to focus sales in the areas IBM considered strategic.

Some examples from the 1989 list of 21 payment plans were:

• Account Manager... responsible for not more than three named enterprises... responsible for the sale and installation of the complete IBM product range, except as excluded by the Sales Plan.

- Telecommunications Specialist... overlay territory on specified accounts, one or more marketing units and/or one or more branches... responsible for selling and installing telecommunications products.

- Software Specialist... overlay territory on specified accounts or marketing units.... responsible for one or more software segments defined in attachment... quota and achievement will be measured in software revenue for licences in the assigned product sub-set.

You can see that each plan type had a different balance of basic salary, guarantee (non-recoverable) and potential for over-performance.

On top of all of these 21 plans, there were some 16 product-related bonuses, and 22 listed performance-related bonuses. During the year more, of either kind, would be introduced to further direct sales activity, especially if there was any risk of missing its periodic targets.

In determining which products to rate as "strategic", and therefore worthy of a bonus, several factors would be important to IBM. But here we will pause to relate a story about "bonuses".

"There's more than one way to...."

Among all the various bonuses and incentives devised to encourage the IBM sales force, the one that always rightly carried the greatest reward was that for winning new business. The exact scale of the reward depended upon the size of the order, but even at the minimum qualifying level the cash reward was significant.

To qualify as a "new name account" three main criteria had to be satisfied:

- First, the equipment installed had to be "designated system". That meant it had to include a processor of some kind. It could not merely be a terminal, or some other system lacking a central processor.
- Secondly, the decision to install the equipment had to be seen to be a "local" decision by independent management, and not imposed by some remote head office, already brainwashed, and "in the pocket" of IBM.
- Thirdly, the installation had to be the first of its kind within the designated site.

These rules were designed mainly for the new business salesperson, often covering a tough new territory with no existing IBM customers. Those who covered large IBM accounts were usually excluded from the new name account bonus pot of gold. By definition, the fact that these were already IBM customers meant that equipment had been installed, so any new sale, however large, would not satisfy all the qualification criteria.

Yet there were corners of most large accounts where IBM had not already reached, and where the selling job could be quite as difficult as the most bleak of new business territories. Indeed the fact that the IBM salesperson came "tarred with the brush" of those "nasty" pro-IBM people in the corporate head office often meant that the IBM sales campaign started several paces behind the competition.

One such area where IBM had minimal presence in the marketplace, yet which it deemed highly strategic in the 70's, was that of telephone switching systems – the world of the PABX. But the new IBM product was not to be a mechanical device. It was to be software-controlled. The IBM 3750 Switching System, announced in 1974, caused IBM to enter a market strongly dominated by indigenous manufacturers, closely linked to that country's PTT utility. The 3750 system was not cheap, and, depending upon exact configuration, might cost as much as a large central processor – certainly in the many hundreds of thousands of £'s. It was deservedly accorded the status of a "designated system" for the purposes of new account bonus considerations.

One or two of the large account teams, mainly in the finance and petrochemical industries, made immediate breakthroughs, but that was usually on the strength of a head office recommendation. The large, often dispersed and heterogeneous, industrial accounts were far more difficult to crack. Local sites jealously guarded their independence wherever they could. Having often been forced to surrender their powers of decision over computing strategy, they were not about to release other areas without a fight.

So this was stony ground, in spite of much effort, for many industrial account teams.

Eventually, however, one such account team, having almost given up trying, did spot a chink of light – indeed, two chinks of light! For having beaten their heads against a brick wall for several years, suddenly two opportunities opened up. Local management, whether out of sympathy we shall never know, accepted IBM's proposals, and in the space of six months two new systems were installed. Given the complexity of a 3750 configuration, and the rules imposed by the UK PTT, this timescale was in itself a minor miracle. However, even more exciting was the fact that, on all criteria, these installations qualified for "new name account" bonuses.

The account team enjoyed a celebratory "bender", duly completed the necessary claim documentation and awaited the expected congratulations from their bank managers.

Silence... nothing happened.

This continued for a while. IBM salespeople were an extraordinarily trusting group, and they had plenty of other things to keep them busy. Of course the system would deliver – eventually. It didn't. The claim was resubmitted, with even more supporting documentation. Local management had approved it. So had regional management. But.... no bonus payment.

This looked like a case for the "open door" (see Chapter 2) to senior management either on the grounds of administrative incompetence or misrepresentation, or both. Eventually, at about the time the account team was preparing its case for "open door", the local branch manager, who fully supported the account team, happened to glimpse the by now burgeoning file on the matter while with his own manager. He perceived several apposite comments: "...the new account bonus budget is badly overspent", and "...can't the claim be managed some other way", and,"...tell the branch to sort it out". And so on, in the same vein.

Probably the branch manager was not supposed to disclose what he had seen to the troops, but he was an decent fellow, and so much the more liked and respected as a result.

He immediately, and contrary to all the guidelines, cancelled two Territory Management Objectives (TMO's are described later in this chapter) already set, and replaced them with another retrospective (an even greater sin!) TMO, along the lines of "Show clear evidence of progress in promoting IBM's switching systems in this account" – worth x per cent of salary. "If country doesn't like this," he said, "I'll tell them I'm recommending the open door case to the account team."

No more was heard. The TMO was paid, for the same value as the original bonuses, and the "planning genius" in head office received retribution for setting the wrong new name account budget! But it was not the way IBM would ideally have chosen to motivate its sales force to "drive the business".

In addition to the new name account bonus there were other bonuses much sought after. First, and probably foremost, were those tied in with IBM's big money generator products – the large systems, where competition from the software compatible vendors (SCV) was fierce. The selling, and installing on time, of such systems carried big rewards for the "prime" salesperson. Likewise, protection of such installed systems was key. One way to achieve this was to ensure that the customer was up to speed with IBM's latest systems software – software that may not have been implemented on the SCV processors. And one way to grow the load on the IBM processor, so that the latest systems software was needed, was to push application growth. That was why IBM, having allowed itself to lose contact with the end-users through the 70's, became so concerned to re-cement that contact. Applications are for end-users. Increasingly, therefore, application selling became another area for Sales Plan attention.

And there you have the cycle: drive application growth (and if IBM itself sold the application software, even better), build the load on the system, create the requirement for the latest systems management software, create even more load (and protect what you've got), and, hey presto, the customer needs an upgrade. Sell the upgrade – and return to stage 1.

If only customers had seen it like that – but perhaps they did!

Too Many Cooks May Spoil the Strategic Broth

So there were increasing numbers of overlay specialist salespeople running around promoting niche "strategic" products. All this could be a nightmare for the "prime" salesperson, who had his own challenging "prime" sales targets to achieve anyway. And it was to him that the customer looked to keep some semblance of control over these nomadic tribes of specialists. There was a temptation on the part of the prime salesperson, unless he needed them to make his own targets, to fend them off and keep them out of the account. Where that happened, it was up to the branch manager to mediate and pacify – and provoke the reaction either from the specialist that he was not being allowed proper access to his prospects, or from the prime that the branch manager would soon be getting a wigging from an unhappy customer systems director who was pretty peeved at all these "freelancers" wandering around his company. Whatever the outcome, one thing was certain – neither salesperson would get reduced targets.

Of course, by the late 80's when things began to get tough, IBM cottoned onto the fact that while all these overlay specialists were scurrying around selling their strategic products, it was costing IBM a small fortune in duplicate commission payments! It was not beyond possibility that five or more sales staff could receive commission for one sale. The prime salesman, and his manager, the specialist salesman, and his manager, sometimes the branch manager, perhaps a region and/or country-level specialist support group, all might be on the gravy-train. One IBM UK senior executive stated that there were examples of up to seventeen people being paid commission for sales of certain products! Apart from reducing the profitability of products thus promoted, it distorted the allocation of funds within a finite commission budget.

A further complication in all of this was introduced by the concept of the Selected International Account (SIA). These were accounts which operated across more than one country, and which sought to impose international control over subsidiary country operations. As long as IBM was satisfied that there was a point of control, and that the account offered sufficient potential, it would designate the account as SIA. Depending upon the classification level, the appointed SIA manager qualified for budget relief for international travel. He also received the support of a US-based staff group, plus, in some countries, the support of an SIA branch committed to promoting IBM's international business rather than that purely of the local country. Needless to say, the SIA manager was overlay, in payment terms, to all the salesmen covering the subsidiary companies around the world.

Yet another layer.

It is noted in this book that IBM sometimes forgot what the "I" meant. SIA was an attempt to address this issue, and it worked, up to a point. However, while IBM was truly international in everything else, it was not international in its marketing. The countries were all-powerful, and since it was the countries that in the end drove the product set, the IBM Corporation was always at the mercy of local country interpretation. The corporation laid very precise financial objectives on the countries. It was more difficult to define rigid country product targets. Of course, it still did, but failure was viewed a little more phlegmatically – only the country product managers got a roasting!

In this context the SIA manager could find, if he weren't careful, quite different solutions being proposed to his customer's subsidiaries, in the various countries, in each of which the local IBM salesperson had a personal interpretation of what was strategic! However, SIA managers, who were usually, and of necessity, experienced IBM salesmen anyway, and had learnt to take the rough with the smooth....

"The international scene"

IBM created the world of Selected International Accounts in the belief that its international customers needed a point of co-ordination for their international systems strategies. This, in turn, would better enable IBM to optimise its own global sales operations.

No doubt some companies did have rigid norms of corporate systems behaviour, and woe betide those who transgressed. For such companies IBM's international role would have been, at least in theory, relatively straightforward. Many international companies, however, saw the IBM SIA system as the lever with which Corporate HQ management, in whichever country they might reside, could prevent local IBM sales staff from implanting treasonable thoughts in the minds of *their own* local management.

This was all very well, and as long as the local IBM people felt that by co-operation, and by not "rocking the boat", they stood to gain something, then they would go along with the recommendations of the SIA manager. The trouble arose when local customer management, always disrespectful of their own alien head office, and finding no sympathy from the local IBM people, decided to open a serious dialogue with competition. That set everybody running around in circles.

The SIA man got it in the neck: "If your local people in Fantasia had given better support, my staff wouldn't have started talking to Control

Uni-Burroughs", complained the International Systems Director. "If you lot in SIA made sure that the International Systems Director got a grip on his overseas staff, this would never happen", whinged the local IBM Branch Manager. It would invariably result in a combined overseas trip. The International Systems Director would threaten his subordinate, and the SIA manager would look for yet more ways in the IBM international bribery system (known as "international sales assistance" credits) to create temporary law and order. Both approaches, equally effective, would be accompanied by a number of exceedingly convivial meals, when all would, hopefully, agree that it had been nothing but a misunderstanding after all.

For the SIA manager, therefore, detailed knowledge of the local IBM Sales Plan in every country where his customer had a presence, was vital. Each country would take its own view of the worth, or morality, of "international sales assistance". Some believed there was no place for it and their local sales staff should only receive recompense for IBM products sold and installed in their home country. Other countries took a more charitable view, and, providing a proper case was made by the SIA manager, then cash could follow for the local staff. So the visiting SIA manager was often seen as someone bringing potential largesse. At the other extreme, of course, where the local sales plan was unfavourable, he might be seen merely as the spoilsport who'd come to prevent local IBM from selling something deemed inappropriate to their local prospect.

Of all the countries an SIA manager might visit, the one that kept him, or her, guessing the most was Italy. Most countries had reasonably clear-cut procedures for working out whether or not to reward local salesmen providing international sales assistance. The Italian sales plan remained unfathomable to outsiders. However, for one SIA manager there was always a great temptation to visit his customer's Italian subsidiary, in the Po Valley.

In the first place the local Italian factory was next door to a truly magnificent cheese shop. The SIA manager could be guaranteed splendid isolation on the return flight from every Italian trip. The concentration of freshly-hewn parmesan and ripe gorgonzola could halt an airline steward at 50 paces.

Secondly, there was the IBM "canteen". Well, it wasn't really a canteen. The IBM branch office, responsible for the account in the Po

Valley, was based in the city of Parma – gastronomic Utopia. It was a small branch, and could not justify its own in-house canteen, or so it was claimed. The branch personnel had, therefore, successfully presented a case to their Italian management for using a local restaurant for this purpose, with, of course, a "modest" IBM subsidy. The local restaurant turned out to be one of Parma's best! Every lunchtime the indigenous IBM population was swollen about four-fold by visiting IBM'ers, customers and general hangers-on (like SIA managers). Indeed, talk of local IBM customer support was superfluous in this account. All the customers ever wanted were regular invitations to IBM seminars – in Parma!

It was not difficult to understand why the Italian systems manager at the Po Valley account used to object to attending his companies international systems meetings in the UK. How could a Coventry canteen compare with the fleshpots of Parma? His general misery was, however, lifted somewhat on one trip which happened to coincide with the annual customer versus IBM cricket match. Pietro, the Italian systems manager, was not fully familiar with the mysteries of cricket. Since the rules of this match dictated that all ten fielders must bowl two overs each, Pietro had to be given some urgent pre-match tuition.

The essentials of batting were quickly grasped by someone used to watching American baseball. Bowling was not so easy. In the end – for Pietro had served his country in the Italian army – the procedures required for throwing a grenade seemed most apt. It was disconcerting for the batsman, however, when the bowler, having released the ball in a gentle lob, threw himself to the ground with his arms covering his head. So disconcerted was the SIA manager, indeed, who otherwise fancied his cricketing prowess, that he was bowled first ball!

Thereafter the SIA manager, on every subsequent trip to Italy, had to view the offending ball, now proudly spotlighted in Pietro's office, while his staff were again reminded of his moment of glory.

Another Wrinkle – the TMO

Having for many years grappled with the refinements of the Sales Plan, and its natural extensions, IBM introduced yet another subtlety in the 70's.

This was the Territory Management Objective (TMO). The concept of the TMO began to emerge in the US in the early 70's, in response to two very lean years for the US sales force. Unbundling had not been well-received, PCM competition was severe and the US economy was not prospering. How to ensure that the sales force did not go collectively bankrupt? Eureka!

On introduction, the TMO was an almost metaphysical concept. Given that IBM had laid upon its sales organisation a bewildering set of numeric targets, here was something that set out to answer the question, "Is he/she doing a good job... in the circumstances?" What circumstances? Well, those like the US suffered in the early 70's, and where depleted commission payments based purely on numeric targets might lead to hardship.

The TMO system required several (usually about three or four per salesman) non-numeric objectives to be set. These objectives might be such things as "Ensure that the chief executive of your customer attends a Directors' Computer Concepts course." Or "Arrange for the IBM Director of Manufacturing to call on Mr. ABC of Company XYZ." These objectives would be rated as worth a certain percentage of salary.

The total TMO contribution was in the range 10-12 per cent of total salary "equivalent". The term "salary equivalent" meant expected earnings on attainment of 100 per cent of numeric targets. It was of further crucial importance that TMO achievements were to be paid "outside guarantee" – that is, IBM would pay TMO earnings even though the salesperson had not secured sufficient business to cover the guaranteed portion of total earnings. TMO's, therefore, offered a limited lifeline to the hard-pressed. The TMO was to be set at branch level, and its initial non-numeric nature implied a high degree of discretionary authority on the part of the "setters". It was quickly, therefore, and somewhat scurrilously, nicknamed the "brown pound" by an ever-attentive sales force.

Most agreed that the TMO principle was a good one. It was a way of directing the activities of the sales force, more subtle than the bludgeon of numeric targets. Alas, however, IBM quickly learned that anything not precisely defined soon attracted the concentrated probing of the argumentative. While few IBM salespersons were Doctors of Philosophy, their end-of-year pleadings for quota relief regularly rivalled the linguistic convulsions of Ludwig Wittgenstein. Of course, with numeric targets such pleadings might fall on deaf management ears, or be readily dismissed; but with non-numeric, interpretable, targets?

Inevitably, but gradually, the TMO system was tightened up. The name was changed, but then, "A rose by any other name...." The terms Territory Performance Compensation (TPC) and Territory Objective Compensation (TOC) spring to mind. The real change, more significantly, was the trend towards including those beloved numeric targets in a different guise. Phrases like "...must be measurable" and "...must be dateable", became regular features of the management guidelines for setting a TMO. The most insidious TMO of the lot, of course, became, "Must make all numeric targets"!

Plus ça change.

Driving the Marketplace

It will not have escaped the notice of the observant reader that so far little mention has been made of "Marketing".

In truth, IBM was never a strong "marketing" company – not in the classical sense of the word anyway. Whenever we use the word "marketing" in this book, we, like IBM, probably mean "selling'; that is, unless we specifically say otherwise. "Marketing" was seen as part of the salesman's job. He was well-educated, well-trained and well-paid, and was the boss of his territory. IBM support was usually of a tactical kind and aimed at specific sales situations. Strategic marketing, marketplace analysis and definition, creating awareness – these were neither well-funded nor well-resourced. Certainly there were departments called, "Product Marketing", "Product Management", "Industry Marketing", and so on, but their role appeared mainly incestuous and focused inwards, towards IBM, rather than outwards, towards the marketplace at large.

Indeed, even advertising, except for recruitment purposes, hardly featured at all in IBM's plans until well into the 70's.

This only began seriously to change when IBM entered the volume product marketplace, initially with the Personal Computer, in the 80's, where other channels were needed to sell these products. Then, for some while, it had to grapple with the very real problems caused by the rivalries between contending channels and IBM's own determined sales force. "Who owns this customer?", was a cry often heard around the corridors of IBM.

A measure of the culture gap between IBM and other companies more used to a classical marketing approach became evident when IBM began preparations for announcing its RISC System/6000 (RS/6000) range of products. The RS/6000 range, announced in 1990, was to be IBM's flagship in the Open Systems marketplace – a marketplace where IBM had neither a seriously contending product before, nor an adequate marketing organisation.

An urgent recruiting programme was put in place to bring on board the necessary skills. Those recruited, from such companies as Sun and Hewlett Packard, were like fish out of water in this new strange world of IBM where "selling" was the name of the game, and "marketing" was an unknown black art. Fortunately for IBM, most stayed to help build a proper "marketing" culture within which sales of RS/6000 might, and did, then flourish.

Had marketing been the established culture throughout the organisation, then the following story would have had a different ending.

"Products for industry"

An example of the need for a clear industry focus (automotive and aerospace in this case) arose in the development of a PC-based product for Electronic Parts Cataloguing. This is a complex and critical application, involving the management of text, graphics and image, with data roots in Product Engineering. Functionally, it is a major influence in achieving customer satisfaction in the consumer products Parts and Service business.

In the era before company cars, when you took personal responsibility for the repair and servicing of your own car, and before the days when you merely handed over the keys of your company car to the garage with a peremptory "Fix it", you may have observed the man behind the parts counter shuffling a microfiche in the x and y axes of a viewer. After standing in the Saturday morning queue for what seemed hours, he would tell you, "You need so and so part", disappear round the racks and shelves and eventually reappear to mutter, "Out of stock".

Or, when you returned the next week saying the part wouldn't fit, he would say, "Oh, that one's for the 1973 model, you need a "xxxx" ". Or "Oh, you need the flanged coupling widget as well. And, by the way, we're out of stock."

Well, that was what this application was about – a much better way!

The need for this new application package was growing with a number of empathetic customers like Renault, UNIPART, Leyland DAF, and others. In the USA, specialist system suppliers such as Bell and Howell, and ADP, were already leaders in the dealer marketplace. However, the IBM Chrysler team were resolute in securing a partnership development with their customer.

To address the European market, a development project named PIPPIN (after the project leader, Mr Bramley) was set up at the IBM Hursley laboratories in England.

The requirement was leading edge, and needed considerable joint working with selected customers on a partnership basis, but unfortunately, this was not reflected in the assignation of overall project responsibility. Control could only be placed with Development or Sales, since there was no true Marketing function.

In practice, control was placed with Development. Thus application specification, scope and architecture became somewhat distanced from the customer. Indeed, the branch offices' prime responsibility was seen as obtaining written agreement from customers to commit to buy application licences. It did not exactly encourage pilot customers to so commit when they were required to pay the full "product" price from the outset in order to meet IBM's onerous cost recovery regime.

The team was assembled. Work commenced. A good team spirit developed, and the manager (Bramley) did as much as anybody to market his future product across the key European automotive companies.

Giving the project to Development guaranteed a further barrier to customer acceptance. Development were bound to base the planned product on IBM's own (pet) OS/2 PC operating system, rather than the marketplace leader – "Windows", from Microsoft.

The project strength waxed and waned with the moons over a period of 18 months or so. Regrettably and inevitably, it became bloated and over-ran both target dates and budgets. The potential customers moved on or away, or, indeed, switched attention to more important financial problems caused by the motor industry recession at the end of the 80's.

Eventually, at an internal meeting held in Paris for the IBM account managers concerned, a European IBM director postulated that the project, which had already cost several millions of US$, would be cancelled unless a customer signed up immediately. Jose, the Renault Account Executive, a highly intelligent man of Portuguese origin, point-edly asked of this director, "Why do you announce over 200 new IBM products that I don't want, and try to cancel the one I do?"

IBM was not used to developing new marketplace products in such a way. Application projects were usually more incremental, with less exposure to the outside world at such an early stage, or with an existing installed customer (as a result of some local development). Most of all, of course, such projects tended to be orientated towards the arena that IBM knew best, computing technology.

With the wisdom of that well-known guarantee of success, hindsight, a pilot customer should have been selected for the product, with equi-table cost-sharing, his ideas formally injected into the project plan, and a phased development and implementation approach adopted.

Strike fast, make it lean and mean.

One would expect any company intent on driving its business never to lift its foot off the accelerator pedal. IBM did lift its foot, regularly, and it helps to explain why, in most IBM companies, and in particular in the UK, the graph describing progress towards the year's targets was invari-ably shaped like a banana – a gentle start, with a suicidally steep finish. Even the Management Control Plan which required the countries to deliver the business, month by month and quarter by quarter, had this same shape. It was rather like a Grand Prix driver lounging in the pits while his competitors began the race, joining them after about four laps, and then driving at increasingly hair-raising speed to finish ahead.

Why was this?

"The New Year doesn't start until...."

It was often said in the British Army, in those far-off days of the Cold War, that if the Russians were ever to attack the West they would do so at dawn on Christmas Day. Most of NATO's front line forces were then likely to be on leave, and those that weren't would probably be suffering from a Class 1 hangover. Russian tanks crews would be dining in Dunkirk within hours.

By the same token, if a competitor were planning to launch a blitzkrieg on a prestigious IBM account the time to do it would be sometime in early January. The reasons were simple.

First, the end-of-year scramble to make targets, to clean out any worthwhile business from accounts due to be handed over to another at year-end, to fit in the appropriate year-end customer and account team lunches... all these things, and more, led to sales force debilitation from which recovery was prolonged well into the New Year.

Secondly, nobody in an IBM branch office could ever believe that the New Year had truly arrived until the branch had held its "Kick-off" meeting. This might take place anytime during the last few weeks of January, or early February. It was one yardstick by which senior management judged to what degree a branch manager was "on the ball". Senior management always attended a branch Kick-off meeting, as if to assess the branch manager's ability to fire up his jaded army.

Of course, the really smart branch manager would get his retaliation in first. He would announce his Kick-off meeting to be held well before the new year's targets had been set. This served at least two purposes – he would not need to devote the whole meeting to explaining how he was going to make the new targets (nobody would believe the explanation anyway), and any criticisms from senior management could be partially deflected by a "plant" in the audience asking why it took senior management so long to set the new targets. It was even once suggested that there was no reason in principle why a Kick-off meeting couldn't take place in the previous December. The answer all really came down to psychology – one's state of mind in December was that of the soldier awaiting demobilisation at year end, whereas in January it would be that of the fresh new recruit about to restart basic training. Mix the two and you'd have total confusion.

The third reason for the slow start to the new year was one that increasingly, and irritatingly, affected all salesmen, and in particular those account managers covering the very large accounts. This was the chore of the account planning session. Over the years this exercise in imposed bureaucracy grew like Topsy. For the large accounts it was embroidered with the grandiose name, the "MAPS" (Major Account Planning System) review. The feeling was that IBM had aimed the adjective "major" at the wrong noun. It would have better deserved the acronym "AMPS", where "major" qualified "planning".

MAPS was a regional level review for the large accounts – that is, the level above the branch. So it was quite a serious business. The degree of information required about the customer almost descended to the detail of the office boy's domestic habits. "Well, we're only asking for information you ought to have at your fingertips anyway," said the regional account planning gurus. "Yes," came the irritated reply, "And I gave it all to you last year, so why haven't you keyed it into a database, whence you can regurgitate it however you like, and I'll tell you what's changed?" "We're working on it," was the usual reply, accompanied by the equally usual whinge, "I've just taken over the job, and my predecessor has left no guidelines for me."

The theory behind MAPS was that if you took the top 100 or so large accounts, analysed them every which way, you could get a very good idea of likely application requirements, industry trends, computing needs, and competitive threats. To achieve this, therefore, IBM produced a vast set of forms requiring details of each large customer's industry, size, turnover, organisation, personalities, locations, workforce – and on and on. Not least, of course, was the information about all computer, and related, equipment installed, whether IBM or competitive. From all this the account manager would derive his "account plan", within which he would reveal, among other things, his plans to achieve his targets for the coming year, and beyond.

He was also required to identify the potential problems and shortcomings that could get in the way. But here you had to be careful. If you described a problem, it would always provoke the executive question, "How are you going to overcome it?" The really brave would reply, "Well, I've told you as much as I know. What do you suggest?" Often, however, you were mindful of Margaret Thatcher's words about one of her Ministers: "I like him," she said, "because he brings me solutions, rather than problems." On that basis, it was better not to mention the problems in the first place.

One area which became the focus for increasing attention was that of the potential for workstation growth. Every employee in an organisation, with few exceptions, was seen as a potential workstation user, whether a clerk in an office, a shop-floor worker, or a chief executive. All used information, and all would gain from using computers. Neither did it matter whether their needs were met from stand-alone systems or terminals attached to mainframes. IBM could supply the lot.

This analytical approach to defining a total potential marketplace became known as "user segmentation", and it could produce alarming results. In a notional organisation of 100,000 employees, where, say, 75 per cent needed some sort of access to information, it appeared that the company should spend the equivalent of its total annual sales revenue on computing equipment! Nice work if you can get it. No doubt the aggregation of all this input from its account managers caused IBM to swoon with opportunity fever.

It is not difficult to understand why, having completed and reviewed all this material, your average IBM large account manager was relieved to be able to go out and start the real year, talking to real customers.

Conclusion

We have talked about the processes, mechanisms and influences that were visible to the front line of the IBM field force, and through which IBM sought to direct its business. There were many other critical forces at work, in Research, in Development and in Manufacturing, aimed at ensuring that the right products reached the marketplace at the right time. But in the end everything hinged around the abilities of those in IBM who faced the customer to deliver the goods.

Those people worked within the framework of IBM's overall personnel policies. Many of these policies are explored in some detail in the next chapter. Suffice to say here that these policies provided the bedrock for IBM's historic cohesion and homogeneity, and allowed the introduction of sometimes disruptive changes to the ways the sales force was compensated.

For many years IBM managed the balancing act of driving the business forward across a bewilderingly large product set, responding to challenges with tactical variations in its pre-eminent tuning mechanism, the sales compensation systems. As each niche-market challenge emerged, IBM responded with a bonus here, an incentive there, a new payment plan, another recognition event. But the sales plans of yester-year, often fondly remembered, were the key mechanisms used by a cohesive and homogeneous IBM to increase its revenues. Whether they represent the core driving forces today is another matter.

2. Managing IBM People

Over many decades, IBM gained a reputation in commerce and industry world-wide as the company that had created and implemented progressive personnel management systems, which were admired, studied, written about and even copied.

There is little doubt that IBM invested much time and money in its people. It paid great attention to recruiting the highest calibre personnel and then provided them with extensive and high-class training – very necessary when the recruitment of one new IBM'er was estimated to cost the company £1 million during his career.

T.J. Watson said: "For any organisation to survive and achieve success, there must be a sound set of principles on which it bases all of its policies and actions. But more important is its faithful adherence to those principles."

For the IBM'er, this meant:

- Respect for the individual
- Single status
- Promotion from within
- Staff mobility
- Pursuit of excellence
- Competitive remuneration packages

As an IBM employee for over 30 years, and as a manager for a large proportion of that time, it was very easy to take these for granted and assume they were the norm. This was certainly not so, and any visit to other organisations soon highlighted the very different approach that IBM had both evolved and continued to develop.

The most fundamental aspect of IBM's personnel policies was the relationship between the employee and the manager. To be an IBM manager was much more than just to undertake the management responsibilities concerning business, customer relations, and processes. The personnel systems required him to take prime responsibility for the career management, development, and direct assessment of each individual's performance.

There were many personnel systems that supported the company's basic beliefs, but none more important than Appraisal and Counselling (A&C).

Appraisal and Counselling

It was the responsibility of the manager and his employee jointly to discuss, develop and agree the prime objectives that would enable the latter to carry out his responsibilities for the position, and to develop and progress his career in IBM.

The employee, the manager and the manager's manager all agreed objectives and plans that were formally documented and signed. Objective setting was always a difficult process, since the need for each objective to be "measurable" was paramount if future assessment was to be non-contentious. A simple objective to a salesman, "Achieve your annual quota", was unequivocal. For a technical support employee, "Develop full technical knowledge of product x", was a recipe for subjectiveness and almost certain disagreement. Well thought out and carefully worded objectives were essential to the success of the A&C programme.

From the point of agreeing objectives to the time of a formal assessment was a 12-month cycle. Yet it is worth noting that, in the dynamic environment of IBM, the good manager would regularly evaluate the appropriateness of re-setting objectives to take account of changed circumstances.

At the end of the 12-month period, the manager and employee would formally meet to discuss the appraisal of the performance against the set objectives. These assessments were assigned a numerical rating between 1 to 5:

1. results achieved far exceed basic requirements in nearly all respects
2. results achieved exceed basic requirements in most respects
3. results achieved exceed basic requirements in some respects
4. results achieved meet basic requirements
5. results achieved do not meet basic requirements

Now, you will have spotted that an averagely performing employee is a "4", not the median number "3". However, an employee performing adequately would be dissatisfied with a "4" rating. Traditionally, "3" was the easy option for the manager; "3"s were OK; "2"s were definitely wanted by the employee, since this rating provided both recognition and the likelihood of a good salary increase at the next review.

The "1"s were for the "superstar" performing at a level that was outstanding in the extreme. There was a resistance to using this rating except in very rare and unusual circumstances. Indeed some managers believed that if it was used why had the employee not already been promoted!

So, you are asking, "What about a 5?". To rate anyone at this level invoked the "Unsatisfactory Performance Report" (UPR) – an unpleasant and bureaucratic process. None the less, this was by no means the end of a career in the company. If someone possessed the ability but was not performing as such, new objectives aimed at producing a "4" performance would be established. An A&C was then conducted approximately every three months to monitor progress. But obviously if he didn't improve, the manager was faced with a decision. Either the individual would be given a further opportunity in the assigned position, or a more suitable role in the company should be found.

More times than not, a satisfactory resolution was achieved, though on occasions a complete parting of the ways did occur. When this happened, it was essential that the manager, the manager's manager and the employee had jointly explored every option. One thing was for sure, there was no lack of paper-work to support the decision. Note this situation and consider the range of "grievance channels" open to the employee (described a little further on), and recognise that the manager had to be right!

A feature, good or bad (depending on your rating!) was that an A&C document and its stated ratings were reviewed beforehand by an employee's manager and his manager's manager. In effect this meant that there could be no change to an assessment during or following the actual A&C meeting – your manager was not going to go back to his boss and admit they had both got it wrong!.

Although objectives should have been set and agreed at the beginning of the annual cycle, sometimes, due to the day-to-day pressures in the field, the employee only got to know of his objectives a few days prior to the review when he was given his A&C form – again, good or bad, depending on what was being said. As with all systems and processes, their success or failure depended upon the manager's commitment and conviction, married with the faith and trust of the employee in the equity of the procedures.

Some managers were very committed to the A&C process, and saw it as a valuable tool. Others would fail to set objectives that were measurable, and would consequently face the problems of subjectivity and opinion.

In a dynamic and ever-changing environment, objectives set at one point in time would be out of date before the A&C review came around. Hence, appraising was often done "on the fly" and the counselling interview could be a little ad-lib. This was not a problem if the next paragraph was a fair representation of the man-manager relationship.

The good manager would conduct a constant appraising process throughout the year with his employee so that, come the formal interview, there were no surprises, no arguments or contention. As one manager put it: "If you cannot discuss anything with me after eight pints, then it is not worth discussing" – an interesting point of view, but at least staff knew where they stood. Perhaps this was the exception rather than the rule.

The rating systems challenged managers to be consistent and strong in their evaluation of people, some were stronger than others. Give a "2" rating, and people were happy and satisfied. To give a "4" would require the manager to be certain that his evaluation was accurate and based on real facts – most important that the employee appreciated and accepted that "4" was OK!

At this point a story to illustrate how the system was used effectively....

"Under good management"

His performance in his first two years as a branch first line manager had been outstanding, transforming his department into an efficient and productive unit. His business numbers were also outstanding, customer relations were superb, and morale amongst his team was higher than ever before. In those two years, his branch manager had been delighted with his contribution, duly recognised this, and rewarded him with a "2" rating and the deserved salary increases. He was a prime candidate for promotion.

Into year 3 with new objectives, he had become less energetic, less actively involved with the day-to-day business. A degree of complacency had set in, with the earlier challenges seemingly overcome, and the job much easier.

The branch manager arranged the unusual step of a mid-year A&C. During this interview, he was advised how his performance was now perceived. He was still meeting the basic requirements of the job, but he now knew that to rest on his laurels was not in keeping with any promotion aspirations. The interview had been frank and positive; he had not been cajoled nor criticised. He now had, however, a new rating – a "4", the first in his career.

Six months later at his normal A&C, he was rated a "2" again, and promoted three months later. That branch manager, through his forthright, positive and constructive approach, making the right use of IBM's processes, had saved, and made, a career.

A natural consequence of using "2's and "3's liberally (and the pressure was to do just that) was that A&C ratings skewed towards the top of the bands, causing problems in turn with salary management.

Given that salary budgets were predicated on an expected distribution of ratings, then if everyone was rated "2" the budgets would not be large enough.

Edicts were occasionally issued to managers to remind them of the company's expectation of ratings distribution. Imagine having to tell an employee with a previous "2" rating, that he had done as good a job as last year, but now he was a "3".

If some of the above observations seem tinged with a touch of cynicism, then it is inevitable that with all systems an element of "imaginative usage" prevails.

Did the system really work?

There is no doubt in our minds that it did, and we assume, still does. To have operated in IBM without the A&C programme would have denied the validity of a "Meritocracy". People management would have been a free-for-all. Inconsistency would have been rife. Like so many aspects of the IBM "way of doing things", there was not only a belief in a system but above all else a determination to make it work and make it work well. It was never perfect but it was better than no process at all.

To miss due dates for conducting A&C's on time was a sin. It was, in the eyes of the IBM management hierarchy, an abuse of the right of the individual. As with all IBM systems there were controls in place that monitored A&C performance at all levels of the company. Any illusion that IBM did not take this programme seriously would have been comprehensively shattered by attending the "Management Committee" (the MC – a regular meeting of IBM senior managers chaired by the Chief Executive).

To hear at this level in the company, the names of your peers being cited on the list of managers overdue in completing A&C's, was salutary indeed. They were soon to hear from on high that their performances were both unacceptable and were under close scrutiny. A black mark indeed!

The over-riding aspect of such a system was that at every level of management and employee it forced everyone to think about the individual, whether it was yourself looking to plan and advance your own development and career, or a manager having to do similarly with a variety of different people with varying talents and abilities. Recognise too that all of this activity was reviewed at the next management level – checks and balances abounded in IBM.

While the A&C programme was the formal representation of the employee/manager relationship, the fundamental basis of IBM's people management record was the day-to-day constant interaction between those people. It was in this area that IBM was unique for so long. An environment where a single status prevailed, no "Mr" or "Sir".... Mr. Edwin Nixon (now Sir Edwin) was Eddie to everyone. To address Mr. Frank Carey, at the time the Chief Executive of IBM Corporation, as other than Frank would have been strange. To some this would have appeared to be disrespectful, but to an IBM'er this was the demonstration of the accessibility of all members of the IBM team.

Communications Channels.

There were other programmes that enabled the employee to air his views or frustrations other than directly with his manager. The objective of such programmes was to enable argument and dialogue throughout all levels of the company, to effect interchanges of views and opinions both up and down the hierarchical chain, and thus cause resolutions of issues standing in the way of progress.

Speak-Up

Any employee could write to the Speak-Up co-ordinator expressing his opinion about any aspect of IBM. The co-ordinator was responsible for maintaining total confidentiality and obtaining an answer for the writer compiled by the IBM director responsible for the subject point. Selected topical "speak-ups" were published in the monthly internal newspaper, *IBM UK News*.

Most Speak-Ups were handled in the UK, but if a sufficient (14) number of IBM'ers submitted a "multiple" speak-up, then this subject would have to be addressed by US Corporate management. Needless to say, UK management did not welcome "multiple" speak-ups.

An example concerned moving offices from Birmingham to Warwick, when it was planned that a sizeable section of the sales force would be located in a sub-office a mile away from all the usual office support facilities. A "multiple" speak-up caused this plan to be overthrown.

Speak-ups covered a multitude of topics from "solid" ones like pay policy, company cars, communications between management and employees, complaints procedures, to others rather more trivial such as car parking, the cost of vending machine coffee or, many years ago, the suitability of IBM females wearing hot pants in the summer!

The programme undoubtedly served its purpose as a barometer of the latest thinking, whether discontented or progressive. It did, however, suffer from a sometimes rather cynical employee view that "They never answer the question".

Open Door

(This was sometimes called the "Open Window" – rumour had it that using this procedure would make you a marked man.)

An employee who found himself in an unresolvable dispute with his manager and his manager's manager could request an interview with the next level of management above – and so on up through regional and country management, eventually to European management and even the Chief Executive Officer at IBM's Headquarters in Armonk. Its power was significant.

Clearly the objective of both "speak-up" and "open door" was to see issues resolved at the lowest level. Here is a story that proves it was used and did work. That this situation had arisen does not speak well of the manager, but we suspect that most of you will have met a similar set of circumstances.

"Under new management"

The young programmer was a very good programmer. He knew it, and so did his peers. He was also a "character", laconic, quiet, a little scruffy, with an unkempt beard. Yet he delivered, and he delivered quality work.

His manager made it clear that he did not like him, nor did he rate him. Following the due processes of A&C's, his salary lost ground to his peers. Despite protestations to his manager and his manager's manager, his position worsened. Yet still he continued to deliver quality output.

Another altercation with his manager resulted in his being asked to resign. He used the "open door" and met with the District Manager. Months later, his new manager rated him "2", and he received a special contribution award for his outstanding work.

Round Table

This was where a group of IBM'ers met a visiting senior manager, thus providing another opportunity for people to air their views directly rather than (filtered) through layers of management.

These meetings were often held as a luncheon, making the overtures relaxed, establishing a relatively calm environment. The protagonist who had worked himself into an emotional state and was ready to "nail the senior man", was usually more equitably disposed when his moment came. IBM senior managers were not naive. They were well briefed and adept at taking the heat out of a situation with a few well chosen and timely observations, thus pre-empting any potential onslaught.

Leapfrogs

This was a more intimate process designed to give an employee the opportunity of meeting privately with their manager's manager. To anyone not familiar with this type of communication channel, it could be construed as an opportunity to "shop your manager". Knowing such interviews would take place was all the more incentive to ensure effective people management was happening.

These sessions were not generally used for whinging and griping, but more as the opportunity to impress senior management. It was a good chance to do this and be talked about afterwards – most good IBM managers had amazing powers of memory and recall.

And finally to the Big Daddy of all the feedback systems – the Opinion Survey.

The Opinion Survey

To describe the opinion survey in all its detail would take pages. Simply imagine yourself in a situation where you can confidentially express your real feelings about the company, your manager, your manager's manager, the country management, your salary, your performance rating – virtually all aspects of the company.

Central to the opinion survey was a set of questions designed to measure the "Morale Index" – a figure which all country management feared. This was the one definitive statistic that was all-important to Corporate.

Imagine also that, as a manager, your reportees were about to judge you and report their feelings, and more, that all the results of the survey would be reported upstairs.

At the highest level, the company would reveal its "Morale Index" performance and highlight those areas in which the most criticism had been voiced. At a lower cut, a first line manager would see exactly what his troops thought of him! A daunting experience.

Following the publication of the results came an inordinate investment of management time to develop "action plans", designed to right all the ills identified – plans which thereafter would be monitored and measured for their effectiveness in correcting out-of-line situations.

Did all these processes and procedures work?

Yes they did. They were not perfect, few systems are. They were (and still are) institutions in the life of IBM. Those involved knew they could not be ignored, they were pervasive, a threat maybe, certainly a constant aide memoir. Certainly, the IBM manager had to become a good manager of people, and equally, the people felt they could influence the company.

How much did an average IBM'er value this culture, this "respect for the individual'? Consider the issue of "strength in numbers"....

Trades Unions

The year 1977 was very significant for IBM UK. It was not so much what did happen as what didn't.

A trade union decided to launch a campaign at the company with the intention of establishing membership as a negotiating obligation in this stronghold of non-unionisation. Those of us who were with the company at this time will vividly recall the strong efforts made by management to present the IBM case. There was no doubt that IBM UK and its parents did not want a change, and made every honest effort to inform the 12,000 UK employees as such..

The union primarily involved, ASTMS (Association of Scientific Technical & Managerial Staffs), made some radical mistakes in their campaign:

1. They focused on the Scottish plant, presumably as if it were a typical British factory where in that era an "us and them" culture prevailed between worker and manager. They did not appreciate that there were no cultural differences between an IBM plant and an IBM administrative office.
2. Further, they failed to understand the IBM culture where the strongest dialogue was between an employee and his manager.
3. They did not appreciate that working conditions and the total remuneration package were good by any yardstick.
4. They ignored the fact that there had been no redundancies, strikes, or go-slows in the 25 years of IBM in the United Kingdom

For two months, IBM management, under the chairmanship of Eddie Nixon, were firmly energetic in their "campaign", yet straight in their representations.

The outcome: a resounding "No" to unionisation – 95 per cent said they did not want a union to negotiate employment pay and conditions. Had the answer been otherwise, no doubt IBM UK would not have enjoyed the next successful 10 years' revenues and profits. Likely, many true IBM'ers would have (gradually) left the company. Some senior management may have experienced an "early bath", being transferred out or sideways.

From an employee (do not forget IBM managers are also employees) perspective this was a short yet very interesting "exercise". No doubt from a management point of view, there were many sleepless nights.

Underneath all of the intensity and focus of this period, there is equally no doubt what carried the day for IBM: the loyalty and conviction for a system and culture, which although not perfect, was considered much better than any untried alternative proposal, especially one involving a third party.

Power to the People.

Why Did Most Stay and Only a Few Leave, Until....

Attending a typical IBM management meeting in the 60's or 70's, you were guaranteed a presentation from Personnel.

At some point in this presentation, our personnel representative would proudly announce that the "attrition rate" for the previous twelve months was yet again below 1 per cent.

"Attrition rate" was an important measurement in IBM. With 12000 UK employees, say, then only 120 employees leaving the company in a year was regaled as cast-iron proof that the principles of the IBM employment practices were vindicated in full.

A job for life, constant training, career development programmes emanating from the rigours of the A&C process, annual (even six monthly) salary increases, regular promotion opportunities in a business that was expanding at an almost uncontrollable rate, led to a legendary phrase – "the golden hand-cuffs".

Imagine being asked the question, "What do you do for a living" and that your response was simply, "I work for IBM". So many people in the 60's and 70's would have given their "eye teeth" to have IBM on their curriculum vitae.

This was the time when IBM was admired, respected, even feared in the data processing industry. Competition, even some customers, viewed IBM as the "American giant", that expensive alternative, that confident purveyor of computers and systems. Yet those who "belonged" were highly satisfied and proud to be fully paid-up members of this exclusive club, while the non-members harboured a wish to join.

If there were some losses of IBM people in those early decades, the reasons were relatively simplistic. The few who were never going to make the grade, the odd head-hunted and a few free spirits. Attrition, was so low that every departure was seemingly a matter of great importance, involving much paper-work, many levels of "exit interview" . Every departure summoned a systematic "post-mortem".

It is well worth noting at this point that IBM had a strict policy that was nigh on sacrosanct. If any employee left the company then the "portcullis", once lowered, could never be raised. There was no re-entry process. To leave IBM was the ultimate "divorce".

Many tried to "resurrect" their IBM "membership", realising that they had made a mistake of monumental proportions, but the system was unforgiving. Good-bye meant Good-bye! Reconciliation was not available.

Some "second marriages" did occur, though they were few and far between. To re-enter was a privilege given to few special cases, and it does not require an Einstein to work out who had the greatest motivation to effect such re-marriages.

Move forward to the mid-70's and early 80's and as the business changed and IBM began to be involved more and more in "business partnerships" – then came the time of increased "courting" of top-notch IBM employees. Were the offers good? You bet they were.

So some did succumb to the temptations and what was the score? We know some who never regretted their gamble and who hit the jackpot. More power to their elbows! (Of course, there were as many who would admit that the gamble did not come up to expectations.) This group are in many ways still to be admired. They had the courage to forgo the "golden handcuffs", even if their adventure was not as successful as they had hoped.

Let us step back a moment and remember our "Personnel representative" proudly regaling that over the past twelve months in IBM the average age of the employee population was very nearly one year older. Stability personified. They were all staying with the corporation. Proof indeed that the "Watsonian" principles were truly working.

The average age of the IBM population was 29, say. Five years later it was 34, and so it continued. With a slowing down in company expansion and the accompanying reduction in recruitment to a mere dribble, the middle-aged spread grew and grew.

The cost of the ageing population became a greater and greater burden upon IBM. Something had to give, and this was a world-wide phenomenon, not singly isolated within the UK. Aged 40, say, with 20 years of pension contributions, a reasonably senior level in the IBM salary structure, a company car and health plan benefits, these were a satisfactory recipe for the continuation of these IBM'ers' desire to see their "jobs for life" through to final fruition.

It took some special offer to entice these people away. Many were old in the tooth, they may have become dissatisfied with their IBM of the late 80's compared to their IBM of the 60's and 70's. They whinged and despaired that their IBM was missing market opportunity, or that it had become over-burdened with bureaucracy. For whatever their discontent may have been, there was nevertheless an inherent security. The Watson principles had ensured that for them. Going through the motions when the very opposite was needed to keep the IBM Company as a major player – somewhat of an impasse.

Then came the first inklings of the revolution, the unthinkable – "down-sizing'!

What occurred thereafter is known not only to those middle-aged IBM'ers but also to many of our readers in other industries.

The early work-force was youthful, energetic, hard-working, highly motivated, top-notch – the very best that could have been recruited and trained to achieve impossible goals in what was the fastest moving industry at that time. IBM was the market-leader; it set the standards in products, services, customer support and respect for its most valuable commodity, its people.

General Management

To describe the processes that were available to the IBM manager is only a small part of what "Managing IBM People" was all about. The style of the day-to-day management of employees, and managers managing managers, was unique to every single relationship. As in any organisation, there were autocratic managers and democratic managers. There were empathetic managers and there were uncaring managers – as many variations as there are folk, after all they were only folk themselves.

This chapter, "Managing IBM People" has stressed the unique relationship between manager and employee that was so essential to all the processes having value. It is vital to remember that we are talking about people and we know that people are all unique characters. Give any group of people the same set of circumstances and you can guarantee they will react differently.

We hope you will enjoy this next story and reflect how you or people you know might have reacted in each of the "dilemmas" that the different characters faced.

"The test"

An accepted fact of life as an IBM salesman was that however aggressive and seemingly impossible your sales quota was in a given year, there was a certainty that like death and taxes the following year's quota would be even more "unachievable". That quotas at the individual and collective level were consistently achieved – nay, over-achieved – year in and year out spoke volumes for the determination and innovation of all branch members.

The best branch offices were a *team* – with a common goal, a collective understanding of the challenge, whether they were Sales, Systems Engineering, Customer Engineering or Administration, each had a fundamental role to play. Sat above all this resource was the Branch Manager, the conductor of this talented orchestra.

One branch manager had a unique style, apparently aloof on occasions, even disinterested (except in his record collection and the latest hi-fi systems). He nevertheless had a track record of never failing to make a branch quota. He never failed to qualify for the "Club" throughout his years in IBM either. Style, presence, confidence, they oozed from him, and a customer call with him was an education in itself. The master of building business relations at any level.

Yet behind the outward charm was a steely determination, a no-nonsense attitude to bureaucracy and indiscipline, a man of single-mindedness. A maverick in the eyes of many. "If you make your quota for the year in three months, I do not mind if you play golf for the rest of the year", was one throw-away line; but beneath that you knew that the real expectation was that 100 per cent, 200 per cent or more was what was really required.

In a particularly challenging year, when the quota was extraordinary, the competition had the edge, the sales resource had more youth than experience, more energy than guile, this branch manager did a fine job in supporting his "troops" through these difficult times.

Five young salesmen in the branch had been struggling to make inroads in the first half of the year, but with support, guidance and cajoling from the branch manager and his more experienced salesmen, each had built a number of promising and closeable situations. The camaraderie was special, and on a hot summer day, with a deal of whooping, hollering and contract waving, the first of what was to become a string of successes was registered on the score-board.

Having no branch manager to share the elation (he was out of the office), the jubilant five retired to the local hostelry to sit in the sun, quaff copious amounts of the local brew, and to debate the lessons learned on how to win.

Came the time to return to the office enough sense prevailed to conclude that an appearance in the branch "under the influence" was not a smart thing to do. So the test match down the road beckoned. "All making afternoon calls" seemed a sensible excuse. Behind the bowler's arm, regular liquid supplies and a happy day concluded at stumps.

The following day dawned, vague recollections of a good time being had by all and symptoms to support the view.

The first of the five entered the branch manager's office at his stern behest. On emerging, with a curious look on his face, he advised the remaining four, "Simply tell the truth, you will come to understand why".

One by one they trooped in, each exited with that look.

The fifth entered, followed the party line in admitting his where-abouts that previous afternoon. His experience was the same as the rest, a withering look of admonishment. Profuse apologies and then the obvious enquiry, "How did you find out?"

"I saw you on TV as the camera panned the crowd behind the bowler's arm. The clock was showing 3.30pm."

"This was on the highlights programme last night, was it?".

"No," came the reply, "I was in Dixons at the time buying a new amplifier. Am I invited to lunch today?"

Suffice it to say, the branch and all its salesmen made their annual quotas and all those five young men went on to bigger and better things over the years. More than one became rather good managers; maybe their "tutor" was quite good too.

IBM placed a lot of importance on recruiting the best possible people. While you may have a "proven" system that produces good overall results, it would be wrong to leave an impression that the process was 100 per cent foolproof. Not a bit of it. There were some people taken on who did not realise the necessary performance levels they were recruited to achieve. As an analogy, ask any football manager if all of his £1 million transfers have been outstanding successes, or has he lost large amounts of money when he sold them on for a much reduced market value.

The next story illustrates how the interviewing process sometimes produced the right results but in different ways.

"Will the real person step forward...."

"Get the people right and the business will look after itself." During the late 60's and 70's, IBM grew at an extraordinary rate from a work-force point of view, and annually had an opportunity to put this motto into practice.

A major source of its new people would come from the universities, and like many major UK companies it would make extensive efforts via the "milk round" and other processes to trawl the student population and identify the very best people.

Much of this work was done by central staff groups and experienced managers from the branch offices. Following initial interviews and aptitude tests, the branches were provided with lists of candidates from which the "lucky" few would be chosen.

Candidates had three interviews with the managers in a given branch, and each manager would record his evaluations on a standard interview check list. All managers would then meet and debate their findings. The system worked well, even to the extent that if an individual branch found more suitable candidates than it had places for, these people would still have the opportunity to meet with other managers at different locations. Never let the good ones go!

Not every interviewing session proved successful and there were many occasions when the specific requirements of the branch were not met by the candidates on offer and the search for people had to be spread. Or was it that in such intensive and time-pressured circumstances the occasional "right" person was not identified. Were the managers not alert, was the candidate unable to impress himself upon his interviewers?

One young man had been interviewed throughout the day. Of the three places available, two were filled, and he and another candidate were vying for the last place. During the latter part of the afternoon he had appeared agitated and uneasy. The management team were undecided and wanted time to get their thoughts straight. Both candidates were advised that they would be contacted again.

It was normal practice that travelling expenses of the candidates were reimbursed by IBM. In administering the settlement, it became obvious that one of the candidates had travelled to the branch office by train, and due to the length of day had missed his last train home.

By pure coincidence, he lived only minutes from the home of one of the interviewing managers. During the one-hour journey home the manager and the candidate had a conversation, embracing many more areas than could ever have been covered during the interviewing. Any doubts were dispelled and the true potentials of the young man were uncovered.

In due course, he began his career with the interviewing branch. The other candidate was offered a job in another branch.

Two decades on, both young men had built outstanding careers with the company in two entirely different career roles.

IBM also paid a lot of attention to intensive and regular education of all its employees. Managers were not excluded from this constant barrage of new teaching, but it did not always go to plan....

"Best know your subject"

A group of IBM managers had had a curious two days on a course directed at teaching them specialised skills in making presentations and the art of public-speaking. The general atmosphere throughout the proceedings was one of disinterest, with the usual attitude that it was all a waste of time. Better to be back at the branch looking after business.

Now, most IBM managers, particularly the marketing sorts, had a way with words anyway. They had not got to be where they were by being shy and introverted. If they wanted to get a message across, few had little difficulty in emulating Billy Graham.

And so to the final exercise, the culmination of two days of "intensive training", how to think on your feet and deliver a spell-binding, five-minute presentation.

One-by-one the managers trooped to the front of the class, selected an envelope containing the subject they had to address, had 30 seconds to formulate the words and then full-flow for five minutes.

They were a class act, word perfect, humorous, forceful and penetrative. Was it the training, or had they come to the course with the ability anyway? Each superb delivery was put across with a venom aimed at proving they were totally competent without two days of classroom meandering.

You had to admire their professionalism, since the subject matters were outrageous, and the inventiveness of each speaker was a joy to behold. You could almost measure the growing sense of pride that pervaded that room. The instructor from the outside organisation was clearly in awe of these masters of the spoken word, though it was clear he was unsure whether his course had worked a miracle on this group or whether they were simply the possessors of a special talent.

It was nearly finished, one final delivery left. The IBM man strode purposefully to the front, collected the last envelope, smiled confidently at his peers with a look on his face that said openly, "Watch out chaps, I am really going to give this some welly."

He opened the envelope, took out the slip of paper and read the following:

"The local Vicar is holding a meeting at the Church Hall where he is addressing a group of young men aged between 18 and 25. He is discussing with them the morals of correct relations with the young ladies of the parish, and the principles of what makes a good marriage and family life. You have five minutes to sell these young men on the benefits of having a vasectomy!"

He was a little taken aback; his colleagues sensed he had a problem, but were confident that once he started he would be OK. They of course knew not of his subject.

His 30 seconds had long since passed, his face was flushed, but he began: "Gentlemen, it is a privilege to have the opportunity to speak to you this evening. I am sure that you found the vicar's words as interesting as I did. What I would like to address this evening is the subject of vasectomy." His audience picked up on the subject matter and intently anticipated his speech – he will be good at this one they knew.

All eyes and ears were at the ready. "I, er, You, er We, er, well I would like to begin by.... Sh** what would I like to begin with?" he said.

There was an embarrassed silence for him as he re-grouped. "Give me a minute to get my thoughts together." Words of encouragement were proffered to him; the "team" was with him. "What is the full scenario?" someone asked. As he read out the brief, suggestions flowed in abundance. He tried desperately to absorb the leads he was being given, but his mind was in turmoil. He just could not think of a benefit; he could not compose a theme to his presentation.

He gathered himself together, faced the audience, took a deep breath... his colleagues were pleased for him, they knew he would succeed. "Regarding the benefits of a vasectomy, I would like to start by saying... oh, bugger this for a game of soldiers, can I sell you a computer instead?"

He walked back to his seat to a great ovation from his colleagues. Later, though, it cost him dear for drinks, and by the time he left, with all the advice and guidance he had received, he would have had little difficulty in selling a vasectomy to a eunuch!

In the same vein, perhaps, the story goes of a course being held during which each participant was required to speak for 10 minutes on a subject of their own choice. Allegedly, a female systems engineer spoke for 10 seconds on "premature ejaculation".

There were two types of training in IBM and the chapter "The IBM Salesman – Fact and Fable" covers these in depth. There was the formal classroom training and the "on the job" training. The latter was often a euphemism for being "thrown in at the deep end'!

Stories about the unexpected outcomes of the sink or swim method are legion and legend. Let us take the time machine back to circa 1962.

"A matter of interpretation"

The young university graduate arrived in the Service Bureau at 9.00 am one Monday morning – the first day in what he hoped would be a long and successful career in IBM. Wanting to make an early impression on his new colleagues and manager, he eagerly awaited his first task.

The Service Bureau Machine Room Supervisor gave him a brief introduction to the "mysteries" of the holes in a punched card, explaining how different combinations of holes represented the characters in the alphabet. He then showed him a rectangular metal panel on the front of which were a knotted tangle of differently coloured plastic-coated wires. The wires had torpedo-shaped metal ends which passed through holes in the bakelite centre of the panel then protruding at the back of the panel.

The Supervisor explained further: "The wired panel is a programmed set of instructions which the machine follows". This specific panel was for a machine known as an IBM interpreter, Model No 557. This machine read the punched cards and then printed selected data along the top of the card.

Opening a slot on the side of the machine, our young man was shown how to slide the panel into position. When closed, the wire-ends on the back of the panel would fit snugly against the internal connectors in the interpreter. The panel was removed and put to one side.

Finally, the supervisor showed our new recruit where to place the punched cards into the reader hopper, and where they would exit the machine into the stacker. Pointing to two trolleys, groaning under the weight of 50,000 punched cards, he explained that these cards were to be "interpreted". Given the speed of the machine, this represented about 2 1/2 days work.

So, with the interpreter available, panel to hand, and 50,000 cards to process, our intrepid young graduate set about his task with gusto – he was clearly enjoying his first foray into the world of data processing and IBM.

Mid-morning on day 3 of his employ with IBM, he wheeled his trolleys of cards to the supervisor and proudly announced that he had completed his task. What would be his next adventure in the bureau?

A "Well done", with a congratulatory pat on the back from the supervisor, was forthcoming. The supervisor picked up a random batch of cards. He checked the printing quality. They were blank! Others were sampled; they too were blank!

The graduate was panicking. "Which way did you put the cards in?" barked the supervisor. "Face down, 9 edge leading, as you told me," came the reply.

The supervisor strode purposefully to the interpreter. He opened the machine to check that the correct panel had been inserted. The panel was there, but all that could be seen were the wire-ends – the panel was in back to front.

That explained the problem. However, the customer engineer was none too pleased when he was asked to repair hundreds of internal connectors, bent by the tangled mass of coloured wires being forced against them.

Our new highly qualified mathematics graduate had thereby experienced his first encounter with the world of data processing, and so developed an early and very healthy respect for the machines that were to shape his career.

Our supervisor learned something too – about supervision.

Here is another story of the trials and tribulations that those early "grey boxes" could bring to the most dedicated and competent employees. We have alluded to the team spirit that so often typified the way in which great challenges were overcome by "the people". This story, and the author was one of the intrepid band for whom you will have sympathy, serves to remind us that an "all is lost" attitude should not prevail....

"Many a slip twixt...."

It was in the same Service Bureau that the following events took place.

It housed IBM's latest range of equipment, the ubiquitous "grey machines", and provided services to companies making their first venture into the "brave new world" of data processing. Although the equipment was archaic by the standards of today's technology, it was a miracle of what could be achieved by the use of punched cards, card sorters, collators, reproducers, interpreters and accounting machines.

After transposing the data into punched cards, these were sorted into the desired sequence at speeds of 600 to 2000 cards per minute. Thereafter, tabulations were printed as fast as 100 lines per minute, providing massive benefits to customers.

A typical bureau ran a strict daily timetable of jobs to done for regular users. Every so often, a one-off job came along. This was the case when a local authority asked IBM to process the results of a major traffic census. This was the biggest job ever undertaken by the bureau to date, involving in excess of 1 million "mark-sensed" cards (similar to today's lottery slips).

To give some idea of the bulk of 1 million cards (which came in boxes of 2000) the bureau had 2.5 tons of punched cards to process. These were to be sorted into the sequence of an eight-digit number. To explain how cards were sorted, imagine you have 99 cards with the Nos. 1-99 punched into two columns on the card. By passing all 99 cards through the card sorter on the "unit's column", they would emerge from the machine into stackers containing all the 1s, all the 2s, and so on. Pass the cards through again on the "10s" column, and your cards would now be in the desired sequence 1-99. A simple physical exercise, but requiring considerable concentration and manual dexterity.

Having to pass each of the 1 million cards through the card sorter eight times (once per each of the eight columns), meant you had 8 million cards to sort. At 1000 cards per minute, plus handling time, you needed 150 hours of "manual labour".

The bureau had three sorting machines and three operators. So, 50 hours each, 10 hours a day – in five days you would be ready to print the tabulations.

Got it? Have a coffee break....

The size of the task can be measured in yet another way – ergonomically. One million cards equals 500 x 2000-card boxes. The cards were normally transported on specially designed trolleys that had three shelves, each shelf holding 4 x 2000-card boxes, so approximately 42 trolleys were loaded and when split for the three operators, each operator had 14 trolleys with 168 boxes of 2000 cards.

The logistics of handling these cards from the boxes into the sorter and back into boxes while maintaining the sequences required can be left to the reader's imagination. This was "high technology'!

Stalwart readers will by now have grasped the magnitude of the task at hand.

To continue with the story.... those sorters hummed, the operators developed muscles they did not know they had, but in five days the job was done. Everything was going to schedule, the customer was pleased, the operators relieved, and so to tabulate the traffic survey analyses.

Some way into the tabulation process, the machine stopped, a red light flashing! Was a card jammed in the reader, or, maybe the paper had jammed in the feeder channel? No, neither of these was the cause.

The analyst who had designed the plugboard control panel was summoned. After a brief examination, he turned to the assembled, very tense gathering and with a tremble in his voice, he announced... "I am sorry, but you have a sequence error."

The enormity of his statement sank in. The 1 million cards, weighing 2 1/2 tons, were out of order – an error in the sorting process had been made.

The offending card was examined by the Machine Room Supervisor and he confirmed the problem. With the card removed the machine was restarted only to stop again. It was clear that a batch of cards had been misplaced during the sorting process, and that they were interspersed throughout the whole million!

An emergency meeting was hastily convened to determine how to overcome the problem.

There were only two options:

1. Run all the cards through the tabulator at 100 cards per minute to find the erroneous cards. Time – 166 hours, or 7 days at 24 hours per day.
2. Re-sort the cards – known time 5 days at 10 hours per day.

The three operators were young men, all less than 20 years old. They were recalled to the office.

The cards had originally been split into three batches, by what was known as a "block-sort". This involved a sort on the most "senior" of the eight digits to produce a split 0-3, 4-6, 7-9. Examining any of the mis-sorted cards, the senior digit identified the operator who had made the original error.

The three young men insisted that they examined the cards. The unfortunate young man whose error it had been was inconsolable, but the other two levelled no blame. They were a TEAM.

It was Saturday morning: the decision was taken, for Option 2, to resort all 1 million cards again.

At 2.00pm on Monday afternoon, the tabulator read its first card.

By 4.00pm, it was still going strong.

Three, exhausted, ashen, but highly elated young men went home to bed. Two and a half days without a break, but the job was done.

Data processing in those days was both character and muscle-building – no easy fast solutions were to hand.

Finally, a brief story that epitomises the unique inter-relationships that existed within the IBM work environment.

"Single status"

Throughout the years IBM had many quite outstanding people who contributed greatly to the success of the company. Ironically, many of these people were "non-IBM'ers" – they were contractors. To this day it is likely that many IBM'ers did not realise that they were contractors. Such was their importance, they became integral to the running of the business.

One such character was a "Mr. Fixit" par excellence. Known to all as Lofty, he could make anything happen. A man of great humour, unlimited invention, he was held in high esteem at all levels of the Company.

The location at which he was based also housed the then chief executive.

So the story goes.... at an important meeting between the CEO and some important UK customer executives, Lofty was charged with making the arrangements for the arrival, car-parking, and problem-free transfer of these IBM guests.

As always, everything went to plan and the CEO met his guests in the reception area of the IBM building. The CEO, the VIP's and Lofty entered the lift.

The CEO, "proud" of his man, took the opportunity to turn to his guests and say, "Gentlemen, may I introduce the man who has looked after you so well, a most valuable member of the team. This is Lofty."

With a mischievous smile, Lofty looked at the CEO and remarked, "name dropper".

Conclusion

In this chapter we have looked at the processes and procedures in "Managing IBM People".

So what are the lessons to be learned?

- Recruit the highest calibre people.
- Provide extensive and continuous high-class training, for both employees and managers.
- Encourage the man/manager relationship through frank and regular ccmmunication.
- Ensure that every employee has a clearly defined and realistic career progression plan.
- Be consistent and, above all, be honest in all performance evaluations.
- Encourage communication channels for problem resolution.
- Encourage flair, innovation and even, measured risk-taking, then reward and recognise consistently.
- Build team spirit.

In Chapters 1 and 2 we have shown how a well-managed field force was developed and motivated by bonuses, commission and sales plans. However, how did IBM operate to keep all this energy on the correct rails – ensuring any wild ducks were not flying too far out of formation?

3. IBM's Business Ethics

The Dream

Imagine a time, some years ago, when the Chairman of the Board of the IBM Corporation, probably a Watson, might have been sitting in his New York office surveying his international sales and marketing organisation. In an idealised IBM world, what might he have expected to see?

Of course there would have been the IBM salesman (or saleswoman, but not many in those days), upright, honest, clean-cut, smart-suited, white-shirted, determined (but fair) and committed in his mission. He would carry a portfolio of leading-edge products (this is before the days when they became "solutions"), software and hardware, all soundly developed, thoroughly tested, of proven value, well-accepted and competitively, yet profitably, priced.

Then, there were the customers and prospects, each successful in their own marketplace, fair in their dealings with their suppliers, well-able indeed to recognise that IBM was much more than just a "supplier", more a business partner and a cut above those other nasty computer companies. Of course, all this would take place in a laissez-faire world where governments recognised true commercial merit and never attempted to meddle with market realities.

We can all dream....

The Reality

The real world of IBM was always somewhat different, and became ever more complicated. Salesmen might on occasions stray off the straight-and-narrow. Products might not always live up to expectations. Customers and prospects might not always behave "reasonably". And IBM's own phenomenal success would lead to corrective interventions by governments, sometimes to try to ensure fair play, but often, it seemed, out of spite or malevolence towards IBM.

The Solution

For all these reasons it had become clear that IBM needed something a bit more than the customary company legal department. This "something" emerged in most countries in the form of departments variously named Business Practices, Contract Practices, or Commercial Relations. Whatever the names, the main division was between matters of business behaviour by IBM representatives, and those of contract interpretation. Without doubt, the main Aunt Sally for IBM field personnel was the Business Practices department, the "Thought Police", whose job was to ensure that the good name of IBM was not prejudiced by the "misguided" actions or comments, spoken or written, of IBM staff.

IBM's legal departments were staffed largely by personnel tasked with providing legal advice. The overall process was driven by the Business Practices departments, staffed largely by professionals and managers with field experience. There was a temptation to assume their backgrounds might make them more sympathetic to the problems of the sales divisions. If that was true, they certainly concealed it quite well!

The year 1956 was climactic for IBM. Whatever else may have happened in that year, it was the time when a "Consent Decree" was agreed between IBM and the US Government. This brought to a (temporary) conclusion the accusations of monopoly practice levelled against IBM by the US Government. While not accepting the accusations, IBM nevertheless agreed to monitor vigorously the actions of its sales force, to ensure there was no abuse of a "dominant market position" (which it anyway denied!).

The Consent Decree remained in effect in the US until 1995. From it, all through the 60's, 70's and 80's, IBM derived its "Thou shalt not..." directives to its sales personnel. Though the Consent Decree was a US Government agreement, nonetheless, because so many of IBM's US competitors operated world-wide, IBM imposed the same standards upon its field forces world-wide. It was the mission of Business Practices to enforce these standards.

The Refinement

By the early 80's IBM required every salesperson, each year, to sign a certificate saying he, or she, had read and understood the IBM booklet "Business Conduct Guidelines".

The booklet, first issued in 1977 and some 30 pages long, covered a variety of issues related to the conduct of IBM sales staff, both as employees of IBM, and in their private lives. To quote from the appended certificate:

"I understand the importance to IBM of the rules of conduct set out in the booklet, and my responsibility to comply with those rules of conduct.... It is understood that in signing this document I in no way give up any of my legal rights to protection against unfair dismissal."

How many other companies placed such an obligation on their sales staff? We often wondered.

The Practice

For the most part, things would jog along quite happily. Salesmen were conscious of the rules.... yet would take the challenges in their stride....

"You are where you are"

One of the most important "gospels according to St. IBM Business Practices" was that under no circumstances should any derogatory statement be made about an IBM competitor. As a salesman, you could only sell the features, facilities and benefits of the IBM Product or Service.

While admirable as a way of doing business, this certainly caused much frustration and anguish. In competitive situations it often felt like having a gun but few bullets. More times than not it wasn't a problem, because you knew you had the best solution. The only area where competition was likely to have an advantage was price... but IBM salesmen were trained to expect that.

An example of the dilemma this caused was when the world of the punched card was being threatened by a new technology. the floppy disk. Hundreds of IBM customers had thousands of IBM card punches and verifiers, and the consequent revenue stream was under serious threat. IBM did not have a "floppy disk" system though it was clear that such a product would soon be announced.

Another "Gospel according to..." was that you must not speculate about, or pre-announce, any future IBM products. Customers became impatient with IBM. They wanted "floppy disks". "Floppy disks are good for you," they cried.

To protect the revenue base of "old technology" machines, hour upon hour of selling time was deployed reminding and re-emphasising the benefits of punched cards – they were cheap; you could see the holes, and therefore your data; and you couldn't lose a box of 2000 cards. One of the key advantages was, "You can slip a few blank ones into your inside pocket and use them for notes, messages and aide-memoirs".

All these arguments were designed to counter competition without saying anything derogatory, or implying that IBM had a "floppy disk" product in the pipeline. Many installations were thus protected by re-selling the positive benefits of cards. If it happened to create some temporary doubts about the new technology, well, that was hardly the IBM salesman's fault.

Within a few weeks, however, the same salesmen and customers were debating the clear advantages of the newly-announced "IBM Floppy Disk System".

It was difficult to keep a straight face at times.

Salesmen would consult Business Practices before committing pen to paper where occasions warranted. Every now and again, however, there would be an earthquake which would lead to a rapid, and compulsory, re-indoctrination of all branch offices.

Of the many possible areas where someone from a branch office might put his, or her, foot in it, without doubt one area in particular was guaranteed to set the Thought Police pulses racing. This concerned the increasing competition to IBM from the so-called "Software Compatible Vendors" (SCV). These were companies, mainly Japanese, or Japanese-funded, selling mainframe processors, below IBM prices, compatible with IBM's own operating systems software. The first on the scene, in the mid 70's, was Amdahl, to be followed soon thereafter by Hitachi, National Semiconductor and others.

The issue at the heart of all this, of course, was how much systems engineering (SE) support the customer might expect from IBM if he were to install an SCV processor: "Of course we should continue to use the IBM MVS operating system on our new computer, and we assume IBM would continue to provide the excellent SE support we've come to expect...?" This might provoke an answer from the mortally wounded IBM salesman, along the lines of: "You must be joking, mate...", or, more thoughtfully, "Of course we'd be disappointed if you decided not to choose the IBM solution, but we always assess how we deploy our discretionary SE resources based upon our perception of future business opportunities".

It is not difficult to imagine that, in the heat of the moment, the IBM salesman might lurch towards the one version, rather than the other! And therein lay the rub. For the customer might choose to interpret the salesman's words as a threat by Big Brother IBM. The customer might then lodge a formal complaint... to IBM, or to the Computer Users' Association, or to the EEC, or, if the customer happened to be a subsidiary of a US parent, to the US Department of Justice.

It would be nice to think that on those occasions IBM would close ranks to protect its own. To those in the front line who'd been battling for some while, in a critical competitive situation, knowing that IBM did not take kindly to losing business, it was of little comfort then to be pilloried by IBM itself. An account team in this position could find all its files seized by IBM Business Practices staff, and examined minutely for evidence of transgression.

Sometimes, circumstances were almost laughable, were they not deadly serious for the participants. There was one occasion (faintly ridiculous, in retrospect) when, following a threatened complaint to the EEC by Amdahl, the wrath of God descended on one IBM account team in the Midlands.

There had been a particularly tough competitive struggle between IBM and Amdahl in this account, early in 1978, when all the issues of SE support had arisen. The position taken by the account team had been sustained all the way by each successive, and more senior, visiting IBM executive – by the Branch Manager, the Regional Manager, the Country Sales Director. There were only two further levels to call upon in the UK, then it was over to European and Corporate management. These levels were the UK DP Director and the UK Chairman. It was at the time when the DP Director (there was no reason to suppose that he would not support the existing IBM stance) was to be briefed for a call on the customer on whose behalf Amdahl had threatened to lodge the complaint to the EEC. They had alleged that IBM had used threatening tactics in its sales campaign.

All hell broke loose. Those in IBM who might have been heroes were suddenly villains. Careers were, in some cases, tarnished, in others blighted for all time. The final absurdity was when, at an IBM meeting with everybody and his aunt present, UK and European executive management, legal staff and, last but not least, the wretched account team, somebody put this question to the meeting: "Alright, *you* are now in the customer's office. How would *you* answer when he asks *you* if his IBM SE support will reduce should he install an Amdahl system?"

European executive management promptly leapt in with words to the effect "...you bet your sweet bippy it will!" The legal gurus became ashen. "You can't say that", they squawked. And there ensued the sort of brainwashing of executive management that account teams had endured for years.

But the meeting didn't get any easier. The harassed account manager was finally forced to state that he would no longer submit to continued and aggressive cross-questioning without having his lawyer present.

This was all something of an exception. Things were not normally that bad, but it does serve as an indication of what an unwary IBM salesman might run into if he were not very careful.

IBM sales people were always conscious of the rules as they went about their everyday business. They also became quite skilled, on occasions, at recognising when they weren't rules at all, but merely bureaucratic inflexibility.

On other occasions... well, what the eyes don't see....

"Irresistible forces"

By the 1980's IBM was becoming a pretty big company: 300,000 plus world-wide employees and heading towards $60 billion annual sales.

The UK company likewise was approaching 18,000 employees and £3 billion revenue, and it had its standard ways of doing business – no favouritism, treat everyone the same, and so on.

Now, most large companies, particularly in the UK, had developed a culture that said they were "special". They expected to tell their suppliers how they would do business, what terms they would accept, whether they would agree to price increases, and if so by what percentage. That was not IBM's way.

In fairness to IBM, it was as a result of US anti-trust legislation that this had all come about. Because a company the size of IBM might potentially indulge in "target predatory pricing" to a particular customer to beat off competition, the US government required IBM to set the same price for all. Similarly, IBM was required to offer the same terms and conditions to all its customers regardless of size. The only exceptions were IBM's dealings with governments, in particular the US government, who saw no reason to be constrained by the same restrictions that it required IBM to place on others. Some were definitely more equal than others.

This all meant that the typical sales IBM team responsible for a "large account" would spend a disproportionate amount of its time being bounced between IBM's legal departments and the customer ("I'm not signing that. Who does IBM think it is anyway? We don't accept price increases. We expect IBM to put something to us and we'll advise whether we're prepared to accept it. There's plenty of other fish in the sea you know....").

Eventually, after enough relationship-building invitations to Wimbledon, Open Golf, Covent Garden and the like (and "large accounts" were always likely to be at the head of the queue for these "jollies"), a way of working would be found – and by some intellectual gymnastics both parties would find it acceptable. That is, until there was a change of senior management within the customer, when the key contact would move on and the whole process would start again with the replacement.

One area where the intellectual gymnastics would always be exercised to the utmost was the standard "Contract – for the Sale of IBM Equipment" (or, indeed, almost any IBM contract for that matter) versus the standard Customer X Purchase Order.

This was a particular challenge in the automotive industry where the culture was traditionally one of kicking suppliers all over the floor, and generally putting them in their place. It is refreshing nowadays that there is now a much stronger notion of "partnership" between supplier and manufacturer. However, that's not the way it used to be.

The IBM Contract versus automotive customer Purchase Order was usually resolved along the following lines. After some suitable "event" (where "event" = "jolly"), ideally with the customer's spouse present (female spouses always seemed to exercise a mollifying effect on customer executives; maybe this was because there wasn't the same need to appear "macho" in front of the spouse, unlike with business colleagues!), the issue might be gently raised, along the lines of, "...Perhaps, Fred, we could clear that small issue of the contract exchange which seems to be blocking progress at the moment." The spouse's ears would prick up: "Blocking progress? Does that mean our invitation to Glyndebourne which that charming IBM fellow was just talking about might be in jeopardy? I'll make sure I mention that to Fred when we get back. I'm depending upon Glyndebourne to take that jumped-up Eileen Watkins at the golf club down a peg or two!"

With a bit of luck the IBM Contract might be signed soon thereafter. That was never the end of the story, but thank goodness the potential "end" was rarely if ever tested. You see the IBM Contract contained words something like: "...these terms and conditions shall be the sole terms and conditions governing the supply and installation of this equipment". IBM would then be sent a purchase order from the customer which contained words something like: "...these terms and conditions shall be the sole terms and conditions governing the supply and installation of this equipment". The two documents were kept in separate files! The two legal departments slept soundly and in blissful ignorance, and spouses continued to be invited to Glyndebourne!

And sometimes a little lateral thinking was required to keep one's customers happy....

"Spray it again, Sam"

"Lead time" – two words that to an IBM salesman could mean another obstacle to making a sale. Every product in IBM had its own delivery

lead time, and usually this was never as quick as both the salesman and his prospective customer required.

Now, *"idle inventory"* could sometimes provide the salvation, if the customer's specification could be satisfied. Our new customer's managing director had decided that he wanted an IBM System/34, but he was annoyed that the lead time was so extensive. He wanted to get on with his installation having made his decision (the fact that it had taken him more than twice the lead time to make his decision didn't come into his reckoning). Surely a company the size of IBM could get his system in less than lead time?

Idle inventory was trawled and, behold, a system close to specification was available – moreover, it did not break the rules of sequential delivery. The MD was consulted, and understood that the system would need some extra "bits" fitted to meet the full specification following delivery. With customary empathy IBM always described such "bits" as MES (Miscellaneous Equipment Specification). The fact that these bits were missing, however, did not impair the use of the system for early applications development.

But, there was one more stumbling block: IBM's machine specifications allowed a choice of colours for the "casing" of the various units, including the traditional IBM blue, or red, or yellow, and, from memory, one or two others. In most cases, the customer had no strong feelings on the matter and IBM blue was what was delivered.

This MD however, was adamant that his system was going to be *yellow*. His company's logo was yellow; the letter-headed paper was yellow; the office decor was yellow. Blue or red were out of the question. The machine in idle inventory was...blue.

The salesman made the decision – deliver the machine.

On the day of delivery, the salesman made sure he was on site with the installing customer engineer. As the system was unpacked the offending blue panels were removed and quickly put into the salesman's car.

A few hours later, after a visit to Halfords for an aerosol can of paint, and the careful application thereof, the MD examined his pristine new yellow System 34.

Another satisfied customer.

But you could be certain that the strict interpreters of the law would always be there, scattering tin-tacks in your path.

"With friends like this...."

Few in IBM, and even fewer outside IBM, could begin to understand the convulsions with which IBM would become mired because of its alleged "dominant" market position.

Having a "dominant" market position carried all sorts of nasty implications under US anti-monopoly legislation. The EEC too, as it began to find its feet and uncover new areas in which to meddle, decided, under the influence of the indigenous European computer companies, that IBM was a suitable target.

IBM itself would always argue that the "marketplace" for information technology was so large (covering computers, application and systems software, networking products, office systems, telecommunications, and more) that it could not possibly occupy a "dominant" position. This debate might have been fought to a draw, but the EEC, shrewd as ever, moved the goalposts. It declared that IBM did indeed have a "dominant" market position – in the IBM marketplace(sic)!

It was able to put forward this truism as a serious argument on these simple grounds; IBM had been so successful that it had created a market for suppliers of IBM "plug-compatible" devices (such as disk and tape drives, terminals) and "software compatible" processors. Self-evidently, this market was "dominated" by IBM! The fact that most companies producing such competitive equipment were Japanese, and not European at all, appeared not to influence the argument. It was somewhat like arguing, say, that Ford occupied a "dominant" market position in the supply of Ford motor cars and spare parts. Indeed, "those whom the Gods wish to destroy they first make mad."

While IBM never accepted the accusation of "dominant" market position, it nevertheless agreed to impose restrictions upon its sales staff which often appeared (to the troops) little different from accepting the accusation in the first place. This meant, for example, that IBM, among other things, should not use its size to gain competitive advantage, should not engage in predatory pricing, and should treat all customers in exactly the same way. It also meant that IBM sales staff were strongly discouraged from using military terminology to describe sales campaigns – oops, I mean sales "activities". Phrases like "fighting the competition" or "sales battles" were likely to arouse the attention of the IBM's Business Practices Department.

This little story illustrates some of the lunacies that could result.

By the mid-80's IBM was keen to encourage its industrial branches (that is, those selling into industrial accounts) to gain a presence on the manufacturing shop floor where competition had become a serious threat. To that end IBM had announced the Series/1 (S/1) computer, well-equipped to attach and control the many and varied devices that may sit on the industrial shop-floor, such as robots, sensor devices, and weighing machines. Every IBM industrial branch was given a target to sell and install a challenging number of S/1's. Account teams were likewise tasked.

So... we reach December, with the branch having achieved all its targets except that for Series/1, where one more needed to be installed. Account teams were summoned and given their marching orders. A sales opportunity was identified, and the customer agreed to install before year-end. Problem solved? Not at all.

First, the rapid installation meant that the system would need to be supplied from idle inventory (assuming there was some) since plant would not have time to manufacture. A system was duly uncovered in "idle".

"Aah," said Business Practices, "IBM's sequential delivery policy means that every UK customer with S/1 already on order must be asked whether they would wish a December delivery. Only if each refuses can we assign this machine to your new customer! And, another thing, if the specification of the system in "idle" is not exactly what the customer wants, then he must advise us of his willingness to take the system "as is", and pay for it(!), while placing on order the additional MES features required."

"But," said the branch office, "IBM can't expect the customer to install and pay for a system that he can't use."

"Oh, yes it can."

Such was the lot of the IBM sales force. Persuading customers was sometimes easy compared to getting IBM itself to see reason.

But, yes, the S/1 was installed in the December, and the branch did make its targets.

The answer to all of this, of course, was to get IBM's "top brass" on your side.

"Jaguar comes first"

The release of Jaguar Cars from the BL umbrella in the early 80's brought independence to many functions, including information systems. Until then, Jaguar's data processing and network management requirements had largely been carried out by ISTEL, erstwhile BL Systems, and a little by IBM's Managed Network Services.

It was obvious from the outset that Jaguar was going to install its own computer and transfer the work from these two suppliers. Assuming that a "real" IBM mainframe (*not* one of those SCV systems) was installed, then IBM would make a net gain. ISTEL could have resisted the transfer, but, to the credit of their management, they mounted a positive campaign knowing that they would gain more in short-term revenues from support work.

Thankfully, Jaguar decided to install a "real" IBM mainframe system. The salesman spent some time getting to understand how their new purchasing function was to operate when ordering the equipment.

Generally IBM wanted to do business its way, and was quite unbending when the "customer" wanted to do business his way. Sometimes this got to the point where each would exchange contracts, describing immutable terms and conditions, and yet neither party would overtly agree to accept the other's rules and legal-speak.

So it was in this case.

In the automotive industry, you knew you'd finally made the sale when the purchasing department gave you an "order number". It didn't have to be on paper. The salesman would still be excited to have "won" the business. The buyer would be just as excited (to provide the order number over the phone) – probably reflecting how difficult it was to move a proposal through his own organisation.

Matters proceeded as follows:

Jaguar's purchasing department duly phoned through the magic order number for business worth more than £1million.

IBM administration refused to accept this order number – "No hard copy purchase order."

The buyer offered to fax the order number, bearing in mind the equipment was needed quickly and the official purchase order would take some weeks to be prepared.

IBM administration would not accept a fax – "A fax could be sent by anybody."

Jaguar offered to have a Board member sign the fax.

IBM administration refused again, saying, "How do we know he is authorised to do so? Can you send a fax with a list of authorised signatures?"

At this point the salesman had had enough, and, frustrated, asked how IBM would know that the sender of this fax was authorised to do so!

This silliness was broken by a timely visit of the IBM Regional Director to the branch. He was asked if he would be the IBM executive contact for Jaguar Cars, and could he announce this at the branch meeting that day. Further, could he state that, "Today, I am pleased to say that we have received an order from the new Jaguar Cars for an IBM mainframe system. Congratulations to all those who have been involved in this important project."

The order was duly processed. Guess what the "evidence" was? Why, a fax from the buyer, of course.

Conclusion

As we have pointed out in this chapter, legal conflagrations with customers were few and far between. Perhaps that was because the penalties for offenders were so severe. Perhaps it was because IBM itself, rather than risk a stand-up row with a customer would usually back down.

IBM senior management was fond of using the term "aggressive selling" when delivering a harangue to the troops. In truth, what was probably meant was selling "with determination". Aggression would too readily lead to confrontation, and Consent Decree really did seem to provide a kind of sword of Damocles suspended over any latent transgressor.

However, the withdrawal of Consent Decree, in 1995, might give rise to a less tractable IBM, less prepared to "turn the other cheek" and less willing to restrain the activities of its own sales force.

To the average IBM salesman, Business Conduct Guidelines, Business Practices, Consent Decree and the EEC equivalents, could appear a delaying, time-consuming pain-in-the-butt. However, salesmen, as has been said, were driven by tactical objectives.

From a strategic viewpoint such constraints may be desirable to maintain the ethics of the business and secure its image.

In the next chapter we look in more detail at those that comprised IBM's sales force, how they were recruited and trained, and how they performed the job of selling for IBM.

4. The IBM Salesman – Fact and Fable

The most popular image of an IBM sales representative has always been that of a uniform appearance, dark pin-striped suit, white shirt, sober tie and well-polished shoes. Entering a lift with any group that included an IBM sales representative, you could identify him immediately.

Our longest-serving author, Bob, met his first IBM sales representative when he joined the company in 1960, and vividly remembers the dark suit with razor-edged creases in the trousers, a starched collar and an old school tie. The ensemble was completed by the bowler hat and rolled umbrella.

Appearance was undoubtedly a major part of the IBM legend. However, the success of an IBM salesman also depended upon three primary factors, namely:

- the business environment... selling to the maturing IT industry;
- IBM's marketplace offerings;
- the salesman's personality and professionalism.

The Business Environment

The selling climate

Though IBM was never quite in the door-to-door selling business, its salespeople certainly required the skills of what is known as "cold-calling", whether face to face or by telephone. One London IBM branch, ironically perhaps, on a summer's day in the early 70's went so far as to mobilise all its sales personnel for a "cold-calling day" – knocking on every door of every prospect company on its territory. The results were outstanding.

Certainly for those salesmen selling IBM's data processing products in the 60's, when there were few IBM customers, it was not at all uncommon to have to explain to the recipient of an IBM cold call, whether by phone or in person, what exactly I-B-M actually meant. And a not uncommon explanation for the uncomprehending might be, "Well, we're a bit like ICT".

Indeed, in those days it was often extremely difficult to secure that first call. This was particularly true when the IBM salesman was endeavouring to make contact with an installed ICT account. There were a number of companies whose chief executives would regard any contact with IBM as little short of treason. The data processing managers of such companies talked to IBM at their peril.

Having made initial contact, you might have found that there was already a existing Request for Tender (RFT). The first task then, was to inveigle yourself onto the short list of potential computer suppliers. Such situations, admittedly rare, were not always welcome. By definition, the RFT was likely to have been put together by people whose only experience of computing was based upon their own (non-IBM?) system. The parameters, therefore, were unlikely to be of IBM's choosing. As any good general would point out, you should avoid fighting on ground chosen by the enemy. In computing terms, you should ensure that technical specifications are not those better-matched to competitive systems.

Of course, there was also the key topic of decision criteria, or, as IBM liked to put it, "What do we have to do, Mr. Prospect, to win your business?"

In the somewhat crazy days of the late 60's, when the big banks really woke up to computing, it seemed very much a question of, "Barclays have got a big one... we'd better get a bigger one". More often, however, the decision criteria would settle around technical issues. That's where the decision criteria were known at all. Quite often it seemed there were no such criteria, the final decision being made on the whim or fancy of the executive with the most power.

But, suppose you'd walked into a company, an existing computer user, happy with what they'd got (and it was not IBM equipment!), and no intention to change? Where to go from there? Well, depending upon the sort of reception you'd got, it could either become a long uphill struggle, leading nowhere, or there might be ways of prising a crack in the defences. The "warmth of reception" was most important. Was the company open-minded and prepared to listen? Or was it closed to further suggestion? If it was open-minded then lots of opportunities might be available.

Even in the 60's, IBM's world-wide customer base was very extensive. It would have been unusual not to have found an example somewhere in the world, and usually in the USA, of a company in an identical industry that could be considered "best of breed". So, for the open-minded prospect, IBM could always dangle the carrot of "Let us tell you about, or show you, how Company X has set up its (by implication, far more successful) computing operations, with IBM". This sort of approach, often couched in terms of the strategic, rather than merely the operational role of computing, was likely to strike a chord with business, rather than just data processing management. Indeed, if played in a really adroit way, it could also be seen by the DP manager as a way to elevate his own visibility in his company. For back in the 60's, computing all too often was nothing more than another way of doing what a few Burroughs, or NCR, accounting machines had done before – and the computer manager was graded accordingly. Give the computer manager a chance to break out and enhance his role, and you'd have a friend for life.

What about the other side of the coin – the companies closed to further suggestion, unwilling to consider change? Well, all you could do was to "hang in there", hoping to be around when they woke up. In the meanwhile, you would issue the occasional invitation to an event, arrange the occasional visit, and all the while search for a glimmer that it was not all wasted effort.

So much depended in those far-off days upon personalities. If a new director was appointed from a company you knew to be a successful IBM account, it could be the breakthrough you were looking for. "Don't force it. Let him settle in. Introduce yourself at the right time. See if there's anything you can do to help him in his new job," and so on. As the business knowledge and experience of an IBM salesman grew, and as the scope and importance of computing increased, so the ability of IBM to support "its man" in the customer boardroom became ever more important. Once you'd got a friend in high places it was critical to ensure that you did all you could to support him. Once IBM was seen as a source for such support, then others wanted the same.

What was this support? Take, as an example, the situation where a newspaper article hostile to IBM appears. Make sure you quickly get a briefing, with IBM's story, to him, so he can put the other side of the story, assuming, of course, he wants to. Likewise, if a similar story favourable to competition appears, then get the IBM counter-arguments to him before the opposition can score. All's fair in love, war and computer marketing!

The IT industry environment

Just as the IT industry, computing technology and suppliers' offerings changed dramatically from the 60's to the 90's, so did the role of the IBM salesman.

The 60's were the days of machines, not systems. In the early part of the decade, punched cards and paper tape were the media of the day, both for data input and for master files. The beasts that handled these were solid, weighing many hundredweights apiece. Real computers were being mainly used for scientific work. The recently-introduced IBM 1401 commercial computer cost many hundreds of thousands of pounds, and therefore was only being bought by large organisations.

A typical card installation had a "punch room" for the primary data entry, a sorter to get the cards in the correct sequence, a collator for merging cards, a calculator for doing sums, and a tabulator, sometimes called an accounting machine, for printing the reports. Such heavy-weights were "custom-programmed" using panels with a knitted mesh of wired instructions.

At that time, use of IT in most countries was biased towards indigenous suppliers – in the UK this meant mainly Powers Samas, ICT, English Electric. Increasingly competition (from their viewpoint) came from the Americans (IBM, Honeywell, Burroughs, NCR) and from France (Bull). Additional competition to all of these at the smaller, office system level, came from essentially "form-driven" systems suppliers such as Kalamazoo. In Britain, ICT, later ICL (after the merger with English Electric), was the dominant supplier.

For the smaller organisations, these were the days when an IBM salesman was generally proficient, expectedly so, in undertaking the technical work – systems analysis and design, form layouts, panel wiring, system testing and documentation. He was *the* customer inter-face. Of course, there were the "elite" – a select band of clever IBM branch people who concerned themselves mainly with scientific computing and "word" machines. They were titled EDPM (Electronic

Data Processing Machine) representatives. The introduction of the "Systems Engineer" (SE) as a specialist technical support function for commercial customers occurred around 1963.

IBM's success and rapid growth in the 60's and 70's caused a shortage of qualified resource to properly manage the consequent workload. To correct this problem, "programmes" (or "programs", as our cross-Atlantic cousins spelt it) were conceived at a goodly rate.

By the 80's, the IT world had become more complex. More players came into the game. No one computer manufacturer could deliver a complete solution to a customer. Our IBM salesman did not possess all the requisite ingredients in his kit-bag – hardware, software, resources and skills. Thus was born the notion of "business partners".

Customers came to regard such agents as both suppliers and primary contacts, rather than IBM, who were progressively seen as the box sub-supplier. Agents were taking a rising proportion of customer spend on services and application software. At the same time, the price/performance battle was driving down box costs. Thus, the IBM salesman walked the tightrope between promoting IBM as the "total solution provider" and at the same time ensuring the success of its partners' business.

Customer ownership

Some customers complained about the frequent changes of their sales and SE representation. From the salesman's point of view, particularly dependent on commission, it was critical not to be saddled with a dead or dying account. However, customer reallocation rarely took place as a result of the salesman's views – there were much better reasons for shuffling the cards. For example:

- salesman being promoted.
- marketing manager being promoted.
- change in branch responsibilities.
- change in district responsibilities.
- because IBM changed from "xx" orientation to "yy" – for example, from geographic.regions to industry districts.

Sometimes this was actually a good thing – for example, when it provided the customer with a higher level of relevant skill from the new supporting team. However, there never was a perfect answer. You never get something (better) for nothing. For example, one "central" team having to represent Rolls Royce nationally, which has operations in a number of locations in England as well as Scotland, could mean that such centralisation involved a lot of travel. Or, an individual member of the team who had to live a long way from the rest of the team, could not therefore contribute to a natural team spirit.

Most times, changes to a customer's support were not discussed beforehand with him. After all, why should he have had anything to contribute in such matters.

There are many theories written on "selling" – you've seen them: "sell at the top", "establish the decision criteria", and so on. IBM in the 60's and 70's was masterful in the pursuit of gaining and securing the business. In the latter part of the 80's, for many reasons, it lost some of its edge.

Do you remember the phrase, "What DP manager ever lost his job by installing IBM?" Well, that changed as well!

Relationships between branch and customer personnel became ever more important as the customer viewed alternatives to IBM as more acceptable, and to be able to talk empathetically with DP and User people was "key" (this was one of the more commonly used IBM-speak words). Ironically some of the personnel recruitment policies of securing highly academically qualified graduates did cause some back-fires. As one customer once said: "Some of your systems engineers frighten my staff."

IBM strove for excellence and a moral and ethical approach to conducting its business affairs. It was strict, for example, about any comment or criticism of competition (really not allowed), and speculation about possible future products (not allowed, even if you knew anything). In image terms, high standards were demanded – when did you last see an IBM salesperson who was not outstanding in his dress and smartness?

A salesman's day

A Data Processing Division salesman would probably spend about an hour a day with his marketing manager, another hour a day with his Systems Engineer, a half-day a month on Branch-and-above meetings, and if he was driving his business, three hours a day with his customer(s)

It is fascinating to note that in the 60's, when a weekly activity report had to be returned each Monday for the previous week, there was a target of five calls a day (not, however, one meeting with five people from the same department from the same customer). The requirement was to cover at least five different functions, either from one or more companies – one seminar for 30 different customers was excellent!

This became more and more difficult to achieve as the business became more complex. However, a GSD salesman was still expected to achieve a much higher call rate – more like those of old!

The field generally liked to operate in a straight black and white environment. Know the targets, the rules, who your customers and prospects are, and very important, who the enemy is. Strains appeared on the faces of sales-people when shades of grey were introduced, such as when IBM disk drives were sold to Siemens for re-badging for their own computer sales market.

Was an agent a customer? What if he collaborates in one sphere of business but sells DEC equipment in another?

When EDS, the giant US Ross Perot systems company, was bought by General Motors, the IBM sales teams throughout the world anticipated (rightly) a difficult period ahead. Who was the customer – EDS or GM?

With its dependence on mainframe business, IBM sales people could find themselves in very murky water. The central DP manager might say, "If you know what's good for you, don't you go talking to the users, creating all sorts of wild expectations." Yet at the same time competitors such as DEC and Computervision had a free rein with no installed business, so no risk of loss.

IBM was always good at defining its customer as an individual company. It fell short when lifting its head to consider levels above, or different from, these discrete entities. Industry sectors were worth real heavy marketing attention. Only in the early 90's did the inevitable IBM reorganisation pendulum swing back (again) to an industry orientation.

The Salesman Himself

So, whence came this army of IBM sales representatives?

Clearly, the aspiring, maybe unsuspecting, IBM salesman would be entering a complex world, and one that became, through the 60's, 70's and 80's, necessarily ever more complex. Selection and training of the right people was all-important. How did IBM go about it?

Recruitment

Selection of the best candidates was all important. These could come from may different backgrounds – engineers, physicists, language students, accountants, merchant seaman, insurance salesmen, to name but a few. Such raw material had to be converted into IBM sales representatives capable of turning barren wastes into verdant IBM pastures.

Training was intensive and thorough. In the 60's, it was mainly course-based in London, reflecting the strong product bias of the industry. Between courses, time was spent in the branch putting theory into practice, helping willing customers. For many recruits, this was the fist time they saw the inside of a factory or customer's office.

"A different world!"

Another of our authors, Tony, after leaving university, worked for the London office of a Canadian insurance company before joining IBM in the early 60's. He had endured life as a London commuter, travelling daily from/to Ilford, Essex: 60 minutes each way on a good day and of infinite duration on a bad day. When offered a job with IBM therefore he opted for a branch in the "provinces"... Birmingham.

Before going anywhere near the branch, however, he had to learn all about IBM's basic unit record products, on an eight-week course in London. That accomplished, he arrived for his first day in the Birmingham branch office as a sales trainee, bursting with knowledge about IBM card punches, verifiers, sorters, collators, interpreters, reproducers, tabulators and calculators.

After a few hasty introductions, he was told that he was to spend the next several weeks helping to prepare for the installation of a computer at a company in the "Black Country". This provoked two concerns: first (for he was a mere Southerner), what, and where, was the "Black

Country", and, secondly, he knew nothing (yet) about computers. Not to worry... his job would be to wire control panels for an IBM 421 tabulating machine (and he was now an "expert" on those) which would provide back-up, in the theoretically unlikely (?) event that the IBM 1440 computer didn't do its stuff. As for the "Black Country", that was the area of smoke, he was told, stretching northwest from Birmingham towards Wolverhampton.

Off he set, from the IBM city centre office, desperately trying to remember his directions amid this alien geography – past HM prison Winson Green, to Smethwick, thence to West Bromwich. These names rang a bell – but Wednesbury, Darlaston and Willenhall?

Eventually, he reached the customer, Welman Smith Owen, a crane manufacturer, in darkest Willenhall. His contact there was the chief accountant, a charming man who took him on a tour of the factory – an eye-opening, smoky world of clanking heavy industry, and a far cry from pinstripe-suited London insurance.

In due course he was taken to lunch in the senior executive dining room. This was most impressive – a nourishing drink or two beforehand, then the Chairman carved the roast. There was followed the sort of apple pie and custard Mum used to make, and then a ceremonial assault on the round of Stilton. IBM was obviously quite a company if its customers treated one of its sales trainees so royally. He was reminded, however, that the normal starting time was around 7.30 am for "executive" staff, of whom he was now deemed to be one – hence the appetite for lunch. The Welman Smith Owen directors were a wonderful bunch, mostly in the 50-60 age range and full of rich anecdotes, especially when reminiscing about the war, in which all seemed to have served. The majority had been born and raised in the Black Country, but given that their company had recently been taken over by a North American group it was a matter of conjecture how much longer the "old regime" would be allowed to last.

About four weeks was spent at this Willenhall company before moving on. It was a most enriching experience – a first introduction to the industrial West Midlands and the world of heavy engineering. With limited data processing skills it had proved possible to add some value to an IBM customer.

Not all customers treated IBM sales trainees, or indeed anybody of whatever level from IBM, quite so generously, as Tony was to find out. But it had been a good start.

Formal classroom training comprising Basic equipment (punched card machines in the early days), Computer and Application schools were common to both Sales and SE. Divergence then occurred as salesmen progressed towards Sales School, and SE's towards SE School. Over time, some of the sequential classroom courses became increasingly modular, and could be studied in the branch or at home.

Another characteristic of the "early years" was that there was little interchange between sales and systems engineering. It was as though each was a different breed from the other. The forehead was stamped at recruitment, and you either passed out (in the military sense!) in that discipline or you left the company. IBM began to lose its way when it compromised its hitherto rigid stance that salesmen were essentially born, not made.

Sales training normally lasted 18 months to two years, and rarely less than one year. There was a case when one individual made it in nine months, but, by definition, he was of such ferocious ambition and determination that he would never conform to IBM's ways of working, and, sure enough, he left the company within a couple of years.

Sales School

Sales School had a mystical significance, where going away for two weeks of isolation would invite others' sympathy and a silent prayer for the soul. This was it – was he/she to be allowed loose, with a pass, to represent IBM, or would it be the early bath, potential humiliation, after a fail? There would be none of the fudges of today's academia, where it's all a matter of degrees of success and "pass/fail" are politically incorrect. Either you passed Sales School, or you did not.

One compensation in those far-off days of the 1960's was that the venue for Sales School was somewhere pleasant – like a 5-star hotel in the London area, complete with all mod cons and a golf course for the odd snatched moments of relaxation. That all changed in time. The hotels' stars diminished coincidentally at the same rate as the recognition of the salesman as someone special became watered down.

Sales School comprised a more concentrated version of the previous 18 months – practice calls, presentations, some instruction. At every turn there would be evaluations and assessments of fitness for sales. Great store was set "in the old days" upon equipment demonstration. This was vital when much of a computer company's product range comprised unit record equipment (punches, verifiers, sorters), but deemed less important, or just less practical, once large integrated computers began to take over. However, many were to argue that the slick demonstration would always be a vital part of the salesman's art.

The practice call was extensively used in the branch prior to Sales School, as well as during the actual school itself. Imaginary (or were they real-life?) situations were used to simulate the types of calls salesmen might need to make when in real "quota-land". The trainee salesman was handed a short brief describing the call he was to "role-play". The "customer", however, had extensive background brief information (well, the prospect or customer was never normally going to make it easy for you, was he?).

The most unnerving aspect of the whole process was that these "playlets" were often performed in front of an audience. The trainee would very often frantically telephone his pals in the branch office seeking information and guidance on how best to handle the call. Their most frequent replies were, "What is the call number?", and "Who is the instructor you are calling on?"

A brief story of a typical practice call....

"Bullish sales calls"

In the 1960's there was often a 50/50 mix of experienced business recruits who did not take kindly to being treated like students (and whose spouses definitely objected to partners swotting every evening) and spotty-faced graduates whose knowledge of business was limited to how to spell the word. It was the task of the IBM training department to knock them both into some common shape and degree of knowledge.

Sometimes, though, even the IBM trainers had a theoretical view, letting slip words and phrases not suited to the real marketplace....

The victim (the recruit) was getting along fine. He was bringing out the salient points in the customer's requirements, handling objections like a good'un and generally progressing so well that he thought he would produce his bombshell. He had heard it mentioned the other day by one of the instructors, and it sounded right out of the latest 1960's textbooks. "Yes," he said with an air of finality, "it's clear to me from all you have said that what you really need is an Integrated Management Information System", and sat back with a smirk on his face awaiting the expected congratulations.

The executioner (the "customer") was one of those rare and experienced visitors from the field, cajoled into "taking a few practice calls" as a way of securing some quid pro quo. He blinked, peered at his victim with total disdain, leaned forward menacingly in his chair – "Integrated management information system? Integrated cock!"

So was another unsuspecting customer protected.

However, neither the extensive two years total training, nor the intensive two weeks Sales School, could cover every twist and turn that might emerge from the catacombs of the human personality, especially if they deviated from the classical call case studies.

"What can one say?"

Well, what would you have said?

The sales representative had established a good rapport over some months with the production manager of a medium-sized component engineering company in the Midlands. It was an interesting system being born, handling the whole spectrum of material planning and workload scheduling – two applications the classicists considered should not be integrated, claiming that either Materials or Shop Capacity should be the "master constraint". Anyway, this was what the customer wanted and we all know that he is always right. The complex system was to be built, and then processed on a bi-weekly basis, at the Birmingham Service Bureau.

Prior to this "repetitive processing" (significant, as it meant the salesman was credited with commission at the time the order was signed) there was a huge task in collecting and cleansing the base master data – part numbers, bills of materials, machines, capacities – then loading this data into the computer. A timely snapshot of dynamic data, such as stock levels and jobs already on the shop floor, had then to be taken before the bi-weekly repetitive processing could be launched. All this data was to be captured on punched cards.

At that time (the late 60's) card punching would often be done for customers in the IBM bureau. However, on this occasion, because of the volumes and the turnaround required, it was agreed that two punches and two verifiers would be installed at the customer's premises. Of course, staff would be needed to operate these machines, so the salesman set in motion the necessary procedures for advertising, polished up the relevant aptitude tests, and agreed the interviewing procedures.

There was a good response to the advertisements. One of the applicants was a stunning chestnut-haired young woman, physically well endowed, and with a very warm smile. She was Welsh, and had the soft complexion that comes from being washed by the frequent gentle rains of the valleys.

At one point of the interview she said to our upright IBM sales representative, "Are you married?", in the very best Gladys Pugh lilting tones. He replied, somewhat caught off guard (what a dumb-bat, did we hear?), "Well, actually, yes."

She then enquired further, again with those soft Welsh vowels, "Are you happileee married?"... and then, "Are you reeeally happileee married?"

Did she get the job?

What would you have said? They don't teach you everything on Sales School.

Back at the Ranch

Those who graduated summa cum laude – and in fairness, they were the majority – now faced the reality of being an IBM sales representative and all that that would entail.

First, the allocation of his territory, ownership of which was equivalent to the intensity shown in the animal kingdom. If David

Attenborough wanted to highlight the degree to which geographic protectionism is a part of human nature, then one day of filming in an IBM branch office would have sufficed.

Next, the "quota", the objectives for the next twelve months. It was fascinating to study the reactions of sales representatives when quotas were allocated; for example, a look of total disbelief, or (rarely) a complacent smile.

To quote illustrious IBM leaders:

Jacques Maisonrouge, Senior IBM vice-president, said: "Poor salesmen always find that their territory has no potential, that competition is too tough, and that economic circumstances are unfavourable. Good salesmen sell whatever the circumstances."

T.J.Watson: "The customer must be given the best possible service"; and also, "Excellence and superior performance must be pursued."

Buck Rodgers, in his book *The IBM Way* averred: "Successful salesmen develop sound and lasting relationships with their customers. They are respectful, thoughtful and go out of their way to be helpful."

No bad messages in any of that.

In practice, selling was very much a team effort, and the best salesmen ensured that all possible resources were aligned with his objectives. Systems Engineers, Customer Engineers and Administration all played their part. However, there was more: Education, Business Strategy Planning, Industry Support, Development Laboratories, were all frequently called on to provide specialist knowledge, engendering that TLC and warm feeling with a prospective customer.

For existing customers, the IBM ethos was not only "getting the order", but equally "account protection". This was particularly true in the earlier decades when most of IBM's revenues came from rental business. Loss of an installed system was both lost revenue to IBM and lost commission to the responsible sales representative. As more sales moved to "purchase", then losing an account did not affect the wallet so much but was still considered a very serious crime and contravened the equivalent of the "Ten Commandments", attracting the wrath of multiple levels of management.

Given all of the aforementioned training and experience, this story illustrates how it was put to good use – perhaps?

"Just the ticket"

IBM sales representatives were generally viewed as smart, professional, well briefed, clear minded, and on top of any situation.

IBM invested millions of pounds in educating its people. There can be little doubt that this investment paid huge dividends for those IBM'ers who ran the whole gamut from basic training, technical training, personal skills development, sales school, management training, business applications, to general business appreciation. They had exposure to the widest range of skills development.

Nevertheless, it seems that it is always possible to "grab defeat from the jaws of victory".

Take the example of the fully trained IBM man who loved his camping, particularly in the Peak District. A dapper, always well-dressed man, with a charming smile and a "chipper" personality.

Camping gear stowed in the trailer, he and some colleagues set off on their long journey – sports jacket, open necked shirt, cravat, slacks, the usual smart appearance, even for a long drive.

It was Friday evening. A white car overtook at speed and indicated that he should pull onto the hard shoulder of the motorway. Seventy five miles per hour pulling a trailer was just not on. It was a "fair cop", and the transaction between the constabulary and himself resulted in a speeding ticket which was duly consigned to his top pocket. The rest of the journey continued uneventfully.

It was Tuesday – the Bank Holiday over, the happy campers began their long journey home. Unbelievably, at almost exactly the same position on the motorway, now going south, a white car overtook and beckoned him to stop on the hard shoulder again: 78 mph towing a trailer was just not on.

Another ticket was handed over, and with more anger, stuffed into the same top pocket of the sports jacket. He walked slowly back towards the car and trailer, inwardly bemoaning his bad luck. Six points in five days.

Then the panic set in. He already had six endorsement points. Six plus that new six – it didn't take Einstein to work out the consequences.

His mind raced; his lifetime of training passed through his brain. Consciously and carefully, the campaign built itself. In seconds the plan was born, formulated, the words chosen, the body language selected.

He turned back to the patrol car and re-engaged in conversation with his "target customer". The sales campaign spilled eloquently from his lips, his audience rapt. Would he get the decision? In his head he yelled "Yes" as the "prospects" indicated that on this occasion a warning would be adequate.

Profuse thanks for the decision, the promise of no further problems, the lesson had been learnt. At their request, he handed back the ticket from his top pocket. A smile, a final thank-you and he turned to return to his car.

"*Sir*" the officer spoke sternly; "your ticket appears to have magically assumed last Friday's date!"

The lesson? Sometimes you must combine bullshit with brains, and vice-versa. Sometimes, of course, you must let your natural personality shine through....

"Close to the brink"

One salesman, a legend in his lifetime, had boundless energy, unbridled enthusiasm and was a master juggler of many balls. Raw honesty, an unshakeable belief in his product set, a simple determination to win a customer and to serve him thereafter. He would promise the world, and against all the odds he would deliver. His customers loved him, and he exemplified the IBM reputation of his era.

A long and tedious campaign to sell a system to a small company had taxed his patience to the limit. Slowly but determinedly he had dragged his prospect from the world of the Luddite to the realisation that computers had arrived. Demonstrations, reference visits, the whole range of his kitbag had been utilised. Competition had been seen off, the Board were with him, but getting the Managing Director to sign the contract continued to elude him. Somehow, this time the normal empathy he developed with his prospects and customers was not there. A final throw of the dice was called for. The Country Sales Manager who was visiting the branch was asked to throw his weight behind the campaign.

At the subsequent meeting, another demonstration of the proposed solution was completed, a reiteration of the benefits elucidated, and one by one the branch management team and the Country Sales Manager were introduced to the Managing Director.

The SE Manager pledged his resources to the successful installation of the system. The Marketing Manager assured him of his commitment to the delivery schedule. The Branch Manager confirmed that he would deploy all necessary support services and...the Country Sales Manager gave the "corporate message".

The salesman in classic fashion produced the contracts and proffered his pen to the Managing Director. Hesitant, uncertain and clearly worried, the Managing Director, outnumbered, searched for an escape.

Undaunted, the salesman asked, "Is there any remaining reason that prevents you taking this important step in the future of your company?"

The Managing Director, searching for a suitable reply answered, "I shall feel such a *prat* if this all goes wrong".

Without hesitation the salesman said, "Don't worry at all, I have sold systems to bigger prats than you."

A deafening silence fell over the assembled gathering, eyes shot to the ceiling or the floor, the whole management team cringing as those words echoed in their ears. All that sales training....

As eyes turned cautiously to the MD, the apologies already being mentally rehearsed, his furrowed brow uncreased and first a sparkle appeared in his eyes, then a huge grin developed which exploded into loud and raucous laughter. He grasped the salesman's hand, shook it vigorously and said, "You've got yourself a deal."

In Summary

Having recruited and trained high-quality people, having provided a set of business guidelines, then recognise that humans come in many different shapes, sizes and characters.

Don't try to mould them all into a straight-jacket.... capitalise on their individuality.

We continue the winning theme in the next chapter, tempered a little by the pain of losing.

5. How We Won (or Lost) the Business

This is it. This is where all that corporate planning, recruitment, ethical guidance and empathetic people management congealed to deliver the revenues that made IBM a $60 billion corporation.

In this chapter, we will look at a number of very real stages in obtaining those increased revenues, with examples of the determination and initiative shown by people in the field. However, before we describe all that dynamic endeavour to secure further business, let us briefly look at two areas that fundamentally affected the "why" and "how" a branch focused its energies – Quota and Productivity.

Quota

Probably the most powerful word in the IBM dictionary. This was the "engine-room" of IBM's success. Quota equalled Target.

The truly professional salesman was not only successful in securing the business, but also was a master at getting the right targets allocated to him.

Not surprisingly, branch people who were on commission spent a lot of time managing next year's quotas. This was indeed a practised art form, as well as a numeric science.

At year end, successful salesmen, if they were keeping the same territory, would assess at the start of the last quarter whether, and how, they would release actual orders to IBM administration. If they were well on target for the year, they might withhold some business. If they had zero chance of making quota, then why would they jeopardise next year's opportunities by securing such business this year?

Well, there might be several reasons....

- Postponement might make the business less rewarding to them next year. This had to be a guess as the new sales plan would not be published till the New Year.

- A sales colleague might be prepared to offer some "inducement" – for example, to swap his *Sales* points for your *Installing* points, or vice versa.

Or, more usually:

- The branch needed the business.
- The branch didn't, but the district did.
- Neither the branch nor the district needed it, but "country" did. Rumour had it that in this event, even bus tickets might be credited.

If they could not "avoid" over-performing, then they had to adroitly influence any quota increase in order not to miss out, for example, on the "Golden Circle".

The successful salesman, if he were not staying with the same patch, would clean up all new business, and hope his quota was not adjusted upwards. Before accepting an account, an assuming salesman would examine the installed, on-order and debt positions with a remarkable degree of thoroughness, and in any case would usually endeavour to cancel any outstanding customer orders on the basis that they were "soft". No less than Jacques Maisonrouge himself cancelled 1200 "points" in this way, against a quota of 1200 points, and subsequently failed to make his first year's targets!

Looking upwards from salesman to sales management, planning numbers extended into resource allocation. Managers in a branch, unless they were maniacally power-driven and looking for the visibility that high quotas would give them, spent a lot of time and effort in negotiating "the lowest quotas for the maximum resource". This was against the IBM planning context of "the larger the target, the more people". A common ploy to assist with obtaining more resource was to argue that a territory or account was dried out, that there was no easy future business, and "investment resource" was the only strategic way forwards. One soon came to recognise the "higher members of the magic circle" who would cast intriguing spells in the practice of this art of misconception, and very often succeed!

Productivity

You will have read in Chapter 1 about the attention IBM paid to helping its sales people achieve their targets. At the same time, productivity was the name of the game. Towards this end, "programs" and "methodologies" flourished to help those in the sales trenches kill two, three or even more target birds with one stone.

IBM in the 70's spawned "programs", like aphids multiplying in a hot summer. "Programs" permeated every business discussion. Some of them were indeed very good, bringing a thought-through structure or process to many aspects of the business. Before the arrival of such programs, there was usually a lot left to an individual to do, both in planning and executing. He not only had to execute a plan, but plan how to do the planning in the first place as well!

One methodology was Intensive Planning.

Intensive Planning

During our time with IBM, many new approaches and ideas for organisation and planning emanated not only as one would expect from the USA, but also from other countries. Canada stood out as a major contributor in this respect.

Late in 1974 a new approach for account sales planning was shipped across the Atlantic: Intensive Planning. Intensive Planning (IP – IBM couldn't talk ideas without spraying acronyms all over the table) was heralded as "major", "significant", "revolutionary", and purported to be somehow "different". It was not explained in any detail. When discussed in the branch office it was enveloped in a mystical cloud and coloured with shades of the unknown.

From on high, it was decreed *mandatory* that every significant (large) account team would undertake (or was it, undergo) an "Intensive Planning" session. Nobody knew exactly what went on in one of these IP happenings, but there was much rumour that it was not a pleasant experience.

It involved the whole account team being locked away in a suitable venue far from home. No contact was to be made with the outside world, including one's family. Much worse, of course, was that the account (customer) was denuded of its usual support from IBM, and had a locum planted to keep the ship afloat. Maybe this was a good thing in one way or another – you know, "absence makes the heart grow..." It was rumoured that each day was virtually endless. A session finished only when it or the participants were totally and mutually exhausted.

While the definition of "team" on an IP covered those directly and wholly involved in securing IBM's revenues with that customer, in the early days it excluded Administration and Customer Engineering. Strange really, in view of the fundamental importance of these functions to customer satisfaction.

In the UK, some large accounts from the Birmingham office were "volunteered" to pioneer this new concept of planning. One team went to Aviemore in the scenic north west of Scotland. The tom-toms and smoke signals back to the branch were not encouraging to future teams, including stories of participants almost suffering nervous breakdowns, but still little was explained by management to future volunteers.

What was it like to be "IP-eed'?

"Rolls Royce planning"

In January 1975, the IBM team handling the Rolls Royce account went to the Imperial Hotel at the south Devon coastal resort of Torquay for their IP. This was RR Aero Engines, not the company producing cars with the lady on the bonnet.

RR had its major sites at Derby, Hillington (Glasgow), East Kilbride (also in Scotland), Bristol, and Leavesden. The main IBM marketing team, based full time at Derby, supported the first three of these sites with two sales representatives and four systems engineers. Both salesmen were very focused and objective, one sharply analytical and the other very good with people – quite a balanced combination.

Equally the Derby SE's were exceptional: bright, positive and, to differing degrees, ambitious.

At the same time, all these people had their feet on the ground and wanted work to be an uplifting experience. This was going to be an outstanding team.

Bristol support came from the Bristol Branch, and Leavesden from Welwyn Garden City. The Derby sales people reported "pay and rations" to a Senior Marketing Manager. The SE's had their own manager. The Bristol and Welwyn people were not full time on RR.

The total contingent, comprising six full-timers from Derby, an SE from Welwyn, plus the Marketing Manager, left their loved ones behind on a Sunday afternoon in January to venture for the next two weeks into this unknown, shielded world of the IP.

The hotel was (and still is) a splendid 5-star overlooking Torbay harbour, with very comfortable rooms. Tennis court, swimming pool, squash court, snooker room, sauna and massage figured in the facilities on offer – but IP's didn't allow time for those!

The hotel also boasted some of the finest cuisine in the country, and indeed it proved so in practice, with the consequence that by the first Thursday nobody had any room left for the main course at lunch, let alone the five-course dinner.

Come Monday morning, 9 am, still the team didn't know what was going to happen on this IP. Enter the conductor; not so much a conductor as what would today be called a facilitator. This was Doug, a very tall IBM'er with sandy wavy hair (remember him in the prologue?), rather laconic and with prodigious stamina.

Doug elucidated gradually on the first morning: "All very straight-forward really. You start off by agreeing what your objectives are, whatever they are. You then agree what the problems are in achieving those objectives. Then finally, you agree what should be done about them."

Notice "agree" is present in each of the above. Unanimity was mandatory – no dissension, even to the minutest detail.

The first two days were fascinating.

We started with the "objectives".

The salesmen believed the objectives were all about IBM revenues and their own sales targets. The SE's wanted to include "career progression" and "technical excellence". The marketing manager wanted "development of top customer contact" high on the list.

Such diversity could have caused endless debate. It became obvious that without unanimity of objectives, an IP could indeed become a nightmare for tiring participants struggling till 2 or 3 o'clock in the morning to make progress.

Once the team discovered that the key to happiness, therefore, was to get a firm bedrock of agreed objectives, this was achieved very rapidly. By a process of democratic discussion, the SE's conceded (sorry, agreed) that without "revenues" there would be no "career paths" anyway. It was also agreed that "top customer contact" was really the individual job of the marketing manager.

So it was agreed between the participants:

- Revenues were to be the objectives for the IP.
- The core group was to be the Derby contingent.
- The "guest" SE from Welwyn would contribute when discussing Leavesden (he didn't mind not participating all the time as he could then improve his putting on the excellent Imperial carpet).
- the marketing manager would set his own plans for "top level contact".

The "six" plus the Welwyn SE also agreed a few house rules:

- The person who knew most about a topic would in effect present it, saving useless guessing and speculation.
- If nobody knew anything about a subject, "it" should be labelled as such and posted for future action.
- The team would work from 9 am till 5 pm; 5 pm to 6 pm would be devoted to refreshing the body through exercise.
- The marketing manager would become an "outside observer" as he had wider and different responsibilities.

In this way the process was very quick and sure, avoiding endless academic or hypothetical debate. An excellent team spirit developed.

Doug gave us some very useful IP process guidance rules and tips such as:

- Be unanimous.
- Think binary – that is, use questions that provoke yes/no answers.
- Don't interrupt.

and

- A problem properly stated is a problem half solved – which one member of the team paraphrased into "a trouble shared is a trouble doubled".

He also tried to explain "confusion" as coming from the Latin "con" meaning "with", and "fusion" meaning "together".... but somehow this didn't seem to quite gel.

This RR Account Team Intensive Planning session was hugely successful, with consequential excellent revenue achievements spanning the next three years. Presumably the customer thought it was beneficial to him as well.

Selected customer management were invited on later IP's for a day or so to provide input – essential in any respect. And other parts of the branch organisation were also included – namely, the aforementioned administration and customer engineering.

IP's subsequently lost the revolutionary "frogs and tar brew" image they first had, and became much enjoyed as a useful item in the sales planning armoury. Follow-up IP sessions were held every six months with somewhat less extreme satisfaction, perhaps due to the fact that as the IBM business grew so did the size of the support team, and that of course impeded and lengthened the debating process.

As budget belts tightened, the mode of an IP was diluted to becoming a few days "off-site" from the local IBM office, and then ultimately to being held "in-house", causing a reduction in the "difference" of the occasion.

Pointers for a successful IP, or any planning session come to that were:

- Team size is critical – six or less is very productive; more than six can be slow or superficial.
- Team members must be wholly focused on the same objectives.
- Numeracy in discussion is essential, particularly for objectives.
- Future actions: tag them with a name and a date. Anything else will mean it won't happen.

Tools for the troops

We were talking about "Productivity". In the early 80's, IBM was spreading its own internal global network throughout the organisation – sometimes called PROFS, sometimes NOSS (PROFS, Professional Office System; NOSS, Networked Office Support System). This was the mainframe-based E-mail system linking everywhere to everywhere in the IBM world, coupled with Note and Document handling functions.

The E-mail part was very good, especially for communicating with IBM'ers in other countries. What used to take weeks of uncertainty as to whether "it" had arrived, or whether the issue (whatever it was) had been fixed, was transformed. The document-handling part was third-degree torture. If any of you ever used IBM's PC-based DisplayWrite, you would never believe it, but this was unarguably worse. Not for IBM'ers "Click and Point" easy to use desktop systems. No, there were plenty of IBM internal mainframes lying around to be used up.

PROFS/NOSS was not the easiest system to grasp.

"Find it if you can!"

The team handling the BL (used to be British Leyland) account was as varied as you could find.

Errol, the Marketing Manager was a bright, chain-smoking individual, liked good wine, was stable at all times, never put on any weight, and was one of those chameleons who could mix very well with people at all levels, either within IBM or with customers.

Nick, one of the salesmen, was shorter, stockier, and displayed a disinclination to get involved in business matters – except when the occasion arose for a financial deal, when he was as sharp as the proverbial razor.

Tony, the other salesman, tall, excellent golfer, very courteous, and deeply committed to see IBM succeed in a fair-play environment.

Brian, the Account Systems Engineer, one of the rare breed who understood computing technology yet who could also relate to "ordinary" people and got on well with everybody.

Denise, one of the SE's, was a determined individual whose fair sex didn't prevent her ruling her customer staff with a rod of steel.

Jonathan, quiet chap, very bright, conveyed a demeanour that erroneously gave the impression he was remote from it all.

Frank, the industry specialist, getting on in years, betrayed a sceptical sense of humour.

And Ronnie. His name wasn't Ronnie at all, but he looked so much a spitting image for Ronnie Corbett, the British TV personality, that it was a natural name for him. Ronnie was the Field Systems Engineering Manager (FSEM).

Apropos of nothing to do with this anecdote: FSEM's came in two flavours. They were either very involved in their customers with the SE's and salesmen, or they settled into the backwaters of arranging annual branch Christmas lunches and SE Awards-of-the-Month. In the same way, the Branch Systems Engineering Manager (BSEM) was either involved with the customers, or was in practice the Personal Assistant to the Branch Manager.

Anyway, it was summer. Errol decided to hold an account meeting and, as it was summer, he decided to do something different. Denise's house was in the countryside, nice place, largish garden, with swimming pool, and the ideal venue for a stuffy account review. As it happened, the weather switched itself on, and the temperature climbed up to the 90's (in old money).

What a splendid day it turned out to be. Most of the team assembled at about 9.00 am. Nick had brought the refreshments, so starters for 10 was copious Buck's Fizz, and the day went on from there.

Like most good planning sessions, there was a melange of happenings. Frank at one point tried to inject numeracy into the planning, but this didn't work as everybody else was being an expert at getting the barbecue working. The team used the pool randomly and frequently during the whole meeting to cool off.

All was going well, when somebody knocked a glass into the pool, and Ronnie (who else?) donned his Jacques Cousteau gear, complete with snorkel, and dabbled up-tails-all to retrieve the fragments, while everybody cheered at his initiative.

An excellent day in building Team Spirit and, by the way, in account planning. The shame of it was, of course, that it had to finish, and why? Well, there was a training session back in the office starting at 5 o'clock. We were being introduced to this new "facility", as IBM liked to call it, PROFS.

It may have been the heat, or the long arduous day, or something else, but the intricacies of PROFS did not readily enter the neuron channels of the reassembled account team. "Aren't you all red," mused the instructress; except for Errol, who possessed an olive-coloured skin even in a November fog.

Next day, Errol held a review of the account meeting to record, as all good managers should, the mandatory follow-up "Action Plan". Errol had a reasonably good technical background; he had been a systems programmer with Tube Investments before joining IBM. He therefore decided to capture the minutes on-line, live, with this new PROFS productivity aid.

Some four hours later at the natural break in the proceedings, Errol pressed the selected function key with the intention of storing the document on disk. After lunch, he logged on to his screen to E-mail copies of the plan to the team. Guess what – yes, we've all suffered it – the document had evaporated into the ether. Somewhere, never to be seen again.

Make sure your productivity aid has been written by a user.

Territory Management

A salesman's lot is to obtain business from his territory. Simple? Yes, unless his world is changed around him.

Setting aside IBM's frequent reorganisations, the essential continuity and bonding unit in the field was the Branch. Within that unit, particularly in the earlier decades, it was reasonably simple to establish one's territory. Named customers and prospects were owned by specific salesmen. Probably the only conflict of interest in the 60's was between a Data Processing (DP) salesman, his equivalent from the Service Bureau (SB), and to a lesser extent with the Office Products (OP) marketers. This was not a great problem, as the first two were usually in the same branch, and the OP people were selling typewriter products – a different ball-game entirely.

However, as OP products became more sophisticated, containing memory, programs and (floppy) disk storage, overlap of marketplace and conflict of ownership increased.

This trend continued to the point where it made sense to include the increasingly sophisticated OP products into the emerging small systems product line of the new General Systems Division (GSD). Now this really gave the territory managers a problem. Soon there were two IBM contending divisions: the traditional DP Division and the new General Business Group Division (formed from the merger of OP and GSD). Both divisions had something to offer to all customers, or so they thought.

As a result, quite often there were two IBM salesmen calling on the same customer, each proffering their boxes and systems as the best solution to his information system needs. It got to the point where customers would ask formally, "What is the IBM proposal. Which of these two solutions is IBM really recommending?" This of course was heaven-sent stuff to competition, particularly small systems suppliers such as DEC.

Jacques Maisonrouge held the view that it was "a good thing for our clients to deal with only one face". And he also asked the $64,000 question: "How could two IBM salesmen propose different technical solutions to one customer problem?"

Well, what was the answer?

Not JM's, as clearly he couldn't convince the then IBM Chairman, who admired the GM multi-divisional product-based model, with Chevrolet, Pontiac, Buick and the others. IBM lost sales to competition because of this, even in the USA, but, as JM added: "Management in Armonk was a long way from Nashville Tennessee."

Demonstrations

There is no doubt that a good demonstration went a long way towards not only showing that the IBM offering fitted the bill, but also particularly to allay any fears that "users" might have. Some of the best IBM demonstrations were to this fraternity, especially with the advent of the PC.

Golden rule: "a user is a person who uses." You know, it is important in any new proposed system to demonstrate that people can actually use the system, since at the day-to-day level they have procedures and practices very often refined and matured over many years.

You also know that there were three major guidelines very often forgotten during the exciting journey towards selling a new computer, and all these concerned the "user':

- Does the proposed system mean he will have a higher workload?
- Will he, for whatever reason, become involved in "unnatural acts", or contorted processes, in his daily sphere of activity?
- Will he, directly and personally – not just the company – derive benefit from the new system?

A good demonstration would go a long way towards helping a potential user gain confidence and enthusiasm.

When IBM became involved with "applications", you could always tell demonstrators who had "done it" from those who had read the manual the night before. There are many memorable demonstrations that come to mind.

"Telling demonstrations"

On one occasion , a bright young engineer was demonstrating one of IBM's CAD/CAM application packages, called CATIA (Computer Aided Three-dimensional Interactive Application), a very complex integrated system with full 3-D, surfaces, NC (Numerical Control), robotics, kinematics, and much more. There were eight customer personnel in the demonstration room. The demonstrator had his workstation screen, keyboard, and dials. The classical demonstrator position is "2 O'clock", on a swivel chair, so that he can face both his workstation and his audience.

On this occasion, a customer asked if the system could do "XXX", a quite complex offset filleting design. Instead of the demonstrator saying simply "yes", and leaving it there, he almost said yes, turned his face to the screen, and proceeded to work his way towards proving, by demonstration, that CATIA could in fact do "XXX".

Half an hour later, he turned back to his audience to find that there was only one customer left in the room, and he wasn't the one who had asked the original question!

Another demonstrator, par excellence, was so laid back when demonstrating, again, CATIA, that he never went beyond getting a single "point" and "line" on the screen, so effective was his handling of people. Sometimes, indeed, he did venture into creating a circle, but this was very rare and special – and a very effective salesman he was, too.

Towards the end of the 70's, in the mid to early gestation days of marketing a key MRP (Manufacturing Resources Planning) package called COPICS (Communications Oriented Production Information and Control System), monthly two-day seminars were held for customers' user and DP management. There were usually two or three IBM'ers running the show, and, de rigueur, there was a demonstration of COPICs' on-line updating capability.

On the first evening of one such seminar, one of the IBM'ers bumped into an old university colleague whom he had not seen for years, and consequently spent some time, and money, reminiscing, as only old students can do. He was still excited and over the top at 10 o'clock the next day. Could he operate his light pen on the VDU screen? No, he could not. The demonstration was an energetic disaster. Yet he was such a personable fellow that the audience applauded his efforts with some sympathy and considerable understanding.

He was known for ever after as "the man who couldn't hit a field with a light pen".

Presentations

Considerable time was spent in IBM bringing a high level of professionalism to presentations. It became almost impossible to hold an internal meeting without the "visual aid" – a good thing in many ways, as we have all experienced the perambulatory meeting with no agenda, no structure and no content. The attendee with the best prepared visual aids usually controlled the meeting. Internal IBM meetings progressively had a very high content of visual aids as it became easier to prepare them.

In the 60's it was the flip chart:

- either big felt tips on paper 4x5 feet – no green prizes would be awarded today. A salesman needed a trainee in tow to lug the board and stand, as most customers would not have one readily available.
- or mini flips – about 12x9 inches. Very good in their way, but obviously only useful for smaller gatherings.

Then came the "foil" as it was called in IBM – the "overhead" or "acetate" in other circles. The first incarnation employed smaller felt tip pens – permanent ones for the brave, washables for the careful. 35 mm slides had a role, but were found to be too time-consuming to prepare, and had to be of high-quality artwork. They remained the medium for large conferences.

With the advent of the PC, keyboard-literate progressives could hold their presentation on the system and project it, either on the monitor or onto a large screen. Sometimes a case of "bullshit baffles brains" hype, the moving dynamic (in the literal sense) PC presentation could hold an audience almost spellbound, regardless of content.

In the early days, branch management rehearsed every customer presentation. You can imagine the pain as the salesman had to alter (frequently) his large flip charts according to different managers' views. In the latter days, such rehearsals faded from fashion. Was this because it was not so much pain for the salesman to alter his artwork?

The Proposal

In the early days, this was one, two or even three chock-full, bright blue ring binders. In the latter days it became a letter or an assembly of diverse papers.

All included the obligatory disclaimer.

The early proposals were statements of how the systems would actually work, plus volumes, timings, and sample print-outs. Often, of course, the trainees in the branch were the actual draughtsmen who meticulously created much of the graphical content. Sample reports were hand-crafted with a scattering of XXXX's showing what and where data would actually print. Application diagrams were created using flowcharting templates with squares, rectangles, oblate circles, and flashes of lightning to represent the movement of data.

As IBM became more cost-conscious, so the thickness of these plastic templates became thinner and they broke quite readily. If you have one of the earlier templates in your possession, you never know, it could be worth a small fortune. In any case, it shows you are a distinguished member of the PTC ("proper template club").

These proposals represented a critical point in a campaign, and they were presented with due ceremony, in multiple sets to the appropriate customer executive. He would distribute them around his company board. It was always interesting on ordinary calls, or even CAPS reviews, to see how much dust had collected on them as they bent the bookshelf.

The effort in writing these tomes, which was considerable, was invaluable not only in showing how a system would actually work, but also in giving a new branch trainee the guiding framework for him to wrestle with panels or programs as a result of a successful sale. Thick proposals were good for you. Rather like today, computer print-outs are (assumed to be) more accurate than hand-written material.

In the latter days, it became easier to print from computer-held standard clauses. In any event, the proposal became more a list of hardware and software, features and prices, still with the statutory disclaimers.

"Savvy" management would drum into lesser mortals that a "proposal is a summary of what has been agreed and sold". This was, and is, an absolute in the salesman's pocket book. If you haven't *sold* it yet, then it's no use wasting time in the office writing about it! On the other hand, woe betide you if you lost the business and you had failed to submit a formal proposal.

The Close

Not much we can say that has not been said already. "Your pen or mine?" "Would you prefer a red one or a blue one?" "Is there a best day to deliver your exciting new system?"

Invariably a customer would "sign" because he had a good relationship with his salesman. This could be built upon a base of personal empathy, business trust, or joint suffering....

"End of year perils"

For most of the time you could rely upon IBM to "talk strategic". Many might argue that this was merely a means to an end, in order to appear a cut above the rest. Nevertheless, IBM retained highly-paid staff to present this strategic face to the world. Information Technology, they said, was not something you could leave to the troops. Least of all was it something you could leave to the data processing professionals.

No, IT must be a key focus for the board of directors. They must take a top-down, strategic view of objectives, opportunities and requirements. They must build a long-term strategic IT plan – "like what IBM does".

For the most part, as an IBM employee, you believed that it was a strategy-driven company. It had to have a clear view ahead. How, otherwise, could it be so successful? Shame to say, however, there was always one time in the year when all notion of strategy was cast overboard in the panic to secure last-minute business before the year-end close-off. It was almost as if the strategy then was to behave "non-strategically". Many a daring deed was done in those last few days.

What about the time when, as a favour to a colleague, an account manager agreed to get a contract signed on the last working day before the Christmas/New Year break? The account manager knew the customer very well. His colleague, an overlay specialist salesman, did not have that advantage. Since the account manager was in any case planning to attend the customer's departmental Christmas lunch, one more little task should not be too difficult.

The lunch was being held at an hotel near Oxford. All the customer staff had taken the precaution of booking a coach for the journey, out and back – they intended to enjoy themselves. The account manager duly arrived by car, and a convivial time was had by all – most of all by the departmental manager who was required to sign the contract. Let's say his name was Geoff.

Our account manager, of course, had to hold back a bit. He had business to conduct, and had to drive back to the office to register his colleague's, hopefully signed, contract. However, Geoff wanted one last brandy before returning to the office. So, having ensured the safe departure of his merry department back to the office by coach, he returned to the hotel with his IBM account manager chauffeur to finish his brandy.

This lasted longer than was planned. One or two key business issues needed to be discussed, including, of course, getting the contract signed. However, that had to be deferred until Geoff got back to his office, as he wanted to discuss a couple of points with one of his managers. What unfortunately went unobserved during all of this was it had begun to snow – not just a few flakes, but tumbling out of the sky and smothering the roads with a thick white blanket.

Finally, the state of the weather was pointed out by a ministering waiter. "No problem," said the account manager, undaunted, "we can take the longer route back on the main roads. They'll be clear." "Aah," said Geoff, "I have to go via the chicken farm to collect the eggs my wife ordered for her Christmas cooking." Needless to say, the chicken farm was on the "country" route back to the office.

So they set off, both peering into the shawling snow, as they skidded and slid their way back. "Tell me when we get to the chicken farm. I've no idea where it is," said the account manager. "Right you are," came the reply, now a little hesitant as Geoff had a tendency to nod off after a more than modest alcohol intake.

Suddenly: "STOP," Geoff bellowed, as he glimpsed the farm on the left through the blizzard. Now, to stop quickly under those conditions would have tested the grip of a tank track. The account manager made a brave attempt both to stop and turn into the farm. He managed, instead, to slide past the farm gate, and finished with the underside of the car balanced on a slight mound, alongside a hedge. But at least it was on the correct side of the road and appeared fairly stable. "Be with you in a second. I'll just collect the eggs," said Geoff, and stepped out of the car into the snow, perhaps reminiscent of Captain Oates in similar weather conditions.

Now, that was where Geoff made his mistake. Between the car and the hedge, on the left, was a ditch, about 5 feet deep, now concealed by the drifting snow. The account manager, himself somewhat startled by the adverse tilt of the balanced car as Geoff got out, was even more taken aback by the sudden total disappearance of his customer. Customers have been known to take evasive action when pursued by contract-wielding IBM'ers, but this seemed a bit extreme. Geoff, however, was made of stern stuff – an ex-soldier and rugby player of some standing. He scrambled from the ditch, sobered somewhat by his immersion in the snow, shook himself like a terrier and determinedly resumed his egg mission, squelching and stumbling across the farmyard.

The eggs having been duly procured, the return to the office was achieved without further ado (after assistance from the farmer to push the car from its hedge-side balance), and the still-merry department was treated to the sight of the two damp, but triumphant, stars drying their clothes by the emergency office fire. All agreed it was a fine start to the festive season.

The IBM contract was signed, and the grateful overlay salesman provided a seasonal reward for the heroic account manager.

Flexible Selling

IBM branch people were nothing if not innovative. Different techniques for opening up an impenetrable territory, making an even better business case, or finding new ways to close the sale, were all latent attributes waiting for the right climatic conditions to germinate the seed. Take for example....

"Virtual reality"

Branch annual sales targets had key measurement checkpoints at the end of each quarter, with associated sizeable bonuses.

A curious fact about IBM's sales performance was that some 40 per cent of the yearly target was typically achieved during the fourth quarter – hence the famous "banana curve". Because of this, the Christmas period was always a hectic time. Whenever this festive season approached, the branch was invariably stimulated to double and redouble their efforts finally to "pass the winning post".

Once, by late May, all the salesmen were way below target, the branch performance was dismal and consequently under intense scrutiny from senior management. The branch management team were bereft of plans to achieve the half-year objective.

At the next tense management team meeting, a manager remarked, "I wish it were nearly Christmas. At least then we would bring in the business."

"That's it," the branch manager expostulated, "we will declare the 25th June as Christmas Day."

The branch office was transformed. Christmas decorations were put up, a seasonal tree erected and posters displayed throughout the office announcing the celebrations. Christmas lunch was arranged and special Christmas bonuses were promulgated for exceptional sales achievements. No more low morale and despair. A real festive spirit flourished. Everyone joined in, including customers and prospects. They changed from a state of puzzlement and disbelief, to sending Christmas cards.

June 25th arrived, the traditional Christmas lunch was consumed – silly hats, crackers, exploding streamers, the full works. You don't need to be told that the half-year objective was achieved – and we still had the real Christmas to look forward to.

Flexible Installing

IBM progressively recognised that the bottom line was best served by actual installs rather than the notional "letter of intent". Heavier emphasis was placed therefore on firm signed contracts, definite instals and receiving the due monies.

"It's good to talk"

In 1974 IBM took the plunge into the world of telephone exchanges – a black art world if ever there was one. The IBM product was a break-through – it was software controlled. No more of the mechanical switches invented by Dr. Strowger generations before. This was the application of computers to telephone switching systems.

The trouble was that the world of telephone exchanges outside North America was dominated by the local country nationalised utilities. These utilities, of which the Post Office was the UK manifestation, had developed a culture that properly belonged to the ark. No telephone exchange could be attached to the national network until it had been given their "type approval". This was a long drawn-out process ensuring that any competitive advantage gained by a new technology break-through would be dissipated in the bureaucratic corridors.

Also of course, IBM was sometimes seen as that dreaded, predatory US Corporation whose sole ambition was to destroy locally developed technologies – better make sure we slow them down a bit.

IBM didn't exactly help its own case. The new product, attractively entitled the "IBM 3750 Switching System", was announced only outside North America, so the very marketplace not dominated by nationalised utilities was excluded. Why was this? Well, one factor may have been that the No.1 supplier of exchanges in that marketplace was the US Corporation AT&T, just about IBM's largest customer! So the rest of IBM's world was required to push out this particular product boat.

Immense pressure was brought to bear at all levels in IBM World Trade to achieve 3750 sales targets. It was a wonderful product to demonstrate. Just think, you could switch calls, you could have three-way conversations, you could automatically call back – the scope seemed limitless. All pretty insignificant today, but in the mid-1970's – Wow!

Our favourite demonstration to car parts distributors was where a customer could phone the distributor, the 3750 itself would fire an enquiry to the local computer, and relate back stock status information directly to the customer in a voice that sounded like a strangulated Dalek.

Yes, demonstrations were wonderful, but as to actually selling anything....

Dedicated teams were set up – with both specialist salesmen and SE's. Account teams, with plenty of other preoccupations, were likely to suffer the management "pounce" at any moment, and woe betide them if their 3750 marketing plan was not at the top of their priorities. It even got to the point where, at the IBM annual sales jamboree, the Hundred Per cent Club, every branch manager who had failed to sell a 3750 was summoned onto the stage to be ceremonially awarded a wooden spoon and told ominously that no branch manager would be awarded a bar to his wooden spoon!

Eventually of course the pressure told: 3750's were sold and installed, usually with great success. Initially sales were to the wealthier accounts – the finance sector, the oil companies. But 3750's were also bought by some of the more cost-conscious industrial accounts, sometimes amid unusual circumstances. One such sale concerned the installation of a 3750 at the Service Division of Austin Rover, some time about 1979.

After many years of trying to sell a 3750 to any part of the erstwhile British Leyland group of companies, IBM had three successes in fairly short order. First, a system was sold to the HQ offices of BL International, a company that had a brief existence, the second to Truck and Bus Division, and the third to Austin Rover Service.

One of the barriers to selling to the UK motor industry was that motor manufacturers seemed not to accept that complex equipment needed time to be made. Purchasing was all-powerful in the motor industry. No one else could place an order, and Purchasing themselves would only order following the customarily tortuous approval processes. Having finally placed the order, delivery was expected within days!

The Service 3750 system had been ordered to tie in with an office move, and was required to be operational as soon as the move was complete. It was part of a radical enhancement of the role of the Service function within Austin Rover. The date for the move was fixed and immovable. The normal length of time for IBM's engineers to install a 3750 was three weeks, following which it would be handed over to the Post Office engineers for connection and test within their network. They specified three months (sic) to complete that task. Because of delays in placing a firm order we had no more than two weeks between delivery and final commissioning! There was only one way this could be achieved and that was for IBM to take one weekend, and the Post Office the rest of the time, to complete their respective tasks.

The plant of manufacture for European 3750's was Montpellier, in the South of France. By emergency-shipping all the related containers we secured delivery for a Friday, about mid-afternoon, thus allowing IBM engineers to do their bit over the weekend.

All went well. Checks were made on the Friday morning. The 3750 had crossed the English Channel (or La Manche, si vous voulez) on time and, having cleared customs, was on its way to Cowley. There was no reason why the customer and ourselves should not all go out for a modest glass of wine.

That done, we returned mid-afternoon and were encouraged to see IBM's transport contractors parked outside the new Service offices. However, the 3750 had not yet been unloaded.

"Any problems?" – we hardly dared to ask.

"Yus, guv, the door is too narrow – the boxes won't go through."

A tape measure was produced, and, sure enough, they wouldn't.

"That's OK," someone piped up, "I'll get Maintenance to take the door and frame out – they'll go through then."

A call was made to Maintenance.

"What's the job number? No job number, so you haven't booked it then? That means it must be emergency, and my Director has to sign off all emergency jobs, and he's gone home for the weekend."

By this time it was 4.15 pm, and Cowley finished early on a Friday.

The IBM account manager could see a large black hole yawning in front of him. "Let's take the door off ourselves," he suggested.

It was as if he'd suggested everybody should take their clothes off and streak through the centre of Oxford. Colour drained from the faces of the Austin Rover cognoscenti. They whispered the one word, guaranteed at that time to bring a chill to the heart of industrial man:

"Demarcation – only maintenance staff can carry out maintenance work – it's in the local agreement. Any breach and there'll be a total shut down. Besides which, we're not even in their union."

The IBM account manager was not to be deflected. He hadn't battled to win the business, secure delivery, persuade IBM engineers to work through the weekend, etc., just to collapse at the final hurdle. "Bugger it – I've got a screwdriver in my car toolkit. The delivery lorry will hide what I'm doing. You all clear off and have a cup of tea. I'll take the door off and you can deny all knowledge. If I get stopped, that's my problem."

To their credit the Austin Rover staff all agreed – a brave move in the totally unionised, totally demarcated, nationalised world of Austin Rover in 1979.

So the 3750 was installed and handed over on time, proved a great success. And nobody said a word about doors.

On the Other Hand....

Surprise, surprise. It didn't always go to plan, or indeed to the IBM business liking. Here are a few anecdotes that show this "other side of the coin".

"The exploding sausage"

The offices of Marsh and Baxter, a meat processing company, were quite imposing really, set on the brow of the hill in Brierley Hill, some 10 miles west of Birmingham in the Black Country. Perhaps from the days when every individual nail and chain maker had his own pig in the back yard, so pork products were big business in that neck of the woods.

The IBM Service Bureau in Birmingham had a 1401 system offering a computing service to local industry and commerce, backed up by the Newman St. Data Centre in London, housing very powerful scientific computers used for number-crunching applications, such as simulating storm-water drainage systems or designing oil refineries.

These were the days when computers were rarely understood in business at large, and indeed were often mistrusted. Frequently the first thing one had to do as a computer salesman was to explain what computerised data processing was all about.

Cold calling, where one has to break in to a prospect from a standing start, was hated by many. The objective was to secure a first appointment with the senior customer manager. If you telephoned, his secretary's objective was usually to stop you getting through to her ward and care. If somehow you did get through, his objective, usually, was to get you off his back quickly, either with a total re-buff (*"No"*) or by relegating you to one of his subordinates. If this happened, it was considered a failure – the IBM ethos was very much "sell to the top".

The local marketing manager at that time, Bruce, was very keen on developing the prospecting and closing skills of his sales force. At one of his regular sales meetings, he decided to focus on cold calling.

We duly went through all the classical related topics, including the complete works of "objection handling", such as, "We've already got one", "I'm too busy", "Call back in six months time", or indeed, "IB who?"

Cold calling is no easy thing to do at the best of times, even when you can secrete yourself in splendid isolation to clinch this all-important appointment. Bruce, however, decided to make it "real", and invited the author to make a telephone cold call on one of his own prospects, in front of the other salesman!

This was a macho situation, equivalent to achieving a 300-yard drive down the middle! To fail to make such an appointment was like shanking this drive in front of the Club Captain.

In front of his peers, the author was definitely not going to fail.

Classically the cold phone call should last no more than three to four minutes. Thirty minutes later, having exhausted the total objection list, and probably the person at the other end, the salesman secured an appointment.

At this subsequent meeting, the senior manager, the commercial director, a mature and pleasant individual, soon invited a member of his staff to the room – we shall call him Paul. Paul was a younger man in charge of administration.

The company had a problem with sales systems; 1000 invoices a day were being prepared with mechanical keyboard machines; sales analyses and ledgers were handled manually. Timeliness and accuracy were the problems with such volumes.

A radical new computer system was designed covering daily

invoicing with downstream analysis, using the Birmingham Service Bureau. Paper tape was to be the input medium – not ideal for punched-card-oriented IBM!

Being daily, it required tight discipline and control. With large volumes, it also represented the salesman's total annual sales target – his eyes glowed and his attention was complete!

It was still only March. The chance of achieving a whole year's target so early was very exciting. It was also the time of the annual IBM Hundred Per cent Club (HPC) when successful salesmen went to a European city for three days of inspirational meetings and retuning by senior European and USA management.

Coincidentally, it was decided that Paul should learn more about computers, and he duly went off on a week's (the same week as the HPC) computer introduction course at the IBM Education Centre in London.

The salesman came back from the Club to find the whole deal was off. On his course, Paul had been told by the IBM educators that "Computers were very clever machines – so much so that they should be used for simulation techniques, management information and decision support applications, and definitely should not be wasted doing mundane things like invoicing".

Message: don't leave your business in other people's hands.

"How many times do you have to win the business before you've won it?"

The mergers, amalgamations and take-overs that finally led to what became known, in 1968, as British Leyland were rationalisations (politically inspired?) aimed at creating an internationally competitive UK automotive industry.

During the course of the 1960's most of the companies that were to become part of this new BL had converted their computer systems to IBM. Subsequently, a centralised systems function was created under the new BL corporate management to rationalise further, and consolidate computing operations. While it was not stated explicitly that the consolidation would be onto IBM, or IBM compatible, equipment, most people assumed this would be the case.

There was one important exception to this (apparently) unwritten rule. The Parts Divisions of the various car companies were to be allowed to keep control over their own computing operations. While this was undoubtedly due to the existence of some strong personalities within those divisions, there were indeed sound business reasons for doing so.

Parts operations have always been a highly profitable area for all automotive companies, and it was always claimed that the tight integration of computer systems with their business operations was critical to continued success. BL was no different from other automotive companies, and with BL's indifferent profit performance it hardly seemed wise to risk one of the few guaranteed areas of profitability.

However, parts operations for the BL car companies were not themselves fully integrated. During 1973 Jaguar, Rover and Triumph had consolidated their computing operations onto IBM equipment at Coventry, under the management of John (now Sir John) Egan. Austin/Morris parts computing operations were based on ICL computers at Cowley, under the management of one of the "strong personalities" alluded to above, Gerry Minch.

At the start of 1974 all car company parts operations were brought under a single management, headed by Allen (now Lord) Sheppard. John Egan was promoted to become the overall sales director. Clearly the plan was progressively to integrate the total business. The key question for IBM was: upon whose computers – ICL or IBM?

Nothing served to concentrate the minds of IBM more than the risk of losing an installed IBM computer – unless, that is, it was to be replaced by a bigger (IBM) one! So the scene was set for a ding-dong struggle, which had some interesting characteristics:

- Parts systems staff at Coventry were convinced they knew best, and would have a certain future if all computing were to be based on IBM.

- Parts systems staff at Cowley were convinced they knew best and their futures would be assured with ICL. They distrusted IBM whom they believed to be in the pocket of BL Corporate systems.

- BL corporate systems longed to take over parts computing, and this would be made easier if IBM were to be chosen.

- Executive management of parts division, mainly now based at Cowley, wanted to be left alone to get on and run their business. They distrusted Corporate staff.

Parts operations was one of the last areas within BL where IBM was not the "preferred supplier". IBM was therefore very keen to win the business, especially since losing meant the displacement of its installed computer at Coventry. ICL were desperate to retain the Austin/Morris parts operations business, particularly as this was one of ICL's few remaining major non-public sector installations.

Moreover, the then British Labour government had declared that computing was an area of "key national interest", and therefore was likely to use whatever influence it could to aid ICL who were still an independent British company.

In truth, IBM itself was in something of a quandary. It knew it somehow had to shake off the image of being "in the pocket" of BL corporate staff, and it had to win the confidence of the senior business management at Parts. IBM was also well aware that it might "win" the business only to find that the corporate staff would move in and, as had happened before, install cheaper IBM-compatible hardware. While in 1974 the so-called "software compatible" vendors (Amdahl and the like) had not yet arrived on the scene, there was an increasing band of suppliers of IBM-compatible peripheral equipment beloved of corporate staff. Interestingly, that problem was well-understood by parts management who were themselves being hit by suppliers of "compatible parts" for BL cars.

Nobody in IBM close to the action thought it was going to be easy, but few thought it would take eight years to sort out! During that time, faces, now famous, came and went. IBM sales campaigns were devised, modified, implemented and abandoned. BL itself collapsed, was rescued by the government (following the 1975 Ryder Report), received an injection of over £3 billion from the taxpayer, endured seemingly endless industrial strife (remember Red Robbo?), before finally re-emerging in the private sector in the late 1980's.

During these eight years IBM "won" the parts computing business on three occasions. Only on the third occasion did it become real. There is much truth in the view that you've never really won until your solution is installed, nailed to the floor and paid for.

The first "win" took place at the end of 1974. After a year of getting to know the key players, understanding better the politics, personalities and requirements of the business, the prevailing view in IBM was that this situation would follow the same path as others in BL. In other words, BL corporate systems would, more or less, tell the users (Parts Division) that they should follow corporate strategy and replace their ICL systems with IBM (just as others in BL had done), and that's that. The assumption was that IBM would ensure a graceful conversion from the one to the other. So, corporate systems staff duly ordered an IBM system in December 1974.

Alas, corporate systems made the mistake of assuming that Parts Division would merely roll over and accept the decision – after all, plenty of others had done just that. Some wiser counsels in IBM knew better. Parts Division were made of sterner stuff and rejected the Corporate systems plan. IBM therefore had to cancel the on-order equipment and was left duly chastened. At least corporate systems had been put in their place, and IBM had learnt that they had to convince the management of Parts Division – if only we could do that then all would be well, or so we thought. How wrong can you get?

After a certain amount of manoeuvring and waiting for Ryder to report, the second campaign commenced seriously in the middle of 1975, and ironically was provoked by ICL, who might have been better advised to bide their time for a bit. There was now a new Chief Executive, John Egan – a first-class salesman himself, who liked nothing quite so much as a sales campaign, whether on the giving or the receiving end.

ICL made a pre-emptive strike by proposing to help develop a new integrated parts system, thus allowing the IBM equipment at Coventry to be displaced, and in addition to provide new systems for BL car dealers to automate their own parts stock control (a "hot button" with John Egan) – and all for a "bargain" price. John Egan must have rubbed his hands with glee. Either IBM was to be dragged into a real Dutch auction or it would need to come up with a better solution. He sat back and awaited developments.

To be continued....

"Make sure your building foundations are sound"

RM Douglas was one of the leading building contractors in the UK, with head offices near to Birmingham. One day, the DP Manager (John) telephoned into the local IBM office to say, "We are looking to upgrade our computer system, would you be interested in proposing?"

A campaign was mapped out and John agreed to a series of presentations, meetings and visits over a period of two months to explore whether an IBM mainframe should replace the installed English Electric System 4/30.

This was an interesting situation. The English Electric System/4 series was acknowledged, even by many true-blue IBM people, to have some sound attributes. For one thing, the company wasn't the arch enemy ICT (later, of course, EE did merge with ICT to become ICL). Secondly, the System/4 was an acceptable "byte" machine, not "words" as with other competitors. It also had an operating system that was well structured. So the usual IBM technical machine-gunning was not going to work easily this time.

Some very good people were brought in to help with the sale. The construction industry specialist, Barry, waved his knowledgeable wand over the prospect. A leading systems engineer, another John, was brought down from Manchester to cover the technical aspects.

The case for IBM was going to be marginal, but the campaign was proceeding well.

Coincidentally, Geoff, another salesman, was running a similar campaign looking to replace a (larger) English Electric System 4/50 at a truck manufacturer in the north west of England. Geoff was an innovative person, and, with an empathetic customer DP manager, built a case "for IBM" with some (at that time) new-fangled concepts, like "return on investment" and "net present value". All this was based on the premise that the DP function would deliver applications faster with an IBM system. Accordingly, they (the truck maker) ordered an IBM System 370/145.

Now, "reference sells" like this were rare indeed. The RM Douglas salesman told this exciting story to the DP Manager, John, including the key theme, "a DP function will deliver applications faster with an IBM system, ROI, NPV and all", and invited him to explore this with his truck-making counterpart.

He made the call.

The outcome wasn't exactly as the salesman expected. RM Douglas did a deal with the truck maker to take their (larger) redundant System 4/50 as their upgrade route, for a very attractive price. Behind every silver lining there is a cloud?

With Patience and Determination...
Sometimes the Clouds Blow Away

You remember in "How many times do you have to win the business?" we left John Egan "awaiting developments"?

"How we all became a bit wiser"

IBM was given just two weeks to return with its counterbid to the ICL proposals in the form of a presentation to the Parts Division Board. The immediate reaction of some in IBM was not entirely unlike that of L/Cpl Jones in "Dad's Army" – "Don't panic...!" ICL clearly had a lot going for it.

First, it was the sitting tenant at Austin/Morris parts operations at Cowley. Cowley had undoubtedly become the HQ for the Division – all the senior management were located there and it could only be a matter of time before parts operations at Canley, with its IBM installation, would be closed down. Secondly, the bankruptcy of the British Leyland parent company at the end of 1974, effective nationalisation by the Labour government and the appointment of Lord Ryder to produce a rescue plan, all meant that political pressure to retain ICL would be mobilised. And, thirdly, any change of computer supplier would require a substantial rewrite of most, if not all, of the programs – a task not to be lightly undertaken without considerable business benefits.

The exact organisation structure within which all this was going on had changed a little from the previous year, and was likely to change much more when Ryder finally reported. John Egan, remember, was in charge of Parts Division. His boss was Allen Sheppard, in charge of Parts and Service Division and reporting to the main board.

The Service component of this business added an interesting, and important, side issue. Service, comprising warranty, owner maintenance handbooks, service manuals, after sales support, also included the complex area of KD (Knocked-Down kits for assembly overseas). Service systems imposed a considerable load on the ICL computers at Cowley, but because this work was closely tied in with engineering, manufacturing and sales, already running on IBM computers, so Service were anyway converting their systems. These would be processed on IBM computers located at Cowley body plant, about a mile away. So the plot was beginning to thicken nicely, thought IBM, and while John Egan might be tempted to say "good riddance" to the Service systems cluttering up his Parts computers, Allen Sheppard might be inclined to a slightly different view.

To that end, and always mindful of the political pressure directed towards chief executives thinking (however modestly) of replacing installed ICL systems, IBM had arranged for its UK Managing Director, Edwin (now Sir Edwin) Nixon, to meet Allen (now Lord) Sheppard to offer some tender-loving-care and firm commitments of IBM support.

Now, back to the plot....

Two weeks was not long to put together a counter-bid. Should we bother? Could we win the business? It would always be a brave man in IBM, however unlikely the chances of winning, who would recommend a "no bid", especially when there was an installed IBM system at stake. However, "Think laterally", "Don't exclude any options" – this was always material for the training classes in which we were all steeped. In this case the "no bid" route was given about three seconds consideration!

Whatever IBM did, it must avoid the risk of a Dutch auction with ICL on who could promise the most support. We would never win that contest. Whatever we did had to be self-evidently well-researched, well-presented, relevant and businesslike. We would have to persuade our audience that they should convert their Austin/Morris parts processing systems from ICL to IBM, while, in parallel, they integrated the existing Jaguar/Rover/Triumph systems – all at a probable cost in IBM computer hardware of some £1 million, plus the hidden costs of deferred benefits from any proposed ICL enhancements.

Now, why would they want to do that? Well, in one sense ICL had solved part of the IBM problem. By making their pre-emptive bid for the business, and by confirming the view that a new parts system was needed (did they know something about their own product line?), they'd probably convinced John Egan that he was faced with a major systems re-write in any case, whichever supplier he chose. So ICL had taken what had looked a very unlevel playing field, and levelled it for us! All we had to do now was make sure we continued the campaign in a professional manner.

There were, in simple terms, two requirements, remember: first, to rewrite, modify, convert (a mixture of all of these) and integrate the internal parts processing systems; secondly, to provide systems for dealer parts stock control.

To address the first, IBM assembled, within 24 hours, a small, highly skilled, technical team, led by the same systems engineer who had worked on the integration of the Jaguar/Rover/Triumph systems two years earlier. He was well-known to John Egan and much respected by him. This team's job was to gain a detailed understanding of every single program (over 100 of them) in the parts processing suite, determine whether each program could be converted or had to be rewritten, what files (we still called them "files" in those days – today they would be "datasets") were used, and what links there were to other programs.

This was a huge task, and it had to be accomplished in less than 10 days. In parallel, and as the earlier task threw up problems and issues, IBM's sales skills were mobilised to resolve every one of these with the applicable Parts Division staff. It was a good example of what could be achieved with a small team (about six people) of highly motivated, highly-skilled IBM'ers with outstanding sales leadership. This was all necessary – we had to do it, and do it well, but we couldn't necessarily claim to have done it better, or with more profound benefits, than ICL.

What would win us the business was requirement No.2 – parts stock control for dealers. We knew that business inside out. We also knew that John Egan was bursting to have a system like the one Vauxhall operated for its dealers – SCOOP (Stock Control and Order Processing). SCOOP had first been piloted on the IBM Service Bureau in 1966, had grown and finally been migrated in-house onto Vauxhall's own computers in the early 1970's.

The advantages to a motor manufacturer of processing franchised dealer parts data are immense: first-hand knowledge of parts sales trends, competitive parts penetration, etc. Furthermore, John Egan was ex-General Motors (Vauxhall were/are a part of GM). We believed he would have loved to be able to say to his erstwhile employers, "Look what I've now got". The automotive industry is, above all, a "macho" industry. Scoring points like that is in the blood. To be able to say to John Egan. "What we did for Vauxhall, we can do for you" was a winner. ICL could never make such a claim.

Through all of this the personality of John Egan emerges very strongly. We knew he would drive this decision, that none of his reporting directors would challenge him (challenging one's boss, uninvited, was always a good route to oblivion in that industry) and, most importantly, we knew he was good at selling. A good salesman likes nothing more than to see his own kind at work. On top of all the technical work, and the unique approach to dealer systems, IBM had to roll it all together into a first-class sales presentation.

So we did, and we won!

This time it took longer to fall apart – perhaps nine months. Why? Well, there were several reasons.

Once the decision had been made, implementation was handed over to others, who, as it happened, still hankered after ICL. To make matters worse, the Corporate Systems staff reappeared on the scene, offering to run these new IBM-based parts systems on the IBM computers already installed "just across the road" at the Cowley body plant. Once again the spectre reared its head that if Parts Division installed IBM computers it would lose control of its computing operations.

Last, but by no means least, the Ryder Report had been published. Allen Sheppard decided the new order of things wasn't for him and resigned. John Egan moved upwards to fill the vacancy, and a new boss moved into Parts Division. The new man was not from the parts business, had no great loyalty to the decisions already made, and did not attach much importance to them. He did, however, allow the dealer systems proposal to proceed, albeit at a much slower pace, and that became quite an important factor when IBM did finally succeed in winning the business – for real!

So what had we now learnt? First, that without a determined executive on the inside supporting the IBM case we were wasting our time. The resistance to change would always wear down an uncommitted implementation. Secondly, in the topsy-turvy world of British Leyland (or Leyland Cars, as it now became) post-Ryder Report, there was such little chance of anyone keeping their job at the top that resistance to change became self-fulfilling. In the torrid industrial relations world of the late 1970's senior management changes at Leyland Cars took place with bewildering regularity. During that time, therefore, IBM pulled back from serious marketing to Parts Division who had their own pre-occupations.

The ICL conversion went ahead – it had to, since ICL progressively withdrew support for their 1900 range of computers and the associated GEORGE operating systems upon which the parts systems ran, and replaced them with the 2900 range, running quite different VME/DME operating systems. The IBM computer at Canley was displaced. IBM winced, but had long since recognised that it was unavoidable. Those Canley staff with IBM skills either resigned, joined the Corporate Systems staff, or, significantly, transferred to Cowley where they continued to support the dealer systems development on IBM. There they provided a vital, small, but critical mass for the time when....

That time came, a little unexpectedly, in 1981, when, unprecedentedly, Parts Division had had the same Chief Executive for an amazing four years – one John Neill. He was clearly unhappy at the way his systems organisation seemed to be getting bogged down and unable to make the kind of business contribution he expected. He therefore appointed a new systems director, a man of considerable determination and intellect.

He was able to provide a new opportunity for IBM to prove its worth. All those dealer systems that had been in development following the "win" back in 1975 had been implemented on IBM computers at the Corporate Data Centre, now centralised at Redditch. The CDC operated as a preferred data centre within the Group, and charged out its computer time accordingly. The new systems director saw the opportunity to save those charge-out costs, and thereby install an IBM computer on site. At the same time he could implement on the IBM computer an important new application (purchasing) that had been, for ages, awaiting development on ICL.

Several birds could be killed with one stone.

Corporate systems staff resisted bitterly – this was good, since on every occasion in the past when they had seemed to be on IBM's side we'd eventually lost! They contended that the dealer systems workload could not be run on the (modest) size of IBM computer proposed. They were wrong. They also contended that there was no way that the new purchasing application could be run simultaneously. Again, wrong.

Fortunately for IBM, those IBM-trained staff who had transferred to Cowley when the IBM systems had been displaced from Canley had held together as a unit, and had enhanced their IBM systems skills while implementing the dealer systems. They were quickly able to form an effective project team, were well-led and totally committed to the success of the project. The installation of a modest-sized IBM computer was well-managed. The applications were transferred from the Corporate Data Centre without a hitch, and the new purchasing applications were implemented on time.

IBM provided strong technical and project management assistance, everybody kept their nerve and, overall, it was the success story we wanted. End-to-end this project had lasted barely eight months, from conception to implementation. As Churchill once said, on a more profound occasion: "This wasn't the beginning of the end, but it was perhaps the end of the beginning." At last, IBM was beginning to be trusted to work in the interests of Parts Division (by now firmly established as Unipart) and no longer seen as the Trojan Horse for others.

There had been some naive assumptions in IBM, back in the early 1970's, that this powerful, and profitable, division would merely "roll over" at the behest of the corporate systems staff. Others had, so why wouldn't they? And wasn't the clear direction in computing in those days towards the formation of large corporate data centres rather than departmental or divisional systems? How refreshing it was, though causing great irritation to other factions, including some in IBM, that users should stubbornly want to keep control over something they considered to be so important to their business.

It was also the custom in IBM that, having fought and lost a competitive bid, IBM would commonly replace the sales team, perhaps in the hope that the next lot would do better. In this case, the main IBM sales contact remained in place throughout the period covered by our story. It was simple to do in a way since he was also responsible for much of the rest of the ex-Leyland businesses. Nonetheless, it was important that the personal contact was maintained, and that opportunities to build mutual trust were not lost. The deep understanding of the customer's business and the friendly relations that developed with most of the customer's staff, at all levels, were undoubtedly key factors in IBM finally winning. People do matter!

The abiding memory of the 10 or so years covered by this story is of three quite different sales campaigns, each in its own way professionally managed, but each leading to quite different conclusions.

The first campaign, in 1974, a clinical attempt to exploit the apparently unstoppable trend towards computing centralisation, ended in stalemate. The second, in 1975, was the supreme example of IBM salesmanship at its very best, but it led to an ultimate reversal of fortunes. The third, in 1981, perhaps born of long experience and more subtly managed, gaining from critical customer executive support and more favourable circumstances, led, within another year or so, to eventual, and conclusive, success.

The partnership between Unipart and IBM has since grown, hopefully to the mutual advantage of both parties. Unipart, under John Neill's alert and innovative leadership, has gained an international reputation. For all the frustrations IBM endured at times, we always found Unipart and its staff, at all levels, a stimulating, though sometimes challenging company with whom to deal. We hope they found us the same. We wish them well.

In Summary

Overall, IBM field people were well-trained and professional, tuned by a variety of skill enhancement programmes and productivity aids. However, the obsession with a mainframe culture meant that many, particularly salesmen, rarely made hands-on contact with other technologies such as personal computers.

The main revenue focus in the IBM field was short range – i.e. *this* year, and the culture and consequent support programmes of the corporation were predominantly "selling" rather than "marketing". Whilst it is always a good thing to have numeric targets, the over-zealous emphasis on annual quotas did not easily accommodate long-range situations which might take years of patience and determination to gain the "win". Again, changing the salesmen frequently, mostly caused an antipathetic reaction from customers.As ever, the system relied heavily on the efforts and flair of the individual. In this context, there is no doubt that the majority of branch people demonstrated these qualities in abundance.

Overlaying (or was it, underlying) all this day-to-day dynamic activity in the field to win business, IBM was clearing the path ahead for its customers by laying down architectures and strategies.These route maps were fundamental to avoid IT U-turns, blind alleys and stop-go systems developments.

Our next chapter looks at these extended horizons.

6. IBM Product Strategies

What's the IBM Strategy For....?

How many times would the poor, defenceless IBM salesman be greeted with this question, as he innocently poked his head through the door of the DP manager's office to wish him a good morning. Too late, the trapdoor had sprung yet again. Should he try to bluff his way out of the ambush? Or should he try that well-honed, and overused, palliative. "Can I get back to you on that one?"

Usually, the fact that the question was asked at all meant that a mischievous competitive salesman (all competitive salesmen are, by definition, "mischievous") had planted the question, and not to have a ready answer meant loss of face. Either that, or else it was a Monday morning and our DP manager had misspent his weekend reading the computer magazines (in most cases, the equivalent of reading a series of anti-IBM manifestos). They could always be relied upon to produce an "awkward question of the week" with which to assail the innocent.

However, not for nothing had our IBM representative attended the competitive marketing seminar, the product strategy meeting, and, even maybe, the pre-announcement workshop. He would be up to the task – well, at least he probably would be if the question related to a "mainstream" hardware or software product. These were "la crème de la crème", IBM's lifeblood, the key mainframe and distributed systems, hardware and software, the key communications products. Anyway, a thoughtful DP manager would probably know better than to risk asking a question about those early on a busy Monday morning – he'd be lucky to escape the verbal clutches of the IBM salesman much before lunch!

A question, however, about IBM's office systems strategy, framed sometime in, say, 1981, or a gentle enquiry, perhaps in 1974, whether it was to be CICS or IMS/DC that would drive IBM's database communications direction – well that really was one down the legside, or a fastball, as our transatlantic cousins like to say. It was on these occasions that "Er... can I get back to you on that one" came into its own.

Where did the strategies come from?

Who invented the notion of product strategies anyway? Why, IBM of course. People didn't ask questions about strategies in the early 60's. If a DP manager demanded to know the IBM strategy on punched card collators and reproducers you'd think he'd either taken leave of his senses or was smoking something much ahead of his time.

It was when IBM announced, bravely and in a fanfare of trumpets, the System/360, that words like "architecture" and "strategy" started to be applied to computers instead of to civil engineering and warfare, respectively. In retrospect, few would argue that System/360 has represented one of the most outstanding examples of "strategy" in any industry. To have put in place, in 1964, in a young and fast-changing industry, a strategy and an architecture, both of which have endured to the present day, is exceptional. The fact that customer programs written back in 1964 can still run today on IBM's latest implementation of the architecture, shows a generous consideration for protecting the customer's investment.

After 1964, we never looked back (here, interested readers may wish to consult the glossary, thoughtfully included with this work); /360 was strategic, operating systems of all denominations (PCP, BOS, DOS, and the mighty OS, to name but a few) were strategic, either in their own right, or as a convenient route to strategic Utopia.

Into the 70's, and we really went to town: OS – (wait for it) – /VS1, /VS2.1 (MFT) and /VS2.2 (MVS), and then the "very" strategic "Systems Network Architecture" (SNA). But let us pause to relate two stories about products and product strategies, both of which occurred before the announcement of SNA.

"Everything under control" (1)

The IBM 370/145 was delivered in 1974, and the customer engineers set about "bringing the system up". Theoretically this was not a long process, but there were peculiarities to this installation that caused one to think it was jinxed. After one long night of working on the system, the engineers discovered that two of the control buttons on the console had been transposed. How this had happened, nobody knew.

Relationships with the customer were not a strong suit.

Part of the plan was to install OS/VS1 – the baby brother of the two major IBM Operating Systems that provided Virtual Storage capabilities. This was an early life cycle installation of OS/VS1, but it was duly accomplished.

Some short while afterwards there were yet more problems.

The Operating System started to produce gremlins – not the straightforward black and white kind, but those mischievous ones that seem impossible to pinpoint to a "cause and effect". "Oh no," thought the salesman, "here we go again."

The IBM software and hardware engineers tried and re-tried to get to the bottom of the problems – with some small, but far from complete, success. IBM possessed a very rapid and efficient escalation system for reporting customer systems problems, but the speed of rectification was not always as fast as the reporting.

A meeting was summoned in the District Manager's office in Richmond. It was a large powerful gathering including the District Manager, his Operations Manager, the Branch Manager, the Marketing Manager, the Customer Engineering Manager, and, last but not least, the workers on the account – the salesman and Systems Engineer. All watched and listened to the (de rigueur) overhead foil presentation about the customer, the "IBM strategy" and so on – and the problems with OS/VS1.

During a recent visit to Detroit, the salesman had heard the IBM people there discuss their approach to the customer's US parent company. The US International Account Manager had described part of this as a "softly-softly" style of gaining acceptance of new concepts and ideas. He had likened it to watching small bubbles coming up from the bottom of a pond and gradually getting larger as they neared the surface.

At one stage in the presentation the UK salesman repeated this analogy. The Operations Manager, a very large powerful man and one not known for his reticence, erupted. "Bubbles? Bubbles? Unless this Operating System problem is fixed, it's more like farting in the bath!"

This prospect galvanised the District Manager, who immediately got on the phone to the US and demanded a VS/1 software developer on the next plane.

Wayne duly arrived, remarkable in that he didn't need any time to get over jet-lag, and proceeded to knock over the list of OS/VS1 problems one by one. He was even bigger than the Operations Manager – 320 pounds he said, 23 stone in old money, and he said he was the smallest male in his family, one brother bending the scales at 26 stone.

It seemed somewhat incongruous to see such a large man manipulating the minutiae of program code, line by line, at microcode level. But fix the problems he did! It was as though the system dared not conceal its secrets from someone of such awesome bulk.

Everything under control.

"Everything under control" (2)

The London South Bank, used to hearing an audience clap after a concert, erupted with spontaneous applause. It was almost unknown for this to happen from a large formal assembly of IBM'ers, such was the enthusiasm with which they received the announcements in 1970.

The sales force had been battling long and hard with competition, such as Memorex, who were increasingly eroding IBM revenues from disk drives and other mainframe peripherals. The System /360 announcement in 1964 had been a brave move by IBM, obsoleting as it did most of its installed computer base. Accompanying it, however, had been the release into the public domain of the channel interface specifications, describing the method of attachment of disks and tapes to the central processor unit (CPU). This enabled competitive Plug Compatible Manufacturers (PCM's, as these companies were called) to offer their own peripherals for attachment to IBM mainframes.

This was a double whammy to IBM. It not only bore the expense of the sales campaign to establish the requirement for a new IBM computer system; it then saw its hard-won revenues eroded by PCM's entering late and offering cheaper attachment units.

IBM reacted well with new products and offerings: small capacity disk drives such as the 2311 were replaced by the larger 2314; these were followed by financial schemes offering rental discounts for customers signing up for longer periods, typically 12 months. But still competition gained ground – their boxes were cheaper.

IBM UK had brought its sales force down (or up, if you're a Southerner) to London. The opening bars of Richard Strauss's "Also Sprach Zarathustra" heralded a clutch of announcements.... new models of the /360, now to be called the /370. These were the 370./155 and

/165, which offered significant price/performance improvements over the replaced products.

However, what really caught the nerve ends of the audience was the announcement of the 3330 disk facility – 100 Mbytes on a single spindle at a price that would wipe the floor with the opposition. Having suffered without sustenance for so long, it was like the relief of Mafeking – a solid, positive, market leading set of new products.

A short time later, yet another set of significant announcements was made to keep IBM competitive: the icing on the cake. This was the provision of virtual storage, and new models of the /370, the /158 and /168 offered this "VS" as an integral feature.

VS was a boon for on-line applications. The technology offered relatively cheap and theoretically unlimited space for large programs where these did not place excessive demands on the horsepower of the CPU.

Customers who had purchased the now obsolete /155's and /165's were offered an attachment device, called a DAT box (Direct Address Translation), for a bargain price commencing at £100,000 for the /155. Inevitably, there was some stiff customer opposition to this offering, along the lines of, "Why did you sell us the /155 in the first place?"

One customer in the Midlands had indeed bought a model 155, and was reluctant to spend yet more on a DAT box so soon after buying his mainframe. The customer was not easy to deal with. Both the Data Processing Manager and the Systems Manager were ex-IBM, so they knew the inside ropes about sales quotas and what made IBM tick.

The DP manager was very entrenched in a view that could see no merit in "on-line" systems. Everything, therefore, continued to be developed as "batch" applications. This was at a time when "on-line" was just beginning to emerge as the direction of the future. At the same time, he was becoming increasingly cost-conscious, and looking (yet again) at Memorex, Telex, you name it – if it was cheaper, it was a likely install. The Systems Manager was more receptive to new ideas, but couldn't get his counterpart to open up the necessary new facilities.

The salesman decided one of his strategies had to be to break the "batch" log-jam. In this way, the customer would need the redoubtable "IBM support", notably Systems Engineering, and this would change the ball-game in IBM's favour when evaluating competitive products.

There was very often a "guru" from the USA visiting Europe,

somebody who was giving the "right message' – laying on the strategic hands. Such a person was Gene Lagubin, from Allen Bradley Co., a large man whose message, which was presented strongly, as most American presentations were, was "Old data is cold data", and hence one had to "go on-line".

The salesman seized the opportunity for him to visit his customer, in spite of resistance from the DP manager, of course. Gene Lagubin had a very forceful personality. Some of the audience, the analysts and programmers present, had never been exposed to Americans other than those of their parent company from Detroit. One analyst, at the end of the positive pitch for on-line systems, asked, "How do you sell them to the users?" The reply was a daunting: "Do you mean you're not paid enough?", which rather made the questioner flinch.

However, it was an excellent event, and with still some reluctance, the DP Manager agreed to trial one on-line system. The IBM Support – that is, the Systems Engineer – wrote virtually the whole application. But it was progress, indeed, a breakthrough. The salesman could see a whole new business relationship developing.

At about this time, things stared to go somewhat adrift on the operations front. The /155 mainframe started to fall over, as the phrase goes. This was fairly sporadic at the start, but soon became a regular daily event, with a serious impact on the customer's operations. Of course, the usual questions were thrown in by IBM branch management: "Are you sure it's not the operators?" or, "Has the operating system been properly configured?"

Senior IBM Management visited for more laying on of hands, and to show that IBM cared. One such visit had a strangely irrelevant outcome, in that the IBM District Manager (the Branch Manager's boss) called on the Systems Director, an American over in the UK on assignment. Reassuring him everything possible was being done, he then persuaded the Systems Director to part with one of his prize pictures from his office wall, saying that this would be displayed in a prominent place in IBM's own offices!

The situation became increasingly fraught. The Customer Engineering manager was replaced by his boss, the heavyweight branch CE manager. This had a valuable effect in terms of resource application, but still the computer was falling over. Rumours started that there was truly a problem with /155's – known as the "yellow peril". Amongst other places, the /155 was assembled in Japan.

After what seemed definitely too long a period, IBM management advised that there was indeed a problem. Sulphur contamination had occurred during chip manufacture, leading to a gradual collapse of the affected circuits. Chip re-population was the only solution, at considerable cost to IBM.

Bad news was usually given to customers by the salesman, good news by senior IBM management. This tradition was adhered to.

Once the re-population was completed, the /155 computer worked fine. But a set-back of no small magnitude to the salesman's strategy had taken place – bad enough for batch systems when the computer fails, disastrous for on-line.

Still, he persisted.... Everything under his control?

You see how "unreasonable" customers could be at times. Why couldn't they just recognise the intrinsic, and substantial, value of the strategies? Why did they always want the products to work as well?

The following story, however, illustrates the difficulties that could follow, for both IBM and its customer, when either a strategy was set aside or, indeed, when there was no strategy at all.

"A tactical cul-de-sac"

For a long while, IBM Service Bureaux in most countries operated somewhat at arm's length from their usual owner and mentor, the Data Processing Divisions. They served a most valuable purpose in introducing companies to data processing when the capital cost of computing might otherwise have deterred them. A Service Bureau could provide everything, from a data preparation facility to sophisticated computer processing services.

In practice, however, Service Bureaux management, who, when all was said and done, had a business to run, did not always conform to the "strategic guidelines" issued by "Big Brother". To have done so would have required more regular changes of hardware and software than was acceptable, and in that sense they behaved somewhat like any IBM customer. It was only when a major hardware or software change was required for their own business reasons that the strategic guidelines came into the reckoning.

Coincidentally, IBM itself did not help its cause. It levied a disproportionately high transfer charge on internal IBM users of newly announced equipment. This was to secure, wherever possible, a rapid claw-back of the development costs from captive internal users. So, Service Bureaux were wary of installing the latest "strategic" products unless the business case was extra-strong.

IBM Service Bureaux had begun to appreciate, during the 60's, the need to enter the interactive computing marketplace and to offer time-sharing services. In parallel, they also saw a need for a commercial batch processing system that might be driven from a terminal in the customer's offices. The customer would enter transactions from the terminal, and would call off volume print-outs from the IBM centre. This system had much in common with what has become known as data base and data communications (DB/DC).

In due course, IBM's key strategic product in this area became Information Management System (IMS). IMS/DB was the data base manager, and IMS/DC the terminal handler. Another terminal handler, Customer Information and Control System (CICS) was available for lower level IBM operating systems, such as Disk Operating System (DOS). IMS itself required a full OS host implementation.

The Service Bureau product was based upon a very early design model of IMS. It was called Terminal Business System (TBS), and was a proprietary product of the IBM Service Bureau organisation. The version of IMS finally released as an IBM program product was not compatible with TBS.

The spare parts operations of the British Leyland Bus and Truck Division had long been a graveyard for computer suppliers. Their shelves were stacked with proposals from all computer companies, none of which had ever been implemented. They'd stuck to what they knew best – tray after tray of stock cards and armies of people endeavouring to keep them updated with spare parts movements.

But the day finally came, in 1973, when they recognised that computers were the answer. Given, however, their dread of installing their own, evidenced by the creaking shelves of proposals, they decided to take it a step at a time by using the IBM Service Bureau, and TBS.

The longer-term issue of DB/DC strategic directions was not accorded much thought.

It was a very big job, and one that earned the responsible IBM Service Bureau team many plaudits. The implementation went well, and the customer was introduced gradually to the disciplines required of such computer systems.

The system grew fast, and the associated costs of using the bureau mushroomed apace. In due course therefore, and after a few years, the customer decided he should now install his own IBM computer, and move the work from the Service Bureau.

But, alas and alack: TBS was not available for installation on a customer's own system (remember, it was proprietary to Service Bureau?), and even if it were, who would support it? The IBM strategic products were IMS and/or CICS, both of which were incompatible with TBS. There followed several months of fairly heated discussions.

The final outcome was that the customer installed an IBM computer but refused to install any of IBM's strategic DB/DC software. Instead two rival products were chosen. Thereafter, and for some long while, any attempt by IBM to grow that account was hamstrung by the presence of some very, for IBM, non-strategic software.

TBS did its job in getting a customer going. Whether the customer would have managed it equally well by plunging straight in to his own installation is conjectural. Certainly, past experience had suggested he would have taken a very long while to have plucked up the courage. Overall, however, it might be seen as another lesson in needing to set the customer's expectations right, at the outset. If you set your store by "strategies", don't be surprised if they turn around and bite you!

SNA was not announced when the TBS decision was taken. Had it been, it would helped clarify to the customer, in a general sense, the consequences that might follow from making a tactical rather than a strategic decision.

Systems Network Architecture

In some respects SNA started to make life a bit simpler. At every subsequent IBM announcement, the guaranteed question from the floor was,

"How will SNA support this latest product?" If the reply was not instantaneous, and along the lines of "Support will be available-at-first-release/in-plan-for-later-release" – or, more usually, "I gave you the details of SNA support in my presentation – you obviously weren't listening", then the speaker had lost his audience. "No SNA support – not even LU 6.2 – can't be strategic", thought the audience, as one.

Indeed, SNA seemed at times almost to be the lynchpin of the whole IBM strategy business. Announced in 1975, it was a brilliant concept, intended to bring order out of the rapidly developing chaos in computer communications and networking. That was its noble, announced, purpose. There was, however, more than a suspicion on the part of our competition that it was intended to lock them out of IBM customer installations by making conformance to SNA standards increasingly difficult. Our customers, too, saw this as a move by "Big-Brother" to restrict their liking for competitive terminal products. SNA therefore had a tough time making headway. But IBM pressed on, and over time eased the SNA device attachment criteria so that even the dumbest products could creep under the qualifying fence. The aforementioned LU 6.2 was, at one stage, the least demanding attachment requirement, but yet one which could still be recognised within an SNA network. SNA still flourishes, 20 years on. The persistence paid off.

It was soon after the announcement of SNA that IBM's strategy machine moved into overdrive. IBM introduced the concept of "Selected Product Line" (SPL) – the preferred product set out of the vast array of IBM options. Everybody in IBM talked "SPL". Booklets were produced by the ton explaining why, what, how and how much. There were configuration guidelines, performance guidelines, pricing guidelines, and a whole new family of "meaningful" diagrams were produced. The triangle came into its own, featuring "Data", "User Interface" and "Network" along the sides of the triangle, and there, lurking in the centre of the triangle, was "Host". No, it wasn't some special feature that served gin and tonic. It was the host computer, and, by implication, it was to be supplied by – guess who? We all became triangular people.

It was also at this time that, suddenly, the letter "E" started to appear everywhere. When you've announced the ultimate strategy, where do you go from there? Easy, you announce "Extended" versions! Thus, in due course we had "Extended" SPL guidelines, and later still OS/MVS SE (Systems "Extensions"). "Extended", just as the sales force were in understanding it, became cemented in the vocabulary of IBM, never to be erased.

But, there was a real world out there, and it was always waiting to pounce on you, even much later, when you were least expecting it.

"It seemed like a good idea, at the time...."

The parent company of some well-known industrial titles, like Massey Ferguson and Perkins Engines, was an industrial conglomerate, then based in Toronto, and soon to be renamed as Varity Corporation. IBM's world-wide marketing activities within this far-flung conglomerate were directed from the UK. That was because the two main Varity data centres were based in the UK, supporting a world-wide network of terminals and distributed systems. This network could be described as a strategic SNA "backbone" with various non-SNA devices attached.

One of the distributed systems was an aged IBM System/7, announced long before SNA was even heard of. This system, based in North America, supported a world-wide emergency parts ordering system. A Varity customer, a farmer, say, could ring a local telephone number in his own country and receive an immediate parts availability status for his Massey Ferguson tractor or combine harvester. The answers came back from the computer in North America, in voice, albeit sounding somewhat unearthly. The trouble was this aged IBM System/7 was not capable of supporting any SNA communications protocols, or, putting it another way, for SNA the System/7 hardly existed at all.

Nothing for it, therefore. The System/7 should be replaced with something more up to date and acceptable to SNA. The replacement product, the IBM Series/1, was clearly made for the task. Followers of Orwell and Huxley, respectively, must have got together to lay plans, in 1984, for this "Brave New World" network strategy.

That was fine. However, the voice facility had not been replicated on the Series/1. It was decided by the IBM development laboratory that customers would prefer to have a Series/1 attachment feature permitting them to attach a wide variety of non-IBM devices. Again, no problem, Varity thought. A Toronto company had the exact answer. Not only that, but their voice attachment device would permit a far more sophisticated set of voice messages to be broadcast.

By this time the harvest was rapidly approaching, when the heaviest load was placed upon the emergency parts replenishment system. The new system needed to be ready in good time. It wasn't!

Meanwhile, the corn harvest threatened to languish in the fields of Europe and North America, while tractors and combines might stand idle for want of spare parts.

Always, it seemed, when these crises arose, it was IBM that was in the firing line. Energetic action by the IBM laboratory responsible for the Series/1 enabled the problems to be resolved. Needless to say, they were not Series/1 problems at all. The Series/1 had performed exactly to its defined interface specification. However, the "voice" system had been less predictable.

The problems were nothing to do with SNA, except, of course, that in the inevitable post-mortem which would follow such occurrences, the question always asked was, "Why did we have to change the old system?" To the uninitiated end-user executive, the answer, "Because SNA does not recognise the System/7 as a logical unit", was so much gobbledegook.

SNA also introduced one or two other little challenges for the IBM sales staff.

At the time of the SNA announcement, IBM was in the early stages of trying to make work the sometimes conflicting demands of the General Systems Division (GSD) and the Data Processing Division (DPD). Progressively, DPD announced products such as the 8100 distributed data processing system, which would, in theory at least, compete with System/34 and its successors from GSD. But, of course, 8100 was a true SNA product, offering wonderful communications capabilities. While it was all in the best possible taste, it would be idle to pretend that there were not some fierce arguments between rival GSD and DPD sales people. The trick was to make sure these took place away from the customers' offices.

As if this wasn't enough, IBM adroitly announced two different, and potentially rival, operating systems for the 8100. Both, of course, were strategic! These were DPPX (Distributed Processing Program Executive) and DPCX (Distributed Processing Control Executive). While there were many subtle technical differences, the main one, simply explained, was that DPCX permitted greater programming independence while DPPX required host programming and program download to the distributed 8100. It was a sure guarantee that, in any customer presentation with a mixed end-user/systems staff audience, once the key difference had been explained, there would be an argument between the two sides. Systems people wanted control, with DPPX. End-users wanted independence, with DPCX! It didn't take end-users long to work out that they could really secure independence with a GSD product, or something from competition!

It was hardly surprising that IBM sales staff, especially those from DPD, regularly confessed bewilderment behind the outwardly relaxed and confident facade.

A Worthwhile Cause?

Herein lay the rub. IBM had, to some degree, got itself hoist by its own strategy, so to speak. Having introduced the concept of "strategy" as all-important and striving manfully, with the key IBM products, to hold to that principle, the world outside formed the view that everything from IBM had to be "strategic". Nobody seemed to ask our competitors much about their product strategies. And yet, here we were:

"What's your strategy on mainframe printers, IBM?"
"What's your strategy on personal computing, IBM?"
"What's your strategy on office systems, IBM?"
"What's your strategy on...."

But so many of IBM's competitors produced systems for a single application. Shove it in a corner, switch it on, and away you go. You don't need a strategy for that, do you? Well, in practice you probably do if you're not to end up with anarchy. That seems to be recognised today, but it often wasn't 15-20 years ago.

It's an interesting philosophical issue: how to persuade customers to recognise an emerging strategy, and buy into it, often at some pain, rather than merely to instal the latest competitive "whizzbang" system, and hang the consequences. One answer is that the first product to implement the new strategy must be sufficiently user-friendly, price-competitive and functional that prospective customers are attracted. If it is not, then the cause may be lost.

IBM struggled for a long while to knit together a credible office systems and publications strategy – something that could give cohesion to such applications as word and text processing, electronic mail, document creation and management, information retrieval and technical publications. IBM was well able to relate the communications requirements of all those applications to what SNA could offer. It was also beginning to understand the necessity for ruling architectures for document content (DCA) and document interchange (DIA).

However, on the ground, back in the late 70's, IBM was being eaten alive by competition. The old IBM Office Products Division, by this time merged into General Business Group (GBG) together with General Systems Division (GSD), competed manfully with its much enhanced versions of the old classical IBM typewriters. But they struggled against the new word processing "minis". Inevitably, with the advent of the "mini", in the mid-70's, it was not to be long before some bright spark developed some smart word processing software. Such a "mini", with its customised cluster of word processing display terminals gathered around, looked like the answer to the long-intoned prayers of the typing-pool supervisor. One of the first, and most successful, entrants to this market was Wang.

"Hold your horses," said the IBM salesman, "Think about the strategic direction", as he rapidly unloaded a hundred foils from his briefcase. But it was somewhat of a lost cause, except in the most loyal of IBM accounts.

Alas, for all the strength of the strategy, some of IBM's early SNA products, including the first SNA distributed word processor, the 3730, lacked a little in terms of user-friendliness. However, not for nothing should the IBM motto have been, with apologies to the SAS, "He who persists, wins", otherwise expressed as "Do you agree, or shall I go through it again?" So word processor 3730 was followed by the scarcely less unfriendly word processor 8100 (likened to a cornered rat);

but IBM had the bit between the teeth. DCA and DIA compatible products began to spill forth, and IBM's kitbag of products today, across the application set described above, must be the equal of any.

So, increasingly, IBM's systems product strategies were framed around its key architecture strategies. It became rare indeed to encounter a systems product (hardware or software) that stood in proud isolation from the rest of IBM's portfolio.

Everything in the garden was not quite so rosy, however, when it came to general application software. IBM might believe it could control its own systems architectures. But there was no way in which IBM could, or should, control the directions taken by 1001 different application software development companies.

There was a time when the question, "What's IBM's strategy for production planning and control?", would have produced an answer framed entirely around IBM-owned application software, from the S/34, S/36, S/38, AS/400 ranges through the entire S/360, S/370 and 3090 systems. Those days began to come to an end by the 90's, and with the massive growth of UNIX-based systems and computing power available on other "open" architectures, such as the PC, IBM, with rare exceptions, began to de-commit from direct responsibility for application strategies. Like others, IBM began to play the field – picking and choosing from those it deemed the best, and giving them a level of IBM accreditation where appropriate.

This somewhat more tactical approach to the marketplace was well evidenced in the world of industrial shop floor systems.

Back in the 70's IBM had announced a range of industrial shop floor terminals, soon to be brought within the beloved 8100 framework. For certain tasks they were ideal, but they were neither sufficiently flexible in function nor price to meet the requirements of this most demanding marketplace. Other companies, like Digital Equipment (DEC), adopted the more successful approach of recruiting third party channels. These systems integration companies could build adaptable shop floor systems around a DEC processor, using whatever other equipment was also needed. The consequence was that DEC mainly, but others as well, built a huge base of shop floor installations. Inevitably, in time, these installations began to spread upwards – towards the IBM central mainframes. Alarm spread in the corporate corridors of IBM.

The immediate knee-jerk reaction was to rush out successive ranges of "strategic" entry-level /370 architecture systems. But this missed the point. Ironically the people in IBM who could have given the competition in this area a real run for their money had been emasculated by IBM itself – that was the General Systems Division with their S/34, S/36 and, in due course, AS/400 products. The threat to IBM from DEC and others among IBM's industrial customers, and elsewhere, had mushroomed for two main reasons: first, because the systems managers of central site IBM mainframes had resisted allowing IBM to sell directly to users, for fear work would be unloaded from the central mainframes (DEC suffered no such restrictions, having no mainframe business to lose); and, secondly, the market had grown upwards and outwards from the shop floor workplace, where IBM had minimal presence, not downwards from the /370 site.

IBM has now realised this, and has developed channels for its products to match anything competition can offer. And IBM is now much more "hard-nosed" about allowing central site management to restrict IBM selling to end-users. But it has a lot of catching up to do.

Let us illustrate the sort of tactics IBM salesmen were forced to employ to maintain a crucial presence on the shop floor, while IBM endeavoured to "get its act together".

"Cupboards full of salient points"

Perkins Engines, a major diesel engine manufacturer in Peterborough, had always been a loyal IBM customer. They even installed both IBM 8100 and 3600 systems for the shop floor – greater love hath no man than this.

The systems had fulfilled a purpose at the time, but would not meet the requirements of the new generation of flexible manufacturing systems emerging in the mid-80's. These requirements were to be satisfied by networked clusters of personal computers (PC's), broadcasting manufacturing information (christened, locally, "salient points") to assembly workers on the shop floor.

These PC's required to be "ruggedised" to withstand the environment of an industrial shop-floor – wide temperature variations, dust and chemical contamination and moisture penetration. IBM did have a product to meet these needs, the Industrial Computer, but that had been designed for the most extreme environments, was built like a tank, and priced accordingly. What was needed was something between the conventional IBM PC, which Perkins used in their offices, and IBM's Industrial Computer. Unfortunately competition, in the shape of Olivetti, had exactly that. To lose this business would cede critical ground on the shop floor to competition, perhaps for ever.

The account manager, therefore, took it upon himself to become a one-man systems integration "facilitator". He uncovered a supplier of compact industrial cupboards of suitable design, and agreed with IBM's environmental test laboratory staff at Hursley, near Winchester, that they should "exercise" an IBM PC housed in such a cupboard. The test was set in motion. It covered all the expected environmental stresses, moisture, heat and contaminants.

The results were spectacular, far exceeding the specifications of the competitive semi-ruggedised product on all counts. The cupboard was simply engineered to provide the necessary window for access and for viewing the IBM PC display. Perkins were impressed that IBM should go to these lengths, and the workers on the line were delighted as well, since the enclosing cupboard gave them somewhere to put their sandwiches, in safety! The whole package was handed over to an IBM PC dealer who sold a large number of IBM PC's to Perkins as a consequence.

IBM retained a presence on the shop floor in this account a little longer. It was hardly strategic, but what are strategies, other than the sum of the tactics?

In Summary

At some stage in this Chapter the reader might be forgiven for thinking that IBM was totally preoccupied with strategies. However, the concluding story served as a reminder that, whatever other strategies drove IBM, the one all-important, never-to-be-forgotten (or forgiven) strategy was to win the business. Nothing was more counter-strategic than losing to competition!

Strategies that were critical in January seemed less so in December when one more sale, or instal, was needed to make the targets. Account reviews in the first half of the year invariably contained the executive question, "What are your marketing plans for these IBM-strategic products?" In the second half of the year it was more likely to be, "When are you going to close the business (any business!)?", and, "What are you doing to secure installation before year-end?"

Experienced customers were, for the most part, smart enough to see through it all. And the strategies did matter for them. We have instanced some of the pains caused by ignoring, or straying from, the strategic IBM direction, once discerned. Most customer systems directors would want to reassure themselves, before placing any major IBM software or hardware order, that the product was truly strategic, that it would continue to be supported by IBM, and that they were not sailing into uncharted waters. Those were the official reasons why so many European systems directors regularly flooded across the Atlantic, for the laying on of IBM corporate hands. It wasn't just that they didn't always believe what their local IBM account managers assured them. Often they seemed to think (rightly) that the ultimate strategic truth was only to be obtained in the US – and it was a nice place to visit – especially in the Fall.

Where are we now, however? Competitive pressures have pushed IBM into a somewhat different stance. Now, more than ever, it must compete product for product throughout the range. It cannot rely as much on those all-encompassing strategies of yesteryear.

And in the even-more-commercially-minded world of IBM who's to deny that, when asked the question, "What's the IBM strategy for...?", the IBM salesman, now unconcerned, may merely reply, "Aah, now that's a chargeable service. If you can confirm your purchase order number, I will arrange an answer."

We go beyond the world of strategy-selling in the next chapter, to look at other ways of winning customers and keeping them happy.

7. How We Retained and Developed the Business

As well as winning this year's new business through the excellent efforts of a motivated sales team, working on very well planned campaigns, we had to develop other relationships with customers to ensure: Non-DP customer management was satisfied with their current IT spend. Directors and user management were empathetic to any new IT investment proposals. Technical support staff was kept abreast of IBM's latest offerings. Non-DP executives were appraised of IBM's activities in relevant advanced industry applications.

In this chapter we explore how IBM achieved these objectives through wider customer contact.

Contact with Customer Executives came in two guises: the obviously business-oriented, and social. For the latter, no doubt IBM's customers were well aware that nothing was entirely free. The trips to Covent Garden, Wimbledon, Glyndebourne, and the like all had to be paid for somehow, and that was from customer revenues. The allocation of invitations was either the reward for past orders received or, more likely, for more of the same in the future.

Some customers were of a size where such invitations might be taken for granted. In those cases, the expected invitations could be traded within the customer: "You take the IBM invitation to Wimbledon this year, Bob, and I'll take the DEC invitation to Henley." IBM'ers would scour the ranks of executive attendees at key events. The absence of a top executive from a major customer was ominous – "What's up, there's nobody here from XXXX Bank.... Amdahl must have got the decision." Slightly unreal, of course. If Amdahl had got the decision, IBM wouldn't have been advised until after the event!

Customers weren't fools.

However, in addition to all the top social events, there were the bona fide "business" events. These included Study Tours, Executive Education Classes and International Customer Executive Conferences for Directors from every discipline. If IBM didn't run an executive course on some topic, then it wasn't worth doing so.

You have to distinguish between a "how" course and a "whether" event. The latter largely remained "free". There was a time when all IBM education was free, but that changed about the same time as "unbundling". The customer could safely bet that if a course was chargeable (a "how" event), then there was a captive audience. If an event was free, (a "whether"), then it was because IBM had a message to sell. Nothing wrong with that. However, even for the free events and courses, international ones would usually attract an internal IBM charge to the "sending" country, and to the branch.

International events were always a matter for disputes. They would be announced well in advance – "International Customer Executive Program – Finance Directors' Course – held at La Hulpe, Belgium".

The first stage for the branch was to secure a place for its chosen customer(s). For the IBM event administrators this was, of course, the wrong way around. The place could not be committed until all the nominations had been received. But no self-respecting IBM branch was likely to risk offending an important customer by offering a place to a VIP and then have that place withdrawn. So the branches always assumed they could commit the places, and the ICX management always assumed they couldn't! This was a recipe for endless squabbles.

International events were generally of the highest quality, and much valued by customers. For companies operating in an international marketplace, the opportunity to meet their peers from other countries was much prized. Many a long-term friendship, indeed many a business relationship, would be cemented over the n'th glass of "the amber nectar" at an IBM customer event.

It was an advantage to have the customer executive accompanied by the IBM account manager on these occasions. Only he was close enough to the day-to-day activities of the account to sense the inner messages of what was being said, and their relevance or otherwise to his customer. Accompanying top people, however, presented its own problems, since international travel in IBM was invariably accomplished on the principle of least-cost. Budgets were finite, and the less each trip cost the more people could go. However, top customer executives often travelled first class. The outcome was inevitable. The IBM'er would offer the excuse that he had to travel early to do some "last-minute arranging", and had to stay on afterwards to do some "tidying-up". So while the top man travelled in first-class luxury, the IBM "squaddie" went steerage.

Executive Contact

The principle rightly promulgated within IBM was "sell to the top". Indeed, folk-lore dictated that there were three people to sell to in an organisation: the Chief Executive, the Chief Executive, and the Chief Executive.

In practice, it wasn't quite like that.

The main contact for an IBM salesman was the customer's Data Processing Manager (not necessarily so for competition, mind). When the relationship was good, it was very good. When it was not, it could be strained, to say the least..

Account reviews by senior IBM management would always include a check on the calling programme of the customer's senior executives, and woe betide you if this was not well covered. Even if there was a good relationship, IBM might not be satisfied that the installation was growing fast enough.

One solution to this was to instigate new ideas and applications. Again a laudable objective, but professional DP managers were usually very concerned to maintain a high degree of control over their own business and not overstretch their resources, so conflict of interests between him and the determined IBM salesman sometimes ensued. The IBM salesman was keen to accelerate the installation of computing facilities, whereas the DP manager was very focused on keeping control of systems already launched.

One avenue for such new application generation by IBM was the CAPS (Customer Annual Progress Survey), where a senior IBM manager made an annual call on a senior customer manager, the main purpose being to review the level of general satisfaction with IBM. Sometimes the customer DP manager resisted such calls, or indeed refused them altogether. One sometimes felt that they were worried about hidden agendas such as "Shopping the DP Manager" or "Sniffing to see if there was a senior job around". In truth, the IBM salesman was 99 per cent focused on achieving his quota.

Determined IBM salesmen were not easily deflected, and sometimes arranged CAPS calls without the knowledge of the DP manager! This route was not designed to encourage a long-term satisfying relationship. Worse, IBM revenues would generally suffer in the backlash

CAPS calls were very good at establishing whether the ship was running a true course, quite good at ensuring the next IBM proposal was approved quickly, but not very good at opening up new opportunities and applications. Even if there were a concluding "glow" to the meeting, with warm handshakes all round, generally nothing new by way of accelerated growth happened. The DP manager could easily retrench to his "original workload plan". It would have been naive to think that there were gaping holes in the customer's plans just waiting for bright ideas from IBM. In time however, the status of a Data Processing Manager became enhanced to that of Information Systems Manager or Director, with consequent better direct Board access for IBM.

The wise salesman certainly sold to the top. The wiser salesman recognised that although the DP manager may not have the power to sign an order, he was the recommender. Likewise his own technical staff recommended to him, and you ignored the chief systems programmer at your peril!

A total contact approach was the only real route to sales success. Quite intriguing, especially in the early career of one of the authors, was how human even the highest executive could be, given the right circumstances.

"Pitting your wits"

Early in the 60's, the National Coal Board (NCB), East Midlands Division, was installing three IBM 1401 computer systems. The first applications were to be Customer Sales Control and Billing. At that time, the NCB employed some 500,000 people, and produced nearly 200,000 tons of coal each year – volumes enough for a computer!

The critical hub of the system was a massive master file, to be held on magnetic tape, structured as DPCCD – Despatch Point (Pit), Consignee, Customer, Destination.

In the spring of 1963, a project team was established in temporary offices in Cinderhill, a suburb west of Nottingham. Not only were these premises on the local trolley bus route (before company cars were business-as-usual, public transport for a new IBM field employee was essential), but also the local pub did an excellent (and calorific) line in spam fritters and chips.

The offices were small, old, with creaky stairs, and army surplus paint on the inside walls. Yet, probably because of this, that most important factor in successful projects was engendered – team spirit.

The team was structured on a flat reporting basis initially, under the guidance of the overall director, Geoff, an elegant man with a small moustache. It included: Eric, a very physically powerful man, who naturally emerged as the project manager; Jim, who drove an enviable Singer Gazelle; Fred, a story-a-minute and an excellent golfer; Les, who smoked a pipe and moved at a very steady pace; and Enid, a well-rounded individual, whom Jim admired.

Later that year the project moved to Mansfield, some 15 miles away, to a bright new purpose-built computer centre, where the three 1401's were progressively installed.

For a few hundreds of thousands of £'s, you could buy a 16k (RAM) processor (characters, not bytes, mind), six tape drives, 1402 card reader/punch, and a 1403 printer. This last machine was formidable (French pronunciation). It was as solid as a rock, with heavy aluminium castings, and weighed the proverbial ton. This model printed at a maximum rate of 1100 lines per minute. Spacing and skipping were controlled by an alarmingly weak-looking, yet effective, piece of paper about 12 inches long glued in a loop. The machine moved to a "new page" by skipping to the channel 1 hole in this flimsy tape – and woe betide if you had forgotten to punch that channel 1: the machine would spew through a box of 1000 sheets of fanfold listing paper in a very few minutes, desperately, but logically, searching for the ordained but elusive hole on the carriage control tape.

In those days one understood the machines. No chance of lasting the race by high-level swotting at a "foil presentation" level. The first programs were written in a symbolic language, only one up from machine-level instructions, and every character of RAM was contested and saved for the rainy days of program corrections, modifications, and enhancements – all this on 16K characters. Compare this with a typical PC today having 8M bytes.

It was a time of fast learning and hard work. Before the computers arrived at Mansfield, program testing was carried out either at the IBM Newman St. test centre in London, or in another NCB centre at Ystrad Mynach in South Wales, where, after working all through the night (Ar hyd y nos?), it was easy to mistake snow-capped slag heaps for scenic mountains.

Came the day when the Board of the NCB were due to visit the Mansfield Centre for a tour d'inspection and to ensure the project was achieving value for money. The team – Eric, Jim, Les, Enid and all – had worked hard and late to get demonstration versions of the applications working prettily.

The visiting executives were indeed overtly impressed with the whole set-up. There was a lot to see. Interestingly, although the machines were very much man-sized by computing standards, they were not so stood alongside some of the equipment used to smash the coal out down below – not that they ever came near to one another!

The demonstrations went extremely well, much to the satisfaction of Geoff, and not without some stage tension in the team. Now, we also wanted the executives to participate personally in some way. A small program, nothing to do with the actual NCB applications, was constructed for this purpose. It tested "reaction times". Turning off the "parity check" feature on the CPU made the program loop towards an erroneous character and caused a red fault light to come on. The visitors' reaction times could then be individually assessed by measuring the difference between that point and when they pressed the "stop" button.

Great fun – it created a competitive atmosphere amongst the executives, and intriguingly turned out to be one of the highlights of the day, lasting almost as long as the "more important" Sales Suite demonstration.

As ever – people are people, and good demonstrations are where the audience get involved personally.

Conferences

Customer conferences were a regular part of the IBM year. For the customer DP manager the content was technical; for senior executives "trends and directions" were the norm, containing more customer case studies. Customers loved them. Rarely did the mandatory post event critique sheets have negatives on them, and even then, attendees turned up again the next year!

Executive conferences were confusingly called ICX's (still "International Customer Executive" but now without the definitive noun at the end). European events were held mostly at the IBM La Hulpe centre near Brussels, where the staff were heavily cajoled to rename ICX's "Customer Conferences" – but bureaucracy ruled, and the term ICX remained. On one conference, one of the authors did have the corridor signs re-worded to "Customer Conference". The customers thought this was clearer, but the IBM La Hulpe staff seemed more confused.

La Hulpe is about 30 minutes from Brussels, and while transport to and from the city centre hotels wasted two hours a day, the popularity of ICX's was enhanced by evenings spent consuming the famous "mussels in Brussels" in the Grand Place. The La Hulpe centre itself was set in pleasant woodlands, complete with running track for the keep-fit fanatics.

The conferences, for the main part, went very smoothly and with expected IBM professionalism. The truth is that behind this, the organisers generally lost pounds in sweat doing the triple jump of chairing the sessions, organising demonstrations and presentations, and hosting the guest speakers.

IBM was about technology, yet new technology can be a delicate matter. Reputedly, one senior manager from IBM Germany, on stage at a conference, suffered not only from a partially damaged audio cable which did wonders for his German English, but he also pioneered the "laser pointer". Obviously thinking it was a microphone, he shone the thing up his nose for the duration of his talk.

The support offered to the conference organiser was good for audio-visuals, yet terrible for demonstrations. No computing hardware was available, and it was only realistic to bring your own when work stations became sufficiently small and powerful.

Likewise, technical support was BYO (Bring Your Own). On site administrative support was incomplete, with attendees lists not even mechanised (in an IT company?), and invariably wrong when they were distributed (late). Yet, all who took part enjoyed the hard work and "getting close to the customer".

There were excellent simultaneous translation facilities, with four languages. This was always a fascinating part of ICX's. Speakers, for example, had to take care when inserting jokes in their text. The translation delay, which varied with the different languages, caused multiple laughter waves to dislocate the next five minutes of his speech.

The most used language was English, generally now accepted as the "common" business language. However, speakers would display their xenophobic credentials:

- Italians sometimes spoke Italian, but usually with English foils.
- The French usually spoke French, but usually with English foils.
- Scandinavians spoke excellent English, and used English foils.
- Germans often spoke German, and sometimes even used German foils.
- Americans spoke American, with American foils.

Some of the English spoken by non-Brits was outstanding, particularly senior customer directors. M. Patrick le Clement from Renault was excellent in this regard.

The British usually had excellent presentations. Highlights from the Automotive Conferences were the speeches of Peter Carpenter, Director of Engineering TRW Cam Gears, describing "Competitiveness Through Quality" from a the standpoint of having actually achieved "it", and Ron Yeomans from ISTEL Automation, bringing reality to the heady topic of "Computer Integrated Manufacturing". Most guest speakers were impressive with their subject knowledge.

Strangely perhaps, there were diverse reactions to some of the talks. One tub-thumping missionary speech by an IBM manager was rated highly by some IBM'ers, but poorly by customer executives. Depends, as ever, on your viewing point. IBM business partners were always very keen to present and demonstrate – no surprise there.

On a wider front, IBM Domestic (USA) held some outstanding

conferences, reflecting the size of the country, its economy, and the breadth of IBM's business. The formal offer from them for non-Americans to attend was variable, understandably, as they were funding the event, but not so in the context of the "I in IBM". The best way, as ever, was for you as an IBM European to establish a working relationship with your counterparts over the pond, and make sure you received pre-announcement news.

We had some great times in industry-oriented conferences, organised by both IBM and, for example, US industry associations, in such unimaginable places as Dallas, Las Vegas, San Francisco. At one such event, the guest speaker was Baroness Thatcher, who was expected to give the keynote address for some 20 minutes and was still going strong after an hour! The Americans loved it. We also received outstanding hospitality from many US customer executives, including short notice invitations to visit their companies while we were out there.

IBM never charged for attendance at an ICX. This was often proposed by one of the authors, but not accepted. Yet they were excellent events, and very highly rated. Why not charge? Subsequent to his time with IBM, one of the authors was involved in very similar conferences where there were attendance fees. There was no adverse reaction and there were good attendances – value for money, as opposed to a freebie?

Euroflights

IBM Europe owned a couple of 16-seater Grumman Gulfstream Executive jets during the 60's and 70's; these were later changed to smaller Falcon 8-seaters. While theoretically they could cross the Atlantic, they were confined to European destinations. They could be booked for a multitude of purposes, but always customers and prospects were on board.

As ever, IBM UK Head Office believed that the natural place to fly from, and return to, was London, but after many arm twistings, they eventually agreed that there were indeed airports in other cities such as Birmingham and Newcastle.

"Package trips"

On one occasion, the Euroflight was used to take some automotive industry executives to visit Volvo in Gothenburg. The trip was an outstanding success, comprising a plant tour, discussions on the use of IT at Volvo, and a new joint venture between Volvo, IBM, and DEC set up to explore new applications and technologies.

The Swedes were always well organised and very good hosts, and this visit was extremely well received. Our courier on the coach from Gothenburg airport, Maria, from the local IBM branch office, was a delightful person. Since we arrived early, she showed us the highlights of the city. This in practice didn't take long, so she then arranged for the coach to climb to the highest land point around. That didn't take long either, as it was only a hundred metres or so high – but she could have shown the UK executives anything and they would have been spell-bound

The Volvo/IBM/DEC CAE research centre was a highlight of such trips, allowing both DP and User executives to explore innovative new applications with their counterparts.

On another occasion, the plane was used to carry, again, automotive executives to the Frankfurt Motor Show one September in the late 80's. This particular show is one of the largest such events in the calendar; even the exhibition centre (Messe) stretches for over a mile.

This flight was a late booking – a slot had become free suddenly. The trip was to be two days' duration. We knew therefore it was going to be tight to organise and, moreover, hotels were going to be difficult to find at such short notice. However find one we did, strangely perhaps, in Frankfurt centre itself.

As a matter of courtesy, the local IBM branch people were advised that a flight was coming in.When they heard which hotel we were staying at, there were many sharp Teutonic intakes of breath, and glottal-stopped "ahs" and "buts". With some nervousness on the part of the organiser, the UK executives were told on the flight over that, as the hotel may not be "top-flight" they may experience an uncomfortable, even sleepless, night. Dunkirk spirits rose again, and they assured the organisers that this would be "no problem".

The hotel turned out to be awful – dirty, get your own breakfast, curtains falling off the windows, terrible. Yet few of the guests complained. Some actually seemed to enjoy it, and rationalised the experience as "saved a lot of travelling" – nothing to do with the fact that the hotel was situated 10 metres from other "city amenities".

In the mid 80's, IBM's European Manufacturing Centre of Competence was based in Munich, the fine capital city of Bavaria.

One Euroflight took some UK manufacturing managers and their systems colleagues to visit this centre. It was traditional on these flights to serve light refreshments but, without reflecting on "taste", champagne and canapés on the plane were probably not everybody's typical repast.

In the evening, the IBM Germany host took us all to one of the finest restaurants in town – live music from a very talented pianist at a real grand piano, immaculate waiters, and food of such "delicateness" that one hesitated to abuse it by eating it. When the meal was finished, half the UK contingent rushed down to the Hofbrauhaus and downed three litres of pils and a healthy ration of Bratwurst and Kartoffelsalat!

The next day was business proper – namely, a visit to the IBM Centre. Installed there was an IBM Series/1, which featured a wide range of interfaces for connecting external devices such as those found on the factory floor. One specific demonstration concerned a package to monitor and control energy consumption in offices and "closed" factories. Considerable savings could be gained, as the rate for all electricity consumed at a company's site was based on peak consumption levels. Turning off, for example, the office air-conditioning for a short period when other facilities made large energy demands, meant that power consumption was constrained to a lower, and cheaper, level.

This trip was early in the year, yet it was a fine day in Munich. The local young German IBM'er gave the obligatory presentation, followed by the pre-cooked demonstration, which, while it worked very well on paper, was rather sluggish on the computer.

With a flourish, as only Bavarians can do, he stated that he would, "Turn down the room ambient temperature, and we should watch the system adjust the air-conditioning appropriately". He twiddled some dials and turned some switches. After some 30 minutes, nothing much seemed to have happened, so we went for lunch.

When we emerged from the IBM Office – applause: it had started snowing! Amazing what can be done with computers (in Germany).

Study Tours

These were typically either one-offs organised for a specific customer, or a group event for an industry (for example, Finance), or an application (such as Manufacturing Control). Most were to the USA, but for those with real stamina they could stretch to "round-the-world" including, say, Japan.

Occasionally a study tour would misfire. A good example that springs to mind of shooting-oneself-in-the-foot was the 1974 IMS (Information Management System – IBM's brave new data base management product) US Study Tour. It was organised by the then Birmingham Manufacturing Branch for the senior systems executives of key Midlands accounts – GEC, British Leyland, Lucas, and others. There was a heavy IBM accompaniment on the tour, and perhaps for this reason the customer executives grouped together for protection.

Having returned to the UK, the customers then formed themselves into a Midland User Group (known as the "MUGS"), which became a thorn in the side of IBM for the next 15 years at least. IBM was not inexperienced in handling user groups, both national and international. MUGS was different. It refused to fit the pattern. Instead, the regular IBM/MUGS meeting was a great opportunity for IBM-baiting – a sport every bit as cruel as the torture of any defenceless animal.

Our Man in New York

To handle the many visits to the USA by "foreign" IBM customers there was a mini-United Nations managing function in New York titled "ISO".

The International Sales Office of IBM World Trade Corporation was located until the mid-70's in New York, initially on East 42nd St, then on UN Plaza, appropriately opposite the UN building itself. In the mid-70's the function was re-located up the Hudson Valley, about 25 miles north of New York, settling down finally in White Plains. This is true-blue IBM country. Even in today's headcount-reduced IBM world, many thousands of IBM employees live and work in this area.

The ISO was an interesting place to work. Its role was not really international sales. The members of the office, mainly assignees from many countries around the world, were there to assist their respective home countries achieve their targets. Specifically their job was to set up, and manage, programmes for visiting customer executives from the home country – programmes tailored to encourage the visitor(s) to invest in more excellent IBM products.

The programmes for UK visitors were developed from briefs sent from IBM UK. Some were impossibly sketchy, some many pages long. Nowadays, of course, everything is whistled across in seconds through IBM's internal telecommunications network. In the early 70's it was all letter, cable and telephone.

The assignees in the ISO then comprised three Japanese, two Germans, two Frenchmen, an Australian, a Brit, a Dutchman, an Italian, a Norwegian, a Swiss and a South American (from memory, a Brazilian). There were several Americans as well to ensure nobody forgot that IBM was after all a US Corporation.

The office was managed from its formation, sometime in the 60's, until 1971, by a distinguished-looking, grandfatherly gentleman, the ex-General-Manager of IBM Cuba. He had decided that discretion was the better part when Castro took over the country. The next manager was an archetypal US manager – keen, energetic, enormous black brogue shoes with trousers at half-mast, and absolutely nothing in common with his predecessor. All-in-all it was quite a culture shock for those used to the previous style. However, this phase was short-lived. To our American manager, the ISO was merely a stepping stone to greater things – in the event as executive assistant to one of the IBM World Trade Vice-Presidents.

The next manager, who subsequently stayed in the job many years and transformed its procedures (for the better), was an enthusiastic Irish-American, with real experience of the workings of the World Trade countries. His Irish-American background, however, nearly provoked an international incident. Soon after he took over, the tragedy of "Bloody Sunday" occurred in Londonderry, Northern Ireland, in

January1972. This was when, as some say, the British Parachute Regiment did what it was trained to do – namely, to attack the enemy.

The following morning, bright and early, our Irish-American, fuming with anger, marched into the office of the UK representative, demanding an explanation. When the UK representative replied that, while not particularly approving what had happened, he felt a little aggrieved to be so accosted by a representative of a country that had either killed, or confined to reservations, its own indigenous population, then fisticuffs seemed possible. Fortunately, common-sense, laundered by IBM indoctrination, took over and oil was spread over troubled waters.

For the UK representative, life was hectic enough anyway. Regular business contact between the UK and the US had long been well-established, and was very informal. While Germany, in particular, and the other countries represented in general would adhere to most of the rules for visits, IBM UK had a frequent habit of dropping some VIP on the office at about three days' notice ("...he'll be in the US on business anyway, and has asked if we can fit in a few things at short notice, so I said we could. Is that alright?"). It was usually alright when it was someone used to informality, or of a level where informality, provoked by the short notice, could be imposed. But when it was the Chairman of Rolls Royce, or a member of the House of Commons Technology Committee, tempers could become strained.

However, the most challenging visitors without doubt were those senior, radical and anti-establishment scientists from universities or research organisations. Some behaved themselves, but you could be sure about one in three would be, in appearance and manner, reminiscent of Rasputin. There was one professor (no names, no pack drill!), a regular visitor, who was always determined to stay in the cheapest accommodation he could find in Manhattan. It would usually be somewhere in the bowels of Greenwich Village, or the sleaziest part of the West Side.

It always caused consternation to our limousine driver (IBM was at pains to look after its customers) to be asked to collect him from these addresses, never the safest areas of New York. After some discussion with limousine head office, the driver would agree (he would no doubt pack a Smith and Wesson, just in case), and the Cadillac would glide to a halt at the appointed place. "Rasputin" would slip from the shadows, like Harry Lime, for a day with IBM.

The trouble with such visitors was that they were really only ever at home with their own kind, and there were not many hirsute Rasputin look-alikes in IBM in the US. There were plenty of capable, white-shirted, clean-shaven and close-cropped American executives, but they were as red rags to a bull. The only place where you could find anyone remotely empathetic was at the Yorktown Heights Laboratory, north of New York. This was the headquarters of the Research Division of IBM, and had much in common with a university. Staff there seemed to be exempt from the normal IBM rules on dress. Modest scruffiness was de rigueur, beards were fairly plentiful, and sandals almost compulsory.

The Rasputins loved it there. A day of sulks and surliness, enlivened only by the occasional bit of IBM-executive baiting, provoking such responses as "...and another thing – don't ever bring him here again!" would be turned around in an instant by a final visit to Yorktown Heights. "Rasputin" would return to the shadows of Manhattan a happy man, and ready to upset CDC, or Burroughs, or Univac the next day. The relieved ISO representative would thankfully retire to the office.

Those were the days when secretaries were called "secretaries". They were not "personal assistants" or anything else politically correct. In the ISO they all seemed to be either Irish-American or Italian-American. The latter were all named "Joan" (they were, after all, of the female gender, but it did seem to suggest some sort of parental single-mindedness). They were all highly efficient. The Italian ladies, indeed, betrayed few of the volatile characteristics traditionally associated with our Latin cousins, other than a tendency to talk too loudly and a preoccupation with marriage.

The Japanese assignees had a torrid time. They seemed continuously harassed either by the efficient band of office secretaries or by the platoon-sized groups of Japanese visitors with which they had to cope. No limousine could handle their numbers. It was usually more a question of a 40-seater coach.

The senior Japanese representative was a Mr. Ohara, pronounced to rhyme with "opera". However, to the Irish-American Coleen, who was his secretary, this must have been some sort of Shinto baptismal oversight. She persisted in the only proper Irish pronunciation, which suggested that our senior Japanese representative was actually related to that well-known Irish-American actress, Maureen O'Hara. However inexact the pronunciation, the dulcet sound of Coleen's voice was always enough to bring him scampering.

The ISO remains in place. For the UK there are now usually two resident representatives – an increase of 100 per cent in manpower from yesteryear. Perhaps the generally harassed appearance of the singleton representative finally registered with IBM UK management.

Meetings

Everybody knows what meetings are, and why we have them.

You might just have the impression that all customer meetings involving "change", such as new applications or new investments, would receive focused management attention and have consistency of purpose and progressive content. Perhaps some didn't exactly fit this image.

"Meetings that are moving"

We were trying to sell one customer a package (sorry, solution) for his problem of a new "Engineering Process Control" requirement. This involved a monthly review meeting held at his premises over a period of about six months. Such a scenario was not atypical in the life of an IBM'er.

The IBM salesman and his application SE (a rare yet invaluable breed in IBM) were consistent in their attendance at these meetings. The customer, however, was suffering from a high degree of unrest and political uncertainty, with all the consequent "twitches" demonstrated by its staff regarding their individual careers, functions and responsibilities.

Over the six months, it was observed that:

- Upon reporting to "reception" (in practice, a telephone at the foot of the stairs) the actual meeting room was not known.
- While there were usually some 12 customer personnel in attendance for each meeting, on average two "fell off" the table and two "new

ones" joined. Thus over the project life of six months most of the customer personnel were new to the subject.
- But amazingly, the secretary brought in the coffee exactly five minutes before the end of the meeting. Amazingly, because there was never a consistent length to a session, nor an agreed duration.

Was the new system installed? We leave that to you to speculate.

For the Technical

Probably the top prize for IBM events, and it was largely free, should go to an excellent gathering of all levels of customer management (mainly systems, but users could also attend) known as DPEI (Data Processing Executive Institute). It was held at Oxford University in September and lasted one week. Since it was repeated successively over four weeks, the throughput of customer staff was prodigious.

The format occasionally changed a little, as did the name. The weeks were sometimes divided between so-called large systems customers and intermediate systems customers, but the flavour remained the same. There was a mix of main tent sessions and electives, as well as an entertaining social programme. The variety was considerable and it is difficult to imagine any other company than IBM having the expertise or span of products to mount such an event. The customers loved it, not least because accommodation was provided for all in several of the Oxford colleges. For those who had (mis)spent a part of their youth at that establishment it was pure nostalgia. For those that hadn't, it was an eye-opening glimpse of Oxford college life. And what a range of subjects.

Plunging our hands into the DPEI barrel for 1981, here are a few topics....

Tuesday
09.30	Central Site Trends and Technology	Exam Schools
11.00	Introduction to MVS/SP	Seminar Room
16.45	Strategic Capacity Planning	Exam Schools

Wednesday

09.15	The Communications Environment	Exam Schools
12.00	Cost Effective Use of Colour Displays	Lecture Room
14.15	Communications Network Management	Exam Schools
	Line Switching Systems	Seminar Room

...and so on, for the week.

A quick count shows 14 main tent sessions, and 30 elective sessions over the week, plus an energetic social programme of punting, real tennis, Oxford Union debates and receptions. And then back to the college bar.... The combination of meaty technical topics with a nostalgic trip back to their university days proved a winner with customers.

All in all, it was an excellent week, in every sense. Over the years many thousands of customers must have enjoyed IBM's hospitality at DPEI, and they always came back for more.

Conclusion

IBM had many excellent events to spread good news among its customers, and within an industry. During our time with IBM, we enjoyed not only planning and managing many such events, but also accompanying our customers. They too, enjoyed these well-orchestrated events.

It is inevitable that "budget" will raise its (ugly) head where overseas trips are concerned. It is essential that the responsible sales representative accompanies his customer on such events. Strong salesmen always manage to find the funding from somewhere. Weaker brethren, well....

The salesman must understand his customer, both as a person and in his professional environment.

One of the signs of a successful field person, whether sales or systems engineer, was the breadth with which he tackled his particular responsibilities. Some concentrated solely on achieving this year's targets. Some wanted to build longer-term relationships with their customers.

The first chapter of this book, "Driving the IBM Business", described the tactical incentives for success in the field. In the next chapter we explore something of the overall IBM strategies, the reference frame within which the branch sought to achieve its targets. These were the market leadership factors designed to "pull" all that innate field energy towards the revenue pot at the end of the golden rainbow.

8. Leading the Field

Leader or Follower?

In many ways, IBM was a "leader in the field". As you have read in this book, its personnel practices were in advance of most other companies.The salaries paid to its employees were up there with the leaders – not the very tops, but being there, or thereabouts, was always the declared objective. It was keen to see its people comfortable; for example, in the 70's, when the UK government imposed a pay freeze, IBM thoughtfully brought forward the monthly pay-day, so helping employees' cash flow.

Its other support and compensation programmes, pensions, private health, share purchase, and, before it became prohibitively expensive, house moves, were all there to help create a (relatively) happy workforce – some would say perhaps too happy. Once, new employees had to fight for a desk, and had to work hard for that exciting first commission cheque to buy their own personal transport.

It took some time for the usual-for-the-UK company car scheme to get off the ground in IBM. At inception, one suspected the vehicles offered, small, 1300 cc models, were more of an inducement to buy your own. But progressively the list was upgraded, even beyond the usual rep's car specification of 1600 cc, grab handles for a coat hanger, and go-faster red plastic lines on the bumpers.

When it became normal, or a legal requirement, to provide dining facilities, many of the IBM restaurants were excellent. North Harbour salads and the Warwick grill bar were near-gourmet occasions. Indeed, some customers commented that eating at IBM was a highlight of the day (we always assumed this was a positive compliment).

Not all is progress, mind. The introduction of coffee machines meant that you could refresh yourselves at all times of the day. However, the emotion of having such machines devour your money without delivering the beverage compared lamentably to the joy of Mrs Burgess and Mrs Francis, with their 10 o'clock trolleys, laden with hot drinks, buns and snacks, imparting a daily ration of wit and humour to their dried-out customers.

When IBM came to downsizing itself, the "early bath" package was good enough to invite/induce many employees to leave – one suspects it also encouraged many to depart prematurely, but, as they say, who's to know?

So, IBM's pay, rations, and general welfare offerings were definitely attractive. But, more than that – what really made IBM people tick, at least the vast majority of its employees who actually did want to "tick", was the satisfaction of working long and hard, not only to gain personal reward, but also to contribute to the overall success of the company. To do this, it was necessary for management to create the right business environment within which the troops could "deliver the goods".

You will remember that the authors were primarily field people engaged in branch activities, sales, management and first-line staff support. This chapter therefore describes "Leadership" from those perspectives.

Creating the Right Environment

Field people looked for leadership from two levels in IBM:

- Their immediate management for setting the right departmental objectives, managing the resources to achieve these, and creating a productive working environment.
- The IBM company to provide the right products, support and pricing.

Leadership is one of those emotive words, especially so in the fast-developing IT industry. In IBM it was always a good thing to show "leadership". Indeed, there was a lot to be gained by displaying this attribute at the right time in the right environment – promotion, money, enhanced career.

There are many different forms, or should we say means, of leadership. Most of the time the IT world was concerned with technology – you know, "We have developed the trillion bit chip", or "Our latest

Version 6.5.4.3.2. Release 27 networking software automatically switches on the kettle for all remote users when they log on in the morning".

Leading doesn't always pay off though. Sir Clive Sinclair created a world leader in the C5 cycle/car, but it didn't sell. You can also be the world's biggest spender on research, but to what end? Marketing leadership – so important: do your potential customers see you as the leader in your chosen marketplace?

Then there is what might be called "midships" – that is, avoiding high-cost research and marketing, concentrating on what you're good at, and getting the terms and conditions right. The classic example of this was Microsoft some 10 years ago with its PC operating systems software, where IBM bore the high cost of creating a market and Microsoft benefited with huge drag-along software revenues. You might of course call this "trailership", since Microsoft's revenues followed the hardware sales efforts by IBM and the PC clone makers.

Of course, Microsoft today is a different company. It is now required to invest in high-cost marketing in order to maintain its dominant position.

Regarding customers

Customers, of course, like to think that their suppliers offer leadership. In reality it may often turn out to be a case of "Just enough – not too much'!

In the field, we found "leadership" issues with customers arose principally at two stages:

- In the sales cycle, it was definitely an advantage to claim lots of it, especially hardware developments and technological vision, as long as what was to be installed was also robust and proven.
- In the implementation stage too much of it could be worrying if it implanted unnecessary risk in the project.

So here lay a dichotomy for the customer. He wanted to be reassured that he was not buying old-hat technology. On the other hand, most times he didn't want to be an out- and-out pioneer – at one time it was (somewhat jokingly?) said, "No DP manager was ever fired for buying IBM". Later, when PCM and SCV products were seen to work, this changed to (less funny for IBM) "You haven't paid the IBM price, have you?"

With the passing years, customer management came to position their projects better. For example, was it a high-yield, competitive-edge, market-facing pioneering project, or did it (merely) address internal efficiencies? Consequently, they were able to assess coolly whether the project required going gung-ho for the latest technological sound-bites or not.

Regarding immediate management

It is very difficult to take "personality" out of this subject, but our collective experiences are that most immediate managers were "good".

Branch managers came in many sizes and personalities, very large to quite small. Many were exciting Technicolour characters, some were not. Some were merely determined, others *extremely* determined.

Systems Engineering management came in fewer guises. FSEM's, on the first rung of the management ladder, were either customer-oriented from conviction (good), or withdrew to organise special awards and Christmas lunches (not so good?). Branch SE managers were generally very competent, mostly mature and helpful.

Marketing managers (really sales managers) varied enormously. Some were ferociously ambitious. Some arrived through competence, some through zeal, others through longevity. Some were good listeners, others were "zero input mechanisms".

One branch manager stood out in the leadership stakes. He was a master at managing the targets sensibly and balancing the resources. He possessed a wonderful knack of involving everybody in his problems (excuse me, opportunities) – you know, "We're all in this together, chaps...." Even more remarkable was his stamina. He could finish the last brandy with a customer at 3 o'clock in the morning, and have a (self-) typed meeting report ready for 8 am that same morning. For a salesman, also with the customer at 3 am, it could be most disconcerting to arrive in the office at the more respectable hour of 9 am, and find on his desk a punched card with the following message in his leader's neat handwriting: "I noted the following action points from our meeting last night...."

By consensus we authors only experienced one out-and-out swine of a branch manager. His was an alligator grin, with an insatiable ambition causing him to chew up the most hardworking, loyal salesperson. His call reports were masterpieces: "I really laid it on the line with so and so (the customer). He will now order £ millions of new kit from us. Joe (the account manager) will fix the details." The calls were never like that. In reality, he was as malleable as warm sticky Plasticene in the face of a customer complaint. He was the same when dealing with his seniors in IBM.

Never mind. There was only one of these in 30 years.

Regarding the IBM company

IBM could display many facets of leadership, though not all at the same time. Such a large profitable corporation could afford to risk where it placed its investment. It could be "in applications" at one stage, then again it could withdraw to a core business of computing equipment. It could be shifting technologically advanced hardware now, and then change to be in the "solutions" game. It could even afford (few) failures, such as the PC Junior, which was closed off as a product in March 1985 less than 600 days after its US marketplace launch.

Each change was presented as though a tablet of stone, but without any sense of duration. Eventually, experienced field people became somewhat cynical, and doubted the validity of many of the new "thrusts".

This chapter reflects on leadership from a field perspective. In this respect, the coal-face job was to convey the IBM messages created from on high about its products and strategies.

What was even more critical to customer revenues was to exploit the skills and expertise of IBM'ers in order to deliver a wide spectrum of benefits to customers. This was a unique form of industry leadership few companies were equipped to deliver: IBM was one of the exceptions.

How? Back to the people (again).

So what went on in the field concerning these leadership issues? Just how did IBM organise itself to maintain its strength in the marketplace? Was it always in tune with its customers?.

The Core Business

Leadership in the sales function was very much to do with knowledge of, and confidence in, the kit bag offerings. (Authority to make your own deals was not part of the IBM salesman's briefcase up to the 90's.)

The early 60's were the days of machines, not systems – the later 60's, hardware systems – the 70's, mostly about getting the customers' application and data strategies on planned rails and the growing importance of the "glasshouse" data centre – the 80's, PC's and distributed processing – and the 90's, communications, networks, infrastructures and collaboration, and the reducing importance of the glasshouse.

Life in the early 60's for an IBM salesman, while demanding and dynamic, was in some senses more defined than the complexities of today's business world. Take the data processing products themselves, punched cards or paper tape being processed step-by-step, machine-by-machine. There was a much more limited range of equipment than today; with punched cards, each process was a single event (sort, tabulate), and each application relied on physically wheeling trays and trays of cards into a "machine room". A far cry from today's array of event-driven, on-line/GUI/LAN/client-server/object-oriented technologies, which sound complicated, but provide to the user a more natural way of working with a computer system.

All of this reflected the lifestyle of a typical IBM salesman: establish contact with a prospect/customer; define his needs and requirements, analyse the processes, design a solution, close the sale, and implement the system. Like the applications themselves, quite procedural really.

Although salesmen made their money from hardware orders, they required an excellent understanding of the customer's whole business to be able to sell, what in the later decades became known as the "solution". This was not easily grasped by new recruits....

"What business are we in?"

In the early 1960's, most sales and SE training courses in IBM UK would be "blessed" on the final day with the arrival of one Mr. Gerrit van der Woude. Although he had but a modest title, DP Sales Manager, he was definitely Mr. Big to anyone working in the field, and all related head office functions. He was perceived as the No.2 to the then Chief Executive, Tom Hudson.

Gerrit van der Woude's purpose in attending the final day of these courses was somewhat akin to that of a duty orderly officer in the army, strolling around the cookhouse in the days of National Service. "Any complaints?", the officer would ask of a table of cowering, square-bashed recruits, while the mess sergeant loomed menacingly in the rear – fat chance that anyone would want to risk saying boo to a goose!

Perhaps it wasn't quite that bad, though Mr. van der Woude was quite a daunting character. He certainly had a presence, always immaculately attired, precisely coiffured and with the relaxed self-confidence that sometimes accompanies the well-heeled – which he certainly was. And then there was just enough of an air of toughness to lend total credibility. Some said he looked a bit like Jack Palance. You could just imagine him as Wilson, the gunslinger in "Shane", zapping anyone he didn't like. Suffice to say, there was rarely a Shane on the IBM training courses of the 1960's.

To break the ice, Mr. van der Woude would often start by asking the question, "Now you've all been in IBM for a few weeks/months, tell me, what sort of business do you think we're in?" Stunned silence. A few feet would shuffle, and finally some brave (or ambitious?) soul would pipe up, "Well, I think we're in the business of selling and servicing data processing equipment" – or something to that effect. There would be a few more comments along similar lines before our leader would offer his answer to his own question. "Yes, all of what you say is obviously correct, but I think that what we're really about, underneath it all, is *offering solutions for business.*"

Now that really was a complete showstopper. "Solutions for Business'? What was that supposed to mean? Nobody had mentioned that in the whole 10-week course. How to wire a panel for a 421 Accounting Machine – yes. How to write a program in 1401 Autocoder – yes. But, "solutions" – surely not. Nowadays, of course, everybody's in the solutions business. Application solutions, network solutions, systems solutions, integrated solutions – you name it, there's a "solution", and someone's offering it. But in the early 1960's?

Coming From the 60's ....

At that time, IBM was probably much closer to being truly able and willing to provide solutions than, say, 10 years later. Why was that? Well, first, by the early 60's, IBM had begun to acquire a wide portfolio of applications software. Secondly, at that time IBM was still "bundled", and could legitimately propose its SE resources, free, to assist customer implementation. Thirdly, and perhaps most importantly, IBM would usually find itself selling to the end user – the one who would stand to gain the most from a successful implementation. By the mid-seventies it had become increasingly difficult to get anywhere near the end-user, especially in large companies, due to the massive growth of this new profession – the systems department, the glasshouse – whose mission was to ensure that end-users were never to be contaminated by contact with nasty computer companies.

After all, what is an effective computer solution? It's a combination of robust hardware and systems software, appropriate applications and enabling software, and implementation assistance. In the early 1960's IBM could, and often did, bid all of these to the person who had most to gain – the end-user director, in those days also the decision-maker. We were well on the way to becoming a solutions provider, par excellence. Then what happened?

Ten or more years later, such an integrated bid would be addressed to the systems department. If the "IBM" bid was successful, then the systems professionals would be let loose. "Suppose we install plug-compatible disks, from, say, Memorex... that would save us some money. Then there's these Data 100 RJE terminals, and Telex tape drives, and of course we could really save a fortune by putting in an Amdahl CPU." Is it any wonder that IBM ceased to bid integrated solutions in such a world?

All the authors were engaged in IBM Business Development activities pertaining to the manufacturing industry. A subjective analysis of the IBM industry revenue streams showed the following broad picture at the end of the 80's:

	product offering	planning/ design	installation	project management	post- installation management	include non-IBM	risk take-on
business system	▒	▒					
application system	▒	▒	▒				
application packages	▒	▒					
programming languages	█	▒					
systems enablers (e.g. database software)	█	▒	▒				
operating systems	█	█	▒				
extrenal networks	█	█	█	█	█		
local networks	▒	▒	▒				
raw DP system	█	█	█	█			
machines	█	█	█	▒	▒		

█ = Standard offerings

▒ = Some offerings available

☐ = Not 'business as usual'

Some observations are:

- IBM was not deeply involved with "services". Yet this was in fact the growing sub-industry.
- The company's natural "gravitation" was towards the bottom-left of the chart – that is, hardware.
- However, "External Networks" stands out as progressive, but, as a separate IBM division, it was not mainstream.

As day follows night, the DP division looked to "mainframes" as its big revenue earner. Similarly, GBG utilised its business partners for accelerated small systems sales.

Both approaches produced the same outcome: IBM'ers knew less and less about applications and packages. The one-year sales plan was also a barrier to developing in-house deeply skilled resources, saleable in their own right, aimed at the "boom segment", the top-right of the chart.

Thus, at the end of the 80's IBM, with its profitability under threat, IBM faced two options:

- Re-skill its people to go for the "boom segment" – this would have taken several years.
- Reduce the cost base – for example, by reducing the number of employees (downsizing). Then, adopt a strategy of contracted skills, bought in as required, as a chargeable resource.

It adopted b).

Global IBM

You might think this a strange one really. After all, "*International Business Machines*" was what it said, wasn't it? Not so.

Equally intriguing was how some IBM senior executives were at pains to promote IBM as "Multi-national" rather than "International".

In the UK we felt that the underlying corporate view was dominated by the "American" view. A large part of IBM's original business was with Federal Systems, i.e. USA government-funded projects; no similarly-sized customer existed anywhere else in the world.

The rest of the IBM sales force was driven by individual customers; some such as GM and Ford in the USA warranted a whole branch. Such companies were, and are, huge – the two mentioned currently have sales in excess of US$100 billion.

However, it was not the same in Europe, where companies were certainly not as large and the industrial and commercial profiles of each country varied considerably, with different national cultures, languages, and currencies. Germany, a strong industrial base; Italy, some large concerns, but many small businesses; UK, considered to be the pinnacle of the financial services industry. IBM did in fact handle some large cross-border projects well, a notable example being the International Airlines Support Centre based near Heathrow.

Each IBM national company had its own uniqueness. Although IBM had a sound policy of appointing "nationals" to manage the country, the European directorate generally had an American assignee in charge.

Internationalism in the general industry sense truly began to take hold as a distinct force in the 70's. Individual companies were forming collective organisations to handle common issues, including IT systems. IBM outside the USA was never strong enough in its marketing organisation across national boundaries to effectively pursue an industry as a "customer".

As an example, it is reputed that a senior director from Allied Signal, a multi-billion-dollar US supplier to the automotive industry said, "Get the I back into IBM!" Consequently, field and front line staff support had to manage industry-wide issues as best they could, with regular, maybe low-key, or reactive, meetings.

The strategic result? well, take for example, one of these meetings....

"I is for IBM"

In 1987, first-line European automotive industry staff support decided to hold an international workshop for key field personnel, with the aim of achieving much greater industry revenues for IBM. Since the volunteer organiser was based in UK, this four-day event was held at the Metropole Hotel in Birmingham, convenient for the international airport, motorway road network, and British Rail.

The UK Automotive Segment Manager, a firm believer in individual ownership of projects, tasked himself with the planning and execution work. The theme and objectives of the workshop, which was to be held in July, were:

- to interchange the status of IT in the automotive vehicle producers.
- to gain agreement on what was needed to increase IBM's revenues from this industry.

An industry guru from Norwich University, Krish Bhaskar, was briefed to give a talk on the international industry. The Engineering Systems Manager of Mazda, Mr Matsumoto, was invited from Japan to address the audience on the use of IT in Product Development, then, as now, a key issue in the industry.

Come May, using the excellent IBM global E-mail facility, PROFS, the targeted account executives, marketing managers and sales representatives were invited.

Sometimes large accounts didn't want to be involved in such events, giving such excuses as "too busy" or "don't need to know". Ironically, smaller accounts usually were very keen to attend, but couldn't get the travel budget approved. On this occasion , the event obviously struck the right chord. Within two weeks, it was clear that new enrolments would have to be closed. IBM people were coming from Europe, USA, and the Far East – some 50 people in total.

All went well in the meeting, with a good "problem" that there was too much to cover, since the audience wished to interact rather more than expected. Bhaskar, with lots of excellent material, over-ran his time (with agreement). Matsumoto was very positively received.

Jaguar Cars, based in nearby Coventry, hosted an excellent visit to their new Engineering Centre. Some of the side issues were intriguing:

- Many participants wanted to take home an XJ-anything, saloon or sports.
- The contingent from that gourmet country France wanted to know where to get the best curry.
- The FIAT Account Executive from Turin, a very attractive Italian woman, considered England in July much too cold and couldn't wait to return to Italy.

The second objective of the workshop was handled by running a "META" planning session. This was an open referendum where two votes were cast, the first asking the question, "What do you need to achieve greater revenues from your customer?", and the second a majority vote on the top 10 issues arising from the first question.

The first META session was held on the Tuesday afternoon, following which all went to Warwick Castle for a tour and dinner, where a senior IBM manager gave a short speech describing computers and vehicles as two of the great people liberators – which is true. He also was well received as he spoke fluent French, thus demonstrating how well the UK handled internationalism. His secretary was presented with some flowers, recognising that there were three important people in Britain.... all with something in common (viz. the Queen, Prime Minister Thatcher, and Shirley).

All, we thought, thoroughly enjoyed the whole evening.

The next day, back in the workshop, the IBM Industry Manager from Germany, furrowing his Teutonic brow, volubly commanded that, "We are not here to enjoy ourselves visiting castles, but to get down to the serious business of...." Naturally, we all then did as instructed.

The overwhelming outcome of the META planning sessions resulted in the priority 1 issue being "Internationalism" (no surprise), requiring IBM to run its activities facing the automotive industry as a global industry – including marketing, world-wide account authority, cross-border industry programmes, and advanced industry-specific product planning .

The results of the workshop were communicated strongly back up the IBM management lines. The effect – one could guess? Well, almost nothing, certainly not for a number of years.

Why didn't IBM pick up the baton and sprint with it?

Perhaps we hadn't got the staff work right before "running it up the flagpole". But IBM did not respond with further advice, and our participants had more than enough to do when they got back to their offices without spending more time on it.

Here was the one major recommendation from a group of people responsible for over $1000 million of annual revenues to IBM. Yet IBM had no means of picking up and moving forward such a recommendation. The "system" only worked the other way: from the top down, not from those at the bottom, who knew.

Much later, certain countries in Europe were appointed as functional flag bearers, providing cross-national coordination for the others – for example, Germany for Manufacturing, UK for Finance, Italy for Small Enterprises. We would like to think that our planning session influenced this decision.

As IBM grew larger and larger, its ability to respond quickly likewise diminished. Jacques Maisonrouge disagreed with Marshal Foch who was quoted as saying, "To kill a project, all you need is to form a committee on it."

In IBM, a project could be delayed in a number of ways, such as putting a "task force" on it; or, making the project proposer check that "...there was or would be no strategy or product conflict with anything else that IBM had in place, or might be considering" (try that in an organisation of 400,000 people).

Our particular proposal never reached the sponsored project stage. However, it is interesting that five years later a UK Director was indeed appointed to head European Manufacturing Business Development, based in Stuttgart. Hope it succeeds – remains to be seen.

What About the Workers?

You can also demonstrate leadership by avoiding "knee jerk" changes. Or, to put it the other way round, by being clear and consistent in your business strategies.

Customers in assessing their selection criteria for a potential supplier or partner invariably measure the expertise of the the other's staff. Time and time again you could see it in his (the customer's) eyes – whether he had confidence in the people he was dealing with. If the answer was yes – sale. If no – no sale.

Most IBM workers were bright, hard-working individuals who wanted to contribute, certainly to IBM's success, but implicitly to the benefit of the customer. What did these workers need to help them in their day-to-day tasks? The CEO's video broadcast about company performance, strategies and directions played a part. More to the point, however, it was a case of "Give us the tools and we will finish the job". But then you have to add: "And let us maintain our expertise through continuity and consistency".

Real expertise can take years to develop. Take the case of "Manufacturing Planning and Production Control applications". This tale relates to the period before the IT world discovered "solutions".

"Skills inventory"

People who joined IBM UK from manufacturing companies such as Joseph Lucas and TI possessed actual "done it" experience. Likewise, those who had come through from the Service Bureau business had solid experience of designing, building, installing and maintaining such applications, *and* in the 60's had developed their own seminal Service Bureau-based package, PRINCE (Production Information Control system), for Bills of Material Management and Material Requirements Planning.

Subsequently, IBM brought together teams to launch internationally developed software suites such as COPICS (Communications Oriented Production Information Control System) for mainframes and MAAPICS (Manufacturing, etc.) for mini-computers.

These were advanced packages. COPICS was an on-line update system. The concept of a company-wide, up-to-date manufacturing system was now a very real practicality. Above all, though, companies invested in COPICS and MAAPICS because they had confidence in IBM and its ability to protect their investment from start to finish.

In 1978, a marketing support group was set up in Birmingham under the leadership of Mike, a dynamic ex-marketing manager. He recruited both application and technical people to build the marketing offerings, including presentations, demonstrations, executive courses and implementation guidelines. His considerable energy and no-nonsense approach meant that anything was possible, and the inevitable budget and bureaucracy hurdles were never going to stand in his way. Thus was formed the MISC – Manufacturing Industry Support Centre.

Mike lobbied and harangued the relevant branch management to recognise the importance of these packages, and put in place branch industry specialists to get out there in the marketplace and sell. He actively encouraged close co-operation between his team and branch industry specialists, systems engineers and salespeople.

The early days were somewhat DIY, particularly as far as demonstrations were concerned, and especially as quite a proportion of IBM personnel and computing facilities in the Midlands was being re-located from Birmingham to Warwick. Nevertheless, an excellent team spirit developed, and there was nothing we couldn't achieve. Indeed, such was the confidence with the COPICS package that it was sold to a local authority to manage council house repairs – determination and imagination!

Sales of these packages attracted what was called "drag-along", or more accurately pre-requisite IBM products and services – computer hardware, terminals and systems software. One enterprising industry specialist demonstrated that, in so doing, greater revenues were consequently achieved for these IBM products, rather than by selling them individually.

Many customers took these packages – BL, Lucas, Sears, Philips, AP, and a positive user group developed. Equally, this was a period when IBM displayed real leadership, measured in terms of customer support. There was a buzz about it all.

Then, within a few years, it all slowed down. Why? Perhaps it was because the IBM organisation changed (frequently). Perhaps it was because the relevant IBM expertise was not nurtured. It was often stated that an SE could better advance his career by being expert in a particular MVS Task Control Block than by understanding applications. Perhaps it was because Computer Integrated Manufacturing (CIM) was born. Followers of fashion will know that CIM meant different things to different people, sometimes all things to some people. This prompted one no-nonsense salesman to ask, "Which bit should I sell first? How much does it cost?" Silly questions to CIM buffs, of course.

Technology also changed: host solutions such as COPICS and MAAPICS were being usurped by first PC's, then Workstations, and then Client/Server systems. Some users, who had long resented centralised computing facilities, now had the means to break free.

How did IBM meet these challenges? Not by focusing on the skills and experience built so far.

In 1981, the MISC was integrated with the CADCAM support organisation GMSG (don't worry) and became IAMG (don't worry) and ultimately ISMD (likewise) – all of which meant a larger and larger organisation (approaching 100 people), a management infrastructure of its own and, at the lowest level, a lack of total clarity as to what "employee Fred Bloggs should be doing on a wet Wednesday morning in ISMD".

The mission and budgets became very focused on this phantom called CIM. Nothing wrong in selling CIM as a concept, as long as you keep your eye on the products that actually deliver revenue – and your staff that understand them.

Internal Conflict

The General Systems Division (GSD) of IBM, formed in 1975, thrived on its smaller-systems mission focusing on minicomputers such as the System/32, /34, /36 and eventually the System/38. Its customers were either existing users of IBM's Service Bureaux or first time users of computer systems. The division was very successful in migrating its service bureau users to these cost-effective systems, despite the fact that competition (ICL, HP, DEC, Burroughs) were well established in this market-place.

It was similarly the case in "new business selling", where the competition was aggressive and prepared to "do deals", something IBM was not able even to contemplate.

For GSD managers, salesmen and systems engineers it was an exciting era in IBM's history. The market opportunity was vast, and the GSD people responded magnificently. Month on month, quarter on quarter, year on year, the sales and installation performances grew and grew.

GSD in the UK enjoyed a good spirit and atmosphere in which IBM's talented work-force deployed its skills and imagination to maximise the business opportunities. Those who were a part of GSD then would unquestionably reflect that this was a moment in the company's history when it was at its very best. There were problems of course, consistent with a fast growing organisation – insufficient resources to match demand, supply shortages, constant battles with "Head Office" who struggled to understand the needs of the field force. The issues were manifest.

However, here was a group of people whose mission was clear, who knew what their objectives were, had nearly unachievable targets, and shared a commonality of purpose. This created team spirit and, at times, a sheer "bloody-mindedness" to succeed.

GSD branches each had a specific geographical sales territory. Branch managers frequently disputed on which territory a specific prospect existed. Post code allocations became the arbiter of these arguments. Even then the debate often became confused as to who owned the "Head Office" of a company. Was the "customer" buying under the influence or control of its central management or was its subsidiary doing its own thing? Left to GSD branch managers to draw a map of the UK, it would not be recognisable as the country we all know!

Yet this was a time when regardless of whether you were in the North, South, East or West, the determination to achieve growth, to beat competition, to surpass your quotas, was paramount.

GSD was a unit, a family, a collection of people who became an irresistible force. When it combined with the Office Products Division in the late 70's, the resulting General Business Group (GBG) continued to be successful.

Within a couple of years, trouble started to brew. As GBG pursued its sales opportunities in this open market-place, it also perceived it had an advantage with its product line to compete in its "Big Brother's" (DPD's) accounts. Now came the moment when IBM began to confuse its customers. The issue came to a head in the so-called large accounts, "owned" by DPD. One day the DPD salesman would extol the virtues of his product offerings, and on the next day the GBG salesman would compete with his offerings.

The dilemma of competing, and incompatible, product lines finally surfaced. For so long, IBM had encouraged its divisions to pursue their own developments, but now the left hand and the right hand were touching – but not with a firm friendly handshake.

The disputes between competing branch managers were intense, but at the end of the day there were two parties who were losing out – that is, IBM and the customer, and a number of parties who were winning – competition. The IBM solution: "Managed Co-operation". Every DPD proposal had to have a pre-requisite GBG element, rigorously enforced by IBM management to ensure this happened.

This was destined to be a failure from the start, as indeed happened. The most successful salesman "owned" his prospects and customers, he sold what he knew, knew what he sold, and was totally motivated by his own quota (targets). Any incursion, however altruistic or beneficial to a wider fraternity, diluted this single-mindedness. The answer – as so often in IBM – another reorganisation, in 1982.

IBM divided its customers into two: those who were large and those who were (no prizes) small. Large customers were to be supported by salesmen and systems engineers providing a full skill set of both DPD or GSD products and services. This division was Information Systems Account Marketing Division (ISAM). Similarly, small customers would be handled by other people bringing the same support services, predominantly GSD-oriented with a smattering of smaller DPD products, to be known as Information Systems Marketing Division (ISM).

This was, in principle, a sound concept, but it lacked one consideration that until this point had been the bed-rock of IBM's beliefs – the respect for the individual.

Soon after the announced reorganisation, the respective stances of the competing ISAM and ISM managers became self-evident. Whichever side you were on, and it did feel as though there were two companies, the edicts were transparent: "You will transfer this number of people with these skills to the other division, and they will transfer this number of people with these skills to you".

This was close to a recipe for disaster. Here was IBM, the corporation universally respected for its management and personnel policies, instructing its divisional management to break apart teams of people who were providing outstanding customer support and apparently with little thought being given to an individual's career plan.

For many IBM managers who had invested their energies in creating and building teams of well trained, extremely able and innovative people, the months following the reorganisation proved to be without precedent. The resistance of the people "selected" for such a "change of career" was pronounced, with consequent inordinate amounts of time being spent in arguing the merits and demerits of each individual's case. The disruption to the business lasted a year. Throughout this time many IBM customers were at a loss to comprehend what was happening.

An over-riding recollection of that time is that IBM needed to neutralise its own ever-burgeoning internal competition, but chose a remedy that showed little consideration for its customers, and, more importantly, its most valuable commodity – its own people.

Eventually of course, the new IBM structure bedded down, and people got on with it.

Business Channels

The large account branches never really wanted other non-IBM companies poking around their customers, whereas GBG's position was that it needed skills and resources beyond its own both to sell and install its products. As improved price/performance technologies provided more "grunt" for lower cost, as applications became wider and more user oriented, as the drive towards on-line applications became relentless, so IBM expanded its marketplace "downwards" into the smaller companies and smaller systems.

The IBM organisation had to change. No longer could the branch handle the width and depth of customer applications needs and potential solutions. Skill-complementing companies were invited to become what today would be called "business partners". Reflecting the discomfort of some at IBM, that it still should be all-embracing, these companies were then mostly called "third parties".

As we all know, some of these third parties have become very large organisations in their own right. Many indeed broke into new markets without IBM. So arrived "Agents" and "Dealers".

There were rather strange discussions at the time with some larger IT vendors as to why they could not be both, i.e. an AS/400 Agent and a PC Dealer – the reason this could not be done was ascribed to the EEC, just as in the 60's it was "anti-trust" that seemed to prevent many, perhaps reasonable, things happening.

Both Agents and Dealers were appointed with particularly stringent checks of financial strength and expertise to ensure the protection of the IBM name in the marketplace. One IBM'er, a master of the pointed presentation, hit the nail on the head by describing the atmosphere as "them and us" – "them" being customers and "us" being – well, there was "us-us" (IBM) and "them-us", being IBM's business partners.

Other channels were created. IBM introduced its own Independent Business Units (IBU's) in the 70's to sell to specified niche markets or very specialised products. From a branch point of view, these were never regarded as "solid" IBM, rather "something else on the side".

So alongside the "normal" IBM branch there were now many organisations selling IBM products or IBM-related services to the same customer: PC Dealers, Value Added Remarketers (VAR's), Independent Business Units, Agents, all with a plethora of different terms and conditions.

Their territories could be geographical, product, or industry type. Not surprisingly, friction did indeed exist in these fraternities. For example, concerning commissions, where a dedicated IBM Agent (who could sell only IBM equipment) might get 8 per cent discount on his IBM hardware, a free-selling PC Dealer (without the same restrictions) could get 30 per cent !

The IBM constitution was also exposed to a whole new marketing world involving retailers, mass marketing and advertising. When third parties first arrived on the scene, responsibilities were not always fully understood. Customers still turned to IBM for support, even though dealers were well trained. However, as time went on, the customer (second party) eventually came to view the Business Partner (third party) as its primary supplier. So the third parties started to "own" the customer. This in turn reduced the essential customer feedback loop to IBM, constraining its role to that of predominantly a hardware company.

As Buck Rodgers himself said: "The customer is the best source of information."

Partnerships

What we've spoken about in the previous section concerning third parties began as informal, ad hoc business arrangements, for sharing responsibilities, resources, and revenues in a known marketplace. "Partnerships" in IBM in the 80's were very different. They addressed some new or undefined business opportunity. This might concern a product, an application, or a marketplace.

Partnerships are a way of achieving business revenues you can't achieve by yourself. Exactly. What is wrong with that? Why allow outsiders to share the profits when you can have the lot?

In his book *The Uses and Abuses of Power*, Richard Thomas DeLemarter claims: "IBM always wanted to maintain a monopoly." This is a quite different matter from engaging in a partnership, but clearly, the degree to which you can control your revenues is diluted by the involvement of other parties.

In the 60's and 70's, partnerships in the true sense were not a recognisable ingredient in day-to-day branch activities. Yes, there were externally designed or manufactured products and applications packages that were either re-badged or "endorsed", but these were never considered in the field as anything other than part of the IBM portfolio. Probably, only when the proposed JOint VEnture between IBM and British Telecom (JOVE) was muted, did the concept of partnerships really enter into the branch vocabulary.

Partnerships between IBM and its customers typically involved very large corporations in the USA and Japan, and more "open styled" companies such as Volvo. IBM and GM collaborated well on a partnership project concerning advanced diagnostics of vehicle electronics for the Buick division, combining the customer's own product knowledge with IBM's computing expertise. In recent times, IBM-customer partnerships have come into being, either for an internal (to the customer) requirement to develop new applications or technologies, or to engage in a (new) external marketplace.

Many customers from the UK and Europe visited the Volvo CAE (Computer Aided Everything) Centre in Gothenburg, where IBM, DEC, and Swedish Telecom were all partners involved in exploring new applications concerning product development, production, commercial and marketing functions. It was housed in a 1000 square metre building with terminals, computers, robots, CAD equipment, LAN's, and a very smart auditorium.

FIAT and IBM formed a joint company, INTESA, to market EDI systems initially to the FIAT affiliated suppliers.

On a smaller, but no less exciting scale, IBM UK and Motor Panels (Coventry) created a joint venture to explore new CADCAM applications.

A joint venture was also proposed between IBM and ISTEL, a systems and application company, to develop a generalised CAD-EDI package. This failed to get off the ground through lack of what seemed a small budget request at that time. The IBM rules were very harsh – pay-back on investment in one year.

In the early, somewhat romantic, days of "Partnerships", some held the naive view that having a partner would provide 100 per cent of the answer to a particular business problem. Those of us who created and implemented such ventures will know that a successful marriage requires considerable realism concerning goals and expectations, resource contributions and results.

Most of the above instances of collaboration are between IBM and one other company. An example of the issues that arise when forming industry marriages concerns Motor Dealers.

Is it a deal? (part 1)

Motor Dealers – not the Arthur Daley's, but genuine companies franchised to vehicle manufacturers, and in the business of selling new and used cars, parts, servicing, and financing – a well-understood breed and industry. In practice the business of a car dealer is reasonably complicated, embracing all the operations of a complete small enterprise, plus interfacing to the vehicle companies. They range from quite small individual companies to large groups with multi-billion pound revenues. Bear with us on this story, which highlights many of the difficult issues facing IBM in the 80's as the mainframe business started to erode with a vengeance.

Car dealers had varying depths of computing to support the local and networked operations; some were content with a PC or two, others required LAN's and WAN's.

The computing business for this sub-industry was estimated to produce annual revenues of some £100m in the UK, and approaching US$600m in Europe – not insignificant sums of money by any measure.

These revenues represented the classic dilemma for IBM, inasmuch as there were hardware, networking, software and services components to these streams. The revenue trend for hardware, which was always going to be "PC" or "minis", reflected the excellent price/performance gains of the IT industry – that is, it was reducing as a percentage of the total. The networking arena was small but growing. However, the software and services revenues were some 80 per cent of the total and were holding their own.

IBM could, in the UK, claim about 50 per cent of the hardware revenues, but very little of the rest.

The prognosis for IBM, gaining only hardware revenues, was not good. The underlying issue facing IBM was that the direct sales and support to the automotive dealers was done by specialist companies. These may have been IBM agents and dealers, but they were the people to whom the "customer" turned for industry, application and technical expertise.

At one time in the UK, towards the end of the 80's, there were seven or more main companies selling to the car dealers, and indeed the vehicle companies for endorsement of their own products and services to the franchised outlets. You may have heard of some of them:

- DCS, based in Leamington Spa and Rochdale – offering packages running on the AS/400 RS/6000, and PC ranges.
- MOTIS in Warrington and Oxford – mainly AS/400.
- VisiSystems in Sutton, near the famous Epsom racecourse and Coventry – PC based.
- Datawork in Portsmouth and Chesterfield – RS/6000.
- Kalamazoo in Birmingham – PC, RS/6000 and the main supplier to the Ford network with Datapoint-based solutions.
- Kerridge, in Reading – who would sell on anything but IBM hardware.
- LSSS in Leamington Spa and London, offering mainframe and AS/400 "Parts" applications, quite successful world-wide.

An internal report was prepared showing that IBM was really represented in the marketplace through business partners/VAR's. The most likely consequence of continuing with this strategy was that over time IBM's market share would decline. The reasons for this were:

- A continuing shift in the marketplace towards open systems.
- The primary open systems suppliers (Kalamazoo and Kerridge) did #not extensively supply IBM-based systems.
- IBM's direct sales force and IVPA arrangements with manufacturers and large groups were perceived as a threat and a loss of profits by the VAR's.
- The VAR's were seeking alternative supplies of compatible open systems hardware that provided them with a more attractive return.
- They also perceived IBM a threat if it launched its own application products.

How could IBM gain extra revenues?

- Buy market share (a VAR company?).
- Improve the terms to the VAR's. This would cause lower margins to IBM.
- Closer collaboration with fewer business partners.
- Pick an AS/400, an RS/6000, and a PC partner(s) and run with it (them).

- IBM own/sell/market its own application product. This would compete with its own business partners, and moreover customers did not rate IBM's industry and application expertise. They wanted one-stop shopping.

To add to the problem (for IBM), some VAR's were already selling their IBM PC's with a non-IBM screen and printer.

Proposals for joint marketing with the VAR's were met with differing views: "Fine, I'll sign, could be good for business"; or, "Fine, I'll sign, what have I got to lose?"; to "Why should I give 25 per cent of my software revenues to IBM – they don't know anything about the business." This proved to be a less than satisfactory approach.

The IBM UK automotive industry support felt strongly that IBM, in order to protect and develop its revenues, should get into bed with one of the above companies, and consequently put together the appropriate business case. This met objections from the Dealer/Agent department in IBM, that: "We cannot be seen to support one partner and not the others". You may say that this should not have prevented it happening, but in IBM it was invariably the case that if your proposal rocked the boat of an already established department, then, forget it!

Another approach suggested that IBM should set up its own specialist marketing team and take on the car dealer industry directly. However, at that time the car dealer companies were customers of different IBM divisions, so that politics were always in play concerning "account ownership". In any event, IBM could never put up the necessary resources to support 7000 car dealers across the UK.

And, bear in mind when considering services revenues, IBM's unit labour costs were too high for this very cost-conscious marketplace.

Is it a deal? (part 2)

Another dimension to all this was what was happening in Europe.

In practice, each IBM country, not surprisingly, was different in its approach. Germany had very strong vehicle production, four million vehicles annually from VW, Mercedes, BMW, Ford, GM and others; France, some three million from Renault, Peugeot and Citroen; Italy, two million from Fiat. On the other hand, Austria produced very few vehicles – likewise Switzerland and Norway. All these countries were facing pressure from non-European imports.

It was amusing (?) to hear the UK being called the "Japanese aircraft carrier off Europe" when first Nissan, then Honda, then Toyota, set up assembly operations in England.

IBM did not have a homogenous marketing approach towards this industry across Europe. Each country did what it wanted. This was particularly true with regard to the car dealer sub-industry. IBM did possess its own Car Dealer Package (CDP) though – PC-based, developed in Austria, and primarily sold in that country and Germany.

During one meeting the question arose as to how to create an IBM Europe-wide marketing strategy for the sub-industry. CDP featured in this debate. But when IBM Germany's top industry man was asked to position this package, he decreed, "CDP is only for dealers selling imported cars!" Here was a subtlety we hadn't anticipated. "Who are *they*?", we all asked. To which the Teutonic response was, "Not Mercedes, BMW or VW!" Clearly without a *European* view, one man's importer isn't another man's.

Is it a deal? (part 3)

What finally happened?

Well, all this was obviously in the difficult pile. As you can see, IBM's development activity for this marketplace was dispersed and uncoordinated, with many, many groups holding many, many meetings over many, many months. Nothing happened.

Meanwhile, the outside world was changing. LSSS formed an alliance with the French CGI Group. Kalamazoo bought first Datawork, and then VisiSystems, giving it close to a 50 per cent UK marketshare. It then formed a collaboration with a Danish company to strengthen its position in mainland Europe.

Within IBM, management became heavily focused on the issues of "re-structuring" and "down-sizing". However, in 1994 IBM bought CGI – a step in the right direction?

Just to add to these observations....

"Focusing clearly"

At the end of nine holes at the RAC Course, near Epsom in Surrey, William said, "How about a fiver on the second nine?"

It was an extremely hot day, with temperatures in the 90's (30's C). William was very appropriately attired in shorts. Bob was not, but was handling the heat quite well.

Bob agreed to the wager. Frank declined, as he was nearly collapsing with the heat, even after many showers under the sprinklers.

This was a critical point in the development of the automotive dealer marketplace in the UK. IBM was stepping up its "Solutions" involvement by entering into complementary marketing with the active third parties. VisiSystems, based just south of central London, was strong in the smaller end of this industry, and was a good company with which to have a joint venture.

IBM'ers Frank and Bob were visiting to clinch the deal. Bob, whose front nine had not been outstanding, now focused very clearly, reeled off a string of pars, and won his Fiver easily.

Now it was time to quench the thirst. William offered to procure three ice-cold pints of refreshment from the clubhouse. Unfortunately, he was not allowed to enter the portals of this august establishment, as he was improperly dressed (shorts). Team spirit came to the fore, and Bob (usual shoe size 7) donned William's shoes (size 11's) and clattered to the bar (strangely, he was considered suitably attired). Given that William was six inches taller than Bob, the alternative idea of exchanging trousers had been very quickly rejected.

Afterwards, they all retired from the heat of the 1989 summer to William's office for a very pleasant smoked salmon and champagne lunch, and to discuss the other business of complementary marketing.

William, who was a good marketing man, readily signed the agreement. He clearly recognised a good business deal when he saw one. He also was the type who hated losing. It wasn't the £5, but maybe an element of "if you can't beat them, join them".

William was the Managing Director of VisiSystems, and one of the most personable and positive people you could hope to meet. He was satisfied with his new IBM relationship.

Conclusion

IBM most definitely was a leader in looking after its people. It was also definitely a leader in ensuring that its customers secured a high return from their investments in information technology.

For too long, its business emphasis remained "machines". Even after "unbundling", revenues from software and services were mainly an adjunct to the big bucks from machines – and big machines = big revenues = big profits. So whilst the mainframe "cash-cow" yielded high-volume, high-grade milk, then it was easy to see how IBM continued (overlong) to rely on mainframes as its major revenue source. However, the need to recognise warning signs, that is, when the cash-cow is becoming a "dog", and take consequent corrective action, was not easily accepted in a very large corporation.

Over-confidence (or arrogance?) in the marketplace prevented IBM recognising the strengthening of competition, and growing customer acceptance of "non-IBM" products. To add to this, other companies were spawning new "standards", for example UNIX, destined to shake the foundations of the mainframe.

The field recognised the signs, but IBM was not a company where "problems" existed – nay, "solutions" only, please. So, it took actual revenue-pain before senior management accepted that there was indeed a big problem out there.

The last remaining and most important player in this whole business equation was the customer. It follows therefore that our next chapter turns the spotlight on IBM providing "Customer Satisfaction".

9. Customer Satisfaction?

The Need

The happy customer is fundamental to business success.

The Volvo Corporation recognised many years ago that "Customer Retention" is the most economic way of (re)generating revenues and profits. At one time it led the automotive field with a 75 per cent retention ratio. Satisfied Volvo customers would buy another Volvo product.

IBM Field people were not in a strong position to change the standard IBM Products and Services. First, it wasn't their job. Secondly, the mechanisms for registering their views on the need for change (whether in a product, a service or a process) did not exist in any formal sense at branch level. Sure, one could highlight a tactical sales requirement, but that was only as strong as the immediate local sales opportunity.

Here, in this chapter, therefore, we will consider some of the factors that influenced "Customer Satisfaction" from the tactical coal-face perspective.

Let us start with a story that would not happen today. This is the 1960's, when IBM UK was growing from infancy through puberty. Compared with the early 90's it only had a few customers, and the product range was relatively limited.

"That may be true, but...."

It was always a pleasant drive from the Midlands conurbation out to Shrewsbury; like going to a different world really, through the countryside, Bridgnorth, the river Severn. It was usually a day trip as well.

The prospect, a subsidiary of a US corporation, was a machine tool manufacturer looking for a new system to mechanise some of their commercial and production applications. The main contenders for the business were IBM and ICT. Local customer management preferred the latter, but US management the former. The main decision criterion was "support" – physical installation, equipment maintenance, and assistance to design and install the applications.

By a short head, the business went to IBM – clearly because of the excellent salesmanship demonstrated!

The installation comprised punched card data preparation equipment, a card sorter, collator, calculator and a tabulator. The machines duly arrived and were satisfactorily installed. The other part of the "support" package did not go so smoothly.

The IBM salesman's quota targets drove him to search for further new business. Yet at the same time he not only had a selling role, he was responsible for after sales support. At that time, this created an overwhelming workload. Installing this Shrewsbury project by himself would have wiped out the salesman for many months and prevented securing any new business. At the same time, the concept of "project planning" was not well understood in those days. It soon became clear that what local customer management meant by "support" was "project ownership by the supplier".

Branch management eventually agreed to assign a "support" person to this account, and soon a new IBM trainee employee arrived, Don, a pleasant fellow from Liverpool.

Don't forget, Shrewsbury, although a nice drive, was a long way from base and generally meant a day out. In practice, Don was not able to work "full time" at Shrewsbury. Consequently progress on the project was slower than anticipated.

IBM had an excellent customer satisfaction programme, Customer Annual Progress Survey (CAPS). Here, senior management from both IBM and the customer met to lift the debate above day-to-day business activities and check strategic progress.

It was time for a CAPS call. Coincidentally the customer's parent data processing director was due to make one of his "visitations" to Shrewsbury.

Came the hour and the day. The IBM marketing director and his salesman travelled to Shrewsbury for the meeting with the local Customer DP manager, his Managing Director, and the US DP Director. The DP manager soon made it clear that he was not satisfied with progress and certainly not with the support he was getting from IBM, and that he wished he had stuck with his original preference of installing an ICT system, and that ICT would have provided all the support he would have needed, and so on in the same vein.

The customer management waited for a positive response from the IBM participants. The IBM marketing director drew a breath, lifted himself emotionally, and responded, "Wait until the end of the year and you will see which company is the most profitable, IBM or ICT."

The discussion experienced what might be called a "quiet period". Some might have called it a deathly silence

With hindsight, the point clearly was an out-and-out truism. The fact that it did not serve to help the much more immediate short-term issue was perhaps missed by the statement donor, but, more important, definitely was not missed by the customer management.

Why was such a statement made? Had the salesman not briefed the director clearly enough? He thought he had warned him about "project ownership and resourcing". Did the director feel he was in a corner, and had to fight back aggressively? One thing for sure, in those days a junior did not criticise his senior, so the point was not fully aired on the return journey.

The good news, not too long after: the first application was indeed satisfactorily implemented.

This had been a stunning introduction to the salesman of the difference between confidence and insensitivity. It was also a rare occurrence. Senior IBM management invariably demonstrated excellent judgement in most customer face-to-face situations.

It is interesting to note that as the IT industry matured, so IBM CAPS calls became much more complex, requiring a far deeper understanding of the customer. This in turn created a better "listening" meeting, on both sides.

IBM always valued its customers highly. Cynics might have you believe that in the past this was only because they provided the ever-growing revenues and excellent profits that IBM enjoyed for such a long time.

Not so – the IBM Corporation was always of the view that business extends into the community, beyond simply generating shareholders" dividends.

For example, at one time the Manager of the Sindelfingen plant in Germany was also the local Mayor. In the UK, IBM had a "Resident Director" programme for geographic areas with an intense IBM presence, such as Hampshire or Scotland. It also cared about the community it was operating in, endeavouring not to "swamp" a locality through over-IBM-ising.

The same extended-caring approach was true concerning the customer, and nowhere was this more so than in the Branch. The IBM philosophy was that it wanted good relationships with its customers, and definitely would not let them down in their use of systems supplied by IBM.

Most sales people and systems engineers were keen both to establish real working business relationships with their customer counterparts, and, moreover, to extend that relationship to "fun" activities as well – like the "us vs. them" cricket match (some of which were anything but purely-for-the-playing!).

There were a few occasions when one felt that the career ambition of some IBM managers made them aggressive and somewhat insensitive to particular customer situations. This usually manifested itself in the first instance by an immediate attempt to bat a "problem ball" back into the customer's court. Clear analysis and hard work by the workers usually prevailed in resolving the real problem.

Branch people cared about their customers. What they often felt, however, was that achieving a satisfied customer rested over-much on their individual efforts, and that there was not the same degree of attention from those not in the field. This was especially the case as productivity drives created an ever increasing workload on the Branch, without the same pain being felt elsewhere in the organisation. But then, that was the Field view!

In the early 80's, from a corporate standpoint, things looked rosy. Revenues and profits were up. The main drives by IBM were inward facing – for example, to be the "lowest cost producer" through the extensive use of plant automation.

From the field perspective, however, there were already signs that things were going wrong. In the industrial marketplace in particular, the IBM portfolio did not totally match market requirements. For example, some customers were looking for low-cost PC-based package solutions, whereas IBM only offered mainframe versions. Others required large-scale project management and integration by the supplier, not IBM business-as-usual at that time.

The point was that IBM could not shake off the image of a hardware (mainframe) purveyor, whereas the marketplace saw the need for "the solution", of which hardware was only a part. Either IBM's vision was not that of the marketplace, or it did not see it as necessary to change this image.

Of course the branch's job was to sell what was in the kit bag, not to whinge. However, if the product is not right, the support isn't skilled, the price is too high, then it is a waste of time measuring "Customer Satisfaction" in abstract. You can guarantee that "wrong offerings" equals "fewer customers", and "fewer customers" means "lower customer satisfaction index ratings".

This underlying problem, that this marketplace was diverging from the IBM portfolio, was exacerbated by an unwillingness to accept grass roots complaint or criticism, these being culturally unacceptable, and the machinery to take corrective action was not there or was too slow. IBM seemed to fall down in the actual process of monitoring and measuring wider customer (dis)satisfaction and taking continuous procedural corrective action at a company level, be it concerning marketing, support, new products, services, terms and conditions or whatever.

Customer Satisfaction requires constant attention to many detailed processes and procedures in an organisation. In 1994, the IBM UK "Top 7" Customer Driven Quality projects had as its No. 7 "New process-driven management system". Why No. 7? Why not "New customer-oriented IBM managed processes" as No.1?

For a company to be successful it always needs to listen, and to heed – not just once, not just annually, but always, and at all levels.

The Listening Corporation

What is usually meant by this is whether "they" are listening, and whether "they" want to change things for the better. "They" can be listening about a number of business-critical factors, including overall Customer Satisfaction, Product and Offerings Strategy, Marketplace Positioning, and Long-range Goals. In most businesses today there is a tremendous focus on the first, identifying the symptoms of dissatisfaction and putting corrective measures in place. In practice, the management of the other factors is fundamental to influencing a high Customer Satisfaction rating.

Who is this "they" who should be listening? Well, it is certainly not "you" or "me", because we are always sensitive and caring, and want to make the corporation work like a well-oiled machine. As indeed most people are, and do. "They" is almost certainly executive management – you know, those people with power, authority, the ability to make decisions, and perhaps more importantly, with the budget.

Here is a very apposite story reflecting some of the complexities where a supplier positions his approach between one of knowledge, leadership and confidence.

"The customer's right"

The battle was really hotting up. IBM had been the natural selection for the customer's almost totally mainframe-based data processing equipment ever since the early sixties. A good relationship at the working level had developed between the two companies.

That is not to say the life of an IBM'er on the account was plain sailing; far from it. The manager in charge of IT strategy was, you might say, "different". Physically he was tall, thin, wore spectacles, and had a goatee beard and moustache. When he was intellectually analysing the question of the origin of the universe, he would pace the room like a caged cheetah, fold his arms round himself, and hold his hands round the other side – this was known locally as the "wrap-around-check" posture. He possessed one of those hyperventilating energy levels that left his IBM support completely exhausted after an hour in his company. He never seemed to pause for breath – one systems engineer on the account described the strategy manager's lunch breaks as "pit stops", which is exactly what they were.

There were three mainframes in the installation, and the annual upgrade was being planned. The only thing different this time round was that Amdahl (an SCV company) was being considered very seriously as an alternative to IBM. Consequently there was no small amount of IBM management attention being paid to this multi-million pound business. As with most real campaigns – that is, where the outcome is not pre-determined and known beforehand by the "winner" – there was a lot of fencing in the dark.

Theories learnt from Sales School, or reading books such as "How to successfully sell/shift/motivate/close", provided the usual checklists for the campaign. These rarely worked in practice because the opponent (the customer) wouldn't play properly by providing much relevant information.

Ask him what the decision criteria were, and he would immediately sense he had the upper hand, and had you, the potential supplier, worried. The reply might be something like, "Nothing much different from normal". At least you would then know that what was meant was exactly the opposite. Ask how much "slack" capacity should be included for unforeseen events, and he would reply: "Difficult to say."

All part of the process, and the strategy manager was enjoying all this, especially the attention it was giving him.

The key IBM players in this instance were two account SE's, the two main salesmen. and the marketing manager – all full time on the account. The SE's were amongst the finest IBM had, bright, energetic, sales-oriented, with the ability to relate to people. The salesmen had a good relationship – one was essentially analytic, the other very good with people. The marketing manager, as befitted his IBM status, was known to fly at six feet above ground, landing in the real world about twice a year.

The salesmen were not at all comfortable with how the campaign was progressing, and expressed that view to the marketing manager. Inevitably, the Branch Manager became involved. Bright chap, he wanted to bring cost benefits into the scene, and prove how IBM support helped make the customer's IT more productive and profitable than otherwise possible. The necessary one-pager of circles, squares and arrows was assembled on this topic and presented to the customer. Not much response there.

The salesmen decided to yes-or-no ask the strategy manager where "he was at" in the decision, who was winning, and why, and naturally we should discuss this over lunch. It has to be said that he was somewhat neutral about going. However, a quality, discreet restaurant was chosen, and the three diners duly arrived.

Warning bells started to ring when the chief waiter welcomed the strategy manager like a well-known friend. More – he asked him if he would like the same table "as last night"!

Yes, you've guessed it. He had been wined and dined by Amdahl at the very same restaurant only the night before. More, he had been wined and dined by Gene Amdahl himself, the ex-IBM employee and founder and chief executive of his own-name company.

Still, at least the IBM salesmen had good taste in restaurants.

Not a lot of useful (to IBM) information was gleaned at the lunch, except that it was agreed that the IBM marketing manager and branch manager should have a meeting with the strategy manager and his manager. At this meeting, the senior customer manager eventually explained: "Look, we have a good working relationship with your IBM team, and would like this to continue. However, we are rather tired of the "heavy" approach by IBM that seems to know what's best for us, and keeps telling us what to do, and how to do it, even when we patently don't agree. So, if IBM wants the business, will you do what we ask and stop pontificating and arguing all the time."

It is reported that the IBM response at the meeting was along the lines, "No, that's not right. What you should be doing is this.... and the best way to get IBM working is...."

The order went to Amdahl.

Back to our theme of the "Listening Corporation", and who is the "they" who should be listening..

More recently, IBM UK set up a specially focused section to measure Customer Satisfaction. Customer Relationship Management is today's mission. Before this, the measurement was usually done through an annual questionnaire that the salesman filled in with his customer DP manager – sometimes before a lunch, usually after a good lunch.

A new sub-language arrived with its mandatory set of acronyms such as Market Driven Quality (or, as some cynics renamed it, "Quantity Driven Marketing"). When told that we were all in this Quality business, some confused field people asked, "But, what were we doing before?"

Today, it is very difficult to pick up a copy of the IBM internal magazine *UK News* and not find at least one significant article on Customer Satisfaction. This reflects the current focus by senior management on this important issue. It was not always so. Only towards the late 80's did it become a day-by-day matter for attention. As a colleague from Germany said, "We have re-discovered the customer."

Support and Productivity

The Account SE, particularly for large customers, was the cornerstone for effective customer satisfaction. Up to the 70's, he was in effect the right-hand man of many customers' data processing management, advising them on capacity planning, systems selection, and helping to build a quality installation. He was closely in touch with his customer, and his consequential feedback to IBM was invaluable.

As productivity assumed ever greater significance in the drive to greater revenues and profits, so customers started to see less and less of "their" systems engineer. Consequently the feedback reduced and became more superficial.

Again, following "unbundling", customers started to develop more in-house skills rather than pay IBM for what they had had for free before – with the same consequence.

IBM reorganisations happened frequently. This often meant a change of salesman and SE. Usually this was done quite independently of the customer: he was told in January of his new team. Bearing in mind that it took about six months for any new salesman to fully understand a customer, its practices and politics, then there was a lot of non-productive activity during this period. Indeed, some customers objected to the frequent changes, especially if they already had a "good one" (sales or SE). The occasions when a salesman or SE was given the customer's thumbs down were very few, but did happen.

Yet in 1994, the Customer Satisfaction Survey still had cases of "We are on our third salesman in six months" and "Who is our sales representative?" These may be isolated instances, but continuity of support has long been an issue at the root of much customer dissatisfaction.

Process Satisfaction

Alongside all the issues described above, there were flawed business processes between IBM and its customers that caused severe day-to-day strains on relationships. Fundamentally, it comes back to the line of the old song, ".... do what you do, do well, boy". IBM branches were full of bright people doing just that – "doing it well" (sometimes it seemed, in spite of the back room boys).

Yet, if you had asked any IBM salesman even as long ago as the 60's, he would have told you that one of the biggest headaches for him was IBM "billing". "Why can't they get it right?" Get it right, they could not. The invoices sent each month to customers were frequently wrong and certainly not "user-friendly". An invoice could consist of many pages with errors such as:

- Machines being invoiced but already discontinued.
- Wrong installation dates.
- Wrongly specified equipment.

The salesman was "responsible" for ensuring outstanding customer debt was less than 30 days, so invoices, even when they were fundamentally incorrect, had to be "paid" within that period. The salesman could not change IBM's system. Any IBM representative will remember the happy hours (or days) spent being firm but pleasant, invoking somewhat strange practices to ensure that customers paid within the 30 days – even to the customer paying a lump sum regardless of the accuracy of invoice detail. This in turn made the next month's invoice even more "wrong".

All this was obviously a major barrier to good customer happiness. But while the salesman spent his time tactically fixing it, the IBM backroom boys did not seem to be able to do likewise strategically, and get the billing system working properly.

More to the point: customers were extremely annoyed by all this. Not only did it take an inordinate amount of their time in checking and cross-checking, but they also, one suspected, exposed themselves internally through by-passing their own company's practices.

This type of activity relied heavily on an excellent relationship between the IBM salesman and account SE (if there was one), and the key individual in the customer. If anything went seriously wrong with the product or service quality, then even this relationship was sometimes insufficient to paper over the cracks.

Even as of today, IBM is still working on improving its billing system.

Accurate Measurement

What should "they" measure ? Ultimately, all systems need feedback to operate satisfactorily. Herein lies a difficult human problem. Of course, any action needs a positive response in order to gauge whether it is producing the right results. Equally, however, for a system to be under control, requires negative feedback. An example of this is one of those early mechanical machines such as steam traction engines – yes, they were required to go as fast as was practical, but they also had a speed control mechanism, the rotating "governor" This was a negative feedback loop.

But, fundamentally, people are happier with good news. "Negative" sounds, and is, "negative". Could it be another word for whinging, or not constructive?

Now, where there is only positive feedback, systems are inherently unstable, usually ending up like ever-expanding stars, imploding on themselves and becoming black holes. For example, groups who award themselves pay increases based on comparisons with other "like groups" are operating with a positive-feedback, unstable, process. Equally, having the right feedback may not guarantee success. Feedback telling you to reduce the temperature, but then taking a consequent action of injecting heat, is rather silly.

So negative feedback is an essential ingredient to improving control, and hence, quality – and consequent timely corrective action is essential.

Given that everything seems to be going well in a large, and perhaps, career-oriented corporation, the emphasis is usually on "positive feedback" – that is, good news. This is self-perpetuating, and very often becomes apparent only when the end-of-year figures suddenly give the wrong answer. (Was it Lawson's Fifth Law of Finance: "Bad figures take longer to add up than good ones."?)

So most Customer Satisfaction systems look for the good news, whereas there is equal or more mileage in digging out and correcting the not-so-good news. Trouble was, messages of bad news within IBM frequently meant the shooting of the messenger – for example, presentations to visiting IBM US directors always had to be positive, without heavily mentioning any problems.

A recent article in IBM *UK News* showed:

- Customer Satisfaction targets ever higher (naturally);
- but actual Customer Satisfaction rating achievement flat.

It also listed a number of projects that had been put in place to improve matters.

What the article didn't discuss in any consequential way was that the actual "response rate" had fallen from 53 per cent to 48 per cent in two years. The drop was explained that more companies were buying AIX products (IBM's UNIX) through Value Added Remarketers (Agents) rather than direct from IBM. IBM's actual customer set was changing. So what was being measured then? Clearly, proper normalisation, rather than rationalisation, is important in any measurement system.

What Else?

Customer satisfaction is very much a matter of supplying quality products at the right price, etc. It can also be significantly influenced by making the environment conducive to "doing business together". (No, we are not talking about arms sales.) Business relationships are as much to do with issues such as confidence, trust, mutual benefit.

Let us describe a situation that shows how these "extramural" issues are so important to a relationship. What you might call:

"A lesson in shooting oneself in the foot"

IBM, by the early 80's, had become a very big user of company cars. Indeed, it was one of the largest fleet owners in the UK and, as such, a target for Austin Rover's Fleet Sales staff. However, the experience of IBM car users had not been very encouraging for Austin Rover.

IBM would not seek to impose a particular car upon its users, at whatever level. Users could exercise a choice from a range of cars, depending upon their level in the company. In the early days of the IBM car scheme (and IBM had long resisted the notion of "company cars", so it was not till the mid-70's that any sort of scheme was introduced) the Triumph Toledo was quite popular. The Marina and Princess ranges also both shared a brief popularity. However, costs of maintenance, unreliability and lack of appeal to IBM users led to the withdrawal of any Austin Rover car from the basic car scheme. The Rover 2000, in its various forms, clung on in the executive car scheme by the skin of its paintwork.

This situation prevailed at the time when IBM was scoring success after success in selling its CAD products to Austin Rover.

It should be understood that IBM never indulged in reciprocal trading – simply expressed as, "you buy my products and I'll buy yours". However, the account team that had become so closely identified with Austin Rover's expanded use of IBM CAD systems, was keen to give wider visibility to the success of these systems. So, at the time of the public announcements of the fruits of Michael (now Sir Michael) Edwardes' new investment programmes (first the Maestro, then the Montego), where IBM CAD had played a significant role in the development, IBM set up demonstrations and test drives for its staff. Needless to say, this was done with the wholehearted support of Austin Rover Fleet Sales staff. Further, the Montego was "unveiled" at the IBM "Club" in Monte Carlo, in front of many hundred potential customers, and an IBM sales competition was announced (the "Montego Challenge") in which the first prize would be a new Montego.

It had proved difficult to set all this up, particularly as there was resistance from the department in IBM UK that managed the car fleet. However, they were persuaded that this was not reciprocal trading, but merely IBM proudly showing the benefits of using its CAD products. This was something IBM might do regularly with any of its products.

While all this was going on, Austin Rover executive management had set about its own programme of "persuading" British industry of the merit of its own products. Letters had been sent to many UK chief executives encouraging them to increase the Austin Rover component of their car fleets. The letters were frequently followed by a personal visit from the Austin Rover Chief Executive.

The problem was that the style and approach used were not those readily recognised by such companies as, say, Marks and Spencer. When politely advised that their policy was to allow their qualifying staff to choose from a selection of suitable cars, the reaction of the

Austin Rover Chief Executive was predictable, and along the lines of, "Don't give them any choice. Make them take one of ours!"

Needless to say, the tactics were not a resounding success.

However, and to the misfortune of the account team for Austin Rover, IBM went one better. When the letter exhorting him to acquire more Austin Rover cars for his fleet arrived on the CEO's desk, a stern reply, saying that IBM did not do business this way, was drafted by Fleet Management, duly signed, and sent, by the CEO. The account team was not even consulted. While they may not have been able to change the message, there was no doubt they would have found a more diplomatic way of saying it!

The reaction of the IBM Director closely involved in our attempts to win more CAD business, when he saw the CEO's letter, might, at the most polite, be termed unprintable! We were told that the reaction of the Austin Rover CEO was even more expressive!

The episode was accurately described by the local IBM branch manager as "a supreme executive own goal". The trouble was that the goal was scored against his branch.

How about those at the other coal faces in the company, be it in Manufacturing, Design, Development or wherever?

The Toyota Corporation in the 80's claimed they were receiving two million suggestions each year from employees in all departments for improvements to the business. Why as many as two million? One suspects because "they", management, took it all very seriously, and believed their coal-face workers knew more about what went on than "they" did. The scheme was not an incidental box on the wall, nor a way of offering money for inventions. Toyota were very proud to tell visitors about this.

A major barrier in IBM was the "onwards and upwards" culture. You know: "There are no such things as problems, only opportunities." To raise an "issue" in IBM without presenting the solution on the next foil was guaranteed to cause "glazed eyeballs" from your manager at the very least – on one of his bad days, perhaps even the sensitive response: "Don't come here with problems. Why haven't you done your homework?"

"Sod it," you say to yourself resignedly, and perhaps to another loyalist propping up the bar, "...it's nothing to do with me, I was only trying to help."

Yes, there were "Speak Ups" and "Suggestion Schemes", but they were not part of the essential lifeblood of the IBM field culture. Rarely, if at all, did those published refer to ways of improving relations between IBM and its customers.

Of course, there were frequent "Management Meetings". We assume these sometimes addressed customer contentedness, but such meetings reminded one of microcosmic papal selections – without the smoke.

Conclusion

The key focus for customer satisfaction in IBM rested in the branch. Although the salesforce had the specific task of obtaining customer views on the annual survey forms, this was not the driving force as far as the typical salesman or systems engineer was concerned, By their very character, motivation and job, they would move heaven and earth to get the IBM products and services performing 100 per cent for their customer.

Where problems concerned products, then the non-USA IBM companies enjoyed additional hurdles because of their geographic distance from many development centres (predominantly in the USA), the multi-layered communication procedures, and because of the relatively small size of customer compared with those found in the USA.

Customer Satisfaction can be somewhat relative. If the customer has no option to go elsewhere with his business, then in the short term you may get away with it. Dangerous stuff this. No company can control the marketplace, behaving as if a monopoly, for ever. Someday things will change. Then the flood gates of dissatisfaction could open with very rapid and dire consequences.

When things start to go adrift, rapid and highly focused management attention is critical. The question is, on what? Product quality, product set, skills, resources, productivity? To change these is definitely in the "difficult pile". Somewhat easier is "cost cutting". That can have a more immediate effect on the bottom line. This was the IBM approach; but it was not without some considerable pain to the remaining parts of the "whole". Hence in a very few years IBM world-wide released over a hundred thousand employees. IBM UK went from 18,000 to 12,500 in a handful of years.

What were all these people doing before they left, one might ask? Some were probably quite divorced from reality, were living in a protected cocoon and should have gone years ago. Many were very experienced. Many were helping customers.

Now, today, the marketplace still places the same emphasis on the 'foundation' offerings of price and quality. If IBM remains a high price company it will have to prove it has the skills and efficiencies to support small and large projects to the customer's satisfaction.

IBM recognised "Success" in many different ways. Let's explore a few of them in the next chapter.

10. Rewards of the Culture

"I am not appreciated...."
"If only someone would just say thank-you...."
"I get no recognition for my efforts...."

How many times have you heard those kinds of comments made by people in all walks of life?

Less so with IBM, essentially an American company, which very much appreciated endeavour and achievement. Taking aside the recognition that employees were given in their IBM salary increases, and ignoring the Appraisal and Counselling system which gave them a "numerical" performance rating, there were many other ways of rewarding an outstanding performance:

- Dinner for Two
- Salesman of the Month
- Systems Engineer of the Month
- Special Contribution Awards
- Administration Awards
- Customer Engineering Awards
- Staff Awards

Each of these awards recognised outstanding achievements. However, "la crème de la crème" were the Hundred Per cent Club, and the Golden Circle.

The Club

The Hundred Per cent Club (HPC), or just the "Club", was the most legendary recognition event in the IBM company. This institution, developed by our go-getting friends from the other side of the Atlantic, was the American way of recognising sales achievements. IBM companies in

Europe keenly embraced this practice of rewarding with an event of special proportions.

In the early days of IBM, the European Club covered all European countries, and successful sales staff gathered at a suitable, and unsuspecting, European city – Paris, London, Palma, Rome, Monte Carlo. As IBM grew larger and it became impossible to accommodate the numbers, so Clubs became segregated – for example, the Northern Europe Club, the Southern Europe Club. Finally, in the 80's, the major European countries – UK, France, Germany and Italy – held their own Clubs.

The UK convention format was a three-day event beginning with the challenge of ensuring some 1000 delegates arrived on time at the selected venue and registered at their designated, and by now slightly apprehensive, hotels.

Accommodation for the delegates was always of the highest class. Managers who clearly should not mix with the riff-raff were allocated their own rooms. Gregarious salesmen, on the other hand, regardless of their level and status, were expected to share. Not surprisingly this was resented by many senior (non-managerial) delegates.

On arrival you received your convention pack, including as a minimum: your convention gift (more about that later), generally useful, occasionally uninspired; city tour map, showing which areas to avoid (always read very carefully); pocket money – the amount which, while reasonable for tax purposes, was obviously never enough for the free-spenders; tour options; convention program(me).

Formal proceedings started with a first-evening reception in a city centre hotel. Most delegates would attend this briefly to get their bearings, before heading off towards other adjacent attractions.

Business sessions comprised a cocktail of orations, eulogies, diatribes and inspirational tub-thumping from invited celebrities, IBM and other. Like a political party conference, each convention had its theme and the mandatory "banner message" – something like "Time for Excellence".

A diminishing audience of IBM delegates, in varying states of consciousness, were regaled, saluted and plied with accolades. Lunch, which seemed endless, was an occasion for the distribution of more awards for the worthy stars.

The final morning session included a star speaker whose identity was kept secret until announced – for the organisers, their most important mission, for the delegates, a source of constant speculation.

A brief anecdote at this point.

Sebastian Coe, athlete and now Member of Parliament, was jetted to the convention to be guest speaker. Arriving a couple of hours before he was due to speak, shock and horror, his luggage had disappeared. He was rushed to a local gentleman's outfitter. Suit, shirt, tie and shoes were hurriedly purchased. His lean figure secured properly fitting clothes, while his athleticism meant he reached the stage on time to deliver an outstanding speech, suitably attired – and still full of breath.

The Club concluded with a "Gala" evening, featuring an internationally-famous celebrity, such as Ella Fitzgerald, or Cleo Lane and John Dankworth. Though the Gala evening may have finished around midnight it was not unusual for some to board the plane home the next day having not disturbed their bed-clothes.

For most recipients the business sessions were, in the main, tolerably interesting or useful, or both.

However, at one Club held in Palma, Majorca, the first morning was so obviously boring that on the second day the auditorium was nearly empty. Even with the lights down, the low level of snoring must have been a give away! A posse was sent out to round up the wayward from the local hostelries and golf courses.

Agenda items included IBM senior management, guest speakers who were IBM customers, and guest speakers who were not. Always there was a contingent of specially invited senior executives from across the Atlantic, manifesting the American executive appearance of steely-gray (their spelling) hair and stern countenance.

First thing each morning there was always a welcoming group of musicians. Perceptive management knew most attendees would be overhung or deaf at that time in the morning, so the music was amplified to a decibel level exceeding that of Concorde.

The incentive

For those paid on a commission basis, the membership qualification was simply to achieve 100 per cent+ of the assigned quota objectives. In addition to the real qualifiers, there many other attendees selected from other IBM functions, such as Systems Engineering, Customer Engineering, Administration, and Staff.

For all the wrinkles of the Club, there are many who remember with great affection and pride that they had participated. They all remember their first one, even if they needed others to tell them about it!

For the non-attendees back at the ranch there was some solace in what became famously known as the "99 Per cent Club" – a long lunch at which there was much mutual commiseration and bemoaning the unfairness of the sales plan. Make no bones about it, however, being left behind because of non-qualification was the evidence, for all to see, of failure.

Here are a few tales of the Club we feel we can tell.

"Name and number"

There were two main reasons why delegates failed to attend the business sessions. Either the excesses of the previous evening prevented early rising, or the venue itself provided attractions more culturally up-lifting than our corporate leaders.

Two examples of the dangers of non-attendance come to mind.

The Divisional Director addressed the delegates, beginning his speech with an appeal. He had unfortunately broken his wrist before flying out to the convention. His arm was therefore both plastered and in a sling.

He thanked the assembled gathering for the concern each had shown him, and took the opportunity of telling everybody how it had happened, thus saving much later repetition. And the show began.

At the mid-morning coffee break, as he strolled amongst the delegates, snatching brief conversations with as many as possible, a branch manager proudly introduced his "star" systems engineer. "Oh, Fred," she exclaimed, "What on earth have you being doing to yourself?"

Name and number....

On another occasion, a delegate on his umpteenth Club was still certain that there were no new messages for him to hear. He was proud to boast that he had not attended a business session in years; but he never missed the lunches, always getting a colleague to brief him on what of importance had been said.

He was pleased to find a guest senior director sitting next to him on the top table at lunch. The atmosphere was relaxed and conversation lively. "What did you think of the business session this morning?" asked the director. "I thought it was outstanding," he replied with conviction.

"How did you enjoy the celebrity speaker?"

"I have to admit that I was delighted when he was announced. Peter Ustinov has always been a great favourite of mine. I thought he was absolutely tremendous."

He never did trust his colleague's briefings again. How could he? The celebrity had been Michael Bentine.

Name and number....

While on the subject of guest speakers....

"Compering notes"

As well as the clear IBM messages from senior management, delegates were also able to observe in action the real professionals – the comperes, well-known media personalities.

Martyn Lewis, the news-reader, was one. He came over as a very pleasant gentleman, who was surprisingly tall for a job where you don't need legs, yet was still out-stripped by the Director of Marketing, Ian Reynolds at about 6 feet 5 inches.

John Cleese was brilliant.

On the first morning of a Club in Venice, there was a problem with the sound system. The loudspeakers at the back were prone to random periods of silence. After the coffee break, Mr Cleese announced, as only he can do: "I have been asked to apologise about the sound in this hall.... Well, I won't!" Those at the back having a quiet snooze, clearly got the message.

Richard Stilgoe was another. He gave some excellent, spontaneous, musical improvisations. His comments regarding IBM were most perceptive.

Alan Coren was not a compere, but gave one of the best hour-long presentations. He used a giant Swiss army knife as his visual aid – very appropriate as, at that time, IBM was using this symbol in its marketing of smaller computer systems. He also presented both plusses and minuses of computers. He opined that Shakespeare might still be modifying "To be or not to be....", as it was not necessary to get it right first time when using a modern word processor.

Brilliant stuff.

But sometimes, not everything goes to plan....

"Don't perform with children, animals.... or retired surgeons!"

This story concerns the first Club for the Northern European area, in Amsterdam in 1970; 1969 had seen the last of the all-Europe Clubs, in London. The Amsterdam Club hosted qualifying sales staff, and "hangers-on", from UK, Scandinavia, Iceland, Israel and South Africa. Don't ask how the last two could be considered to be in Northern Europe. It was something to do with neither country mingling with others who were either excessively sensitive to racial issues, or had strong Arab affiliations. Besides which, as we now know, there was a strong community of interest between Israel and South Africa – each sold the other arms – so it made sense to keep them together. The Brits could put up with most people – except the Germans... and the French... not to mention the Italians, and also the... (we jest, of course). So about 750 delegates were readying themselves to indulge in an orgy of self-congratulation and serious business discussion.

This story concerns the preparation and delivery of one small part of the programme. The central staff required to run the Club usually numbered a hard core of about 10, with others co-opted as required during the event itself. In addition, there were country co-ordinators to validate the qualifying delegates, and generally make sure fellow-countrymen behaved themselves.

These central staff were usually assigned on a full-time basis for 3-6 months, with duties including administration, programme management, entertainment, transportation, hotel checking and booking, and financial control.

One area always the subject of much agonising was that of

programme management. A professional adviser was hired to help handle the sensitive and fragile "flowers" that occupy the world of stage management – most of whom had names like Quentin or Gervaise (quickly christened "Gerv the perv" by the IBM'ers). This was all quite illuminating to a youthful IBM ex-salesman (one of the authors), fresh from selling to hairy Midlands industrialists, soon to head off to the US on the next stage of his IBM marketing career, but in the interim acting as the administration manager for this Club.

The stage programme was rightly considered to be of great importance by IBM since that was when senior management from the countries, from Europe head office and from the US would deliver their messages. It was therefore the most likely place where they might be upstaged, embarrassed, or just make fools of themselves in front of their troops. And of course the troops, generally pretty hung over from the night before, would always be gleefully awaiting just such an occurrence to brighten the gloom. So the programme would be agonised over, amended, rehearsed, re-rehearsed, thrown out – unendingly. Gervaise regularly had an attack of the vapours, and the IBM'ers would go off glumly to the pub for mutual commiseration.

In this case the miracle had been achieved: the programme had been finalised and agreed by all levels of the senior management hierarchy – with one exception, but that was only a small item and could not possibly cause a problem, could it? There was still a need to fill a short 10-minute slot before the final presentation by the Area General Manager.

Various suggestions were made for this 10 minute slot – a short business film (but we'd already got plenty of those in), another IBM speaker (the audience would be getting pretty sick by now of IBM speakers), a short coffee break (but the delegates wouldn't come back for the GM's final pitch). Then, manna from heaven, our external consultant adviser (remember him?) said he'd heard there was a wonderful speaker who would be just the job. He was a retired surgeon, a Mr. Dickson-Wright, perfect for all occasions, and, well, no, he had not actually heard him speak, but there could not possibly be a problem. The programme management team broke with their habit of a lifetime, and in their exhausted state, agreed that the retired surgeon, "perfect for all occasions", should fill the slot. Yes, his diary was free, but no, he would not be available to rehearse, and, no, he could not send a script because he always spoke unscripted.

So, the great day came. All had gone wonderfully well. The audience were in good humour. The stony-faced US senior representatives, with their trousers at half-mast and massive shoes, appeared to be taking it well. It was all following the Corporate line – happy contented troops, not too raucous, you understand. They could return to the US with a clear conscience and a present for the spouse.

Then came the last-but-one presentation. "Who's this guy Dickson-Wright?" "Oh, he's a retired surgeon, comes highly recommended, first class chap." Indeed Mr. Dickson-Wright was a genial old buffer. But alas, he had not briefed himself on the corporate culture of IBM. Just because the audience laughed with increasing hilarity at his increasingly risqué (and unrehearsed!) script, that was no reason for self-congratulation. He should have concentrated on that audience from "over there", here represented by the now even-more- stony-faced in the front row. The stories poured forth ever more medical, ever more lavatorial –10 minutes went by, 20 minutes. How to stop him? One minute a joke about a crystal-ball gazer patient who was determined to die – out of curiosity. The next minute, suppositories....

Well, much to the troops' disappointment our genial old buffer was escorted from the stage mid-joke, the GM's closing address was abandoned and replaced with a profuse apology to the audience (quite unnecessary, except for the stony-faced).

After the event, a "customer satisfaction" survey was conducted. Delegates were asked, among other things, what they most liked and disliked about the Club. The answers were a foregone conclusion. They most liked the talk by the "genial old buffer". They most disliked the apology thereafter. The results of the survey were not communicated to the US.

Man-years of effort went into the organisation and preparation of the Club. The whole venture was planned and executed with military precision, nothing was left to chance.

Or was it...?

"Eau de toilette"

Convention organisers never ceased in their efforts to be innovative and to give the qualifiers something to remember.

It was in Venice that something special was to take place. At the first morning's session, the stage curtains were to open with a crescendo of music and there would be – a hologram! A sensational start and one that was successfully rehearsed.

The auditorium was full in spite of hangovers, and the front rows glittered with top brass. As the clock ticked to 9.00 am, the lights dimmed, the music began, its decibel level rising by the second, the curtains opened slowly and a spotlight picked out centre stage.

All a bit over the top it must have felt to many, but the show was on the road. There was an unnatural pause, and as the fanfare quickened the IBM General Manager edged slowly to centre stage.

The historic moment came and went – failure.

What had happened?

The equipment that projected the hologram was water-cooled (no better place than Venice, you would think), but no-one had considered that when 1000 IBM'ers hit the toilets between 8.30 and 9.00 there would be a huge drop in water pressure in the Convention Hall.

The staff were not to be beaten, and numerous possibilities were considered to ensure that the hologram appeared the next morning – water pumps, generators, all manner of high-tech options, before the final solution was agreed.

Next morning, the lights dimmed, the music, the curtains, and – to gasps from the audience – the hologram appeared. IBM was yet again demonstrating its leadership in technology. The audience went wild with cheers and applause. A standing ovation.

While comfortable in the knowledge that they worked for an outstanding company, many in that audience were very uncomfortable until coffee break. For some unexplained reason, 75 per cent of the toilets in the convention centre had a hand-written sign saying "Out of Order".

Organisers dreaded the moment when droves of excited and enthusiastic qualifiers descended on them.

"Going down, Sir?"

The delegates, in varying states of travel fatigue, spilled from the air-conditioned coaches into the foyers of their Spanish hotels, home for the next three days. Unfortunately their plane had arrived many hours later than originally scheduled, allowing excess time for the traditional pre-Club refreshment.

Registration proceeded in an orderly fashion, but there is always one problem child, isn't there? Swaying and stumbling to the front of the queue, he was asked for his yellow registration card which should have been completed on the plane. This seemed to cause him great consternation – he knew nothing about a yellow card. The tolerant administrator reached over and plucked it from the delegate's sports jacket. After the formalities, our man staggered off clutching his case in one hand, welcoming package, gift sports bag and room key in the other, with his camera equipment and duty free bag distributed about his person.

Fifteen minutes later, the administrator, by now processing another coachload, looked up to see a familiar face sweating profusely at the front of the queue. "Shyou shaid I was in room 421. Iysh looked every-where and there ishn't one."

Now, this Spanish hotel had a novel design. The entrance to the hotel and the foyer were actually the eighth floor. There was one additional floor above street level (ninth) and the remainder, ground to seven were built into a cliff, overlooking the beach.

The administrator calmly and slowly explained this, and advised the delegate to use the lift to floor four (going down, sir), whence room (4)21 would be easy to find.

"Shyou aren't taking the pish, are you?" asked the delegate.

Pointing in the general direction of the lifts, the administrator aimed him at his target and, together with the now highly amused gathering, watched him tack towards his goal.

Adjacent to the lifts was a plastic telephone booth. It took more than a few minutes for the delegate to get himself, his case, his convention kit and his duty free into this phone booth, but with obvious determination and no little blasphemy he eventually made it.

By now, the foyer was at a standstill. Our poor man pressed every button and protuberance in a vain effort to make his "lift" go to floor 4.

Finally, he lifted the telephone and was heard yelling, "Thish lift ish busted and ish stuck."

Back home, he knew he had enjoyed a good Club – because we told him so!

For some the story didn't really begin until after they'd reached their hotel room....

"Strange the people you meet"

One of the consequences of the growth of IBM was that more and more people began to qualify for attendance at the 100 Per cent Club. Until the early 70's there were quite separate events for qualifying sales people (who qualified through achievement of their sales targets) as opposed to SE's (systems engineers, whose "event" was called the SE Symposium, and for which qualification might be "submitting a paper", some work of technical excellence, or maybe it was just your turn). With the growth in numbers for both events, IBM decided, probably in the interests of economy, to combine the two.

The end product, however, was closer in style to the original 100 Per cent Clubs, than to the SE Symposia. One of the consequences was that there could be quite a mixture of Sales and SE attending each Club. Again, no doubt in the interests of economy, IBM decided that it would introduce, amid much complaining, shared rooms. "Managers", of course, were allowed to retain single rooms. Who said it was a "single status" company? After some initial trials and tribulations the shared system was generally accepted (let's face it – IBM was never a democracy, so there wasn't much choice!) and qualifying delegates were given some time, before the start of the event, to choose their room mates (within the bounds of decency of course), to avoid the obvious problems of smokers and non-smokers, etc. Occasionally, however, due to last-minute qualifying, one could find oneself sharing with a complete stranger.

This story concerns such an occasion, and the players were our hero and his room-mate. Our hero shall be nameless – let's just call him, Doug. The story begins the morning after, when Doug staggered down, late, to breakfast. The hotel restaurant was nearly empty and the buses were already departing to take delegates to the first morning's formal conference session. Doug felt in need of at least a coffee, and as luck would have it, he glimpsed his room-mate sitting with some of his pals, having just finished breakfast, and, more importantly, in possession of a full jug of coffee. Now Doug had only met his room-mate for the first time the previous evening, but not slow at coming forward, he marched over to the table, put his hand on his room-mate's shoulder in greeting, turned to the rest of the table and said, "Hi, my name's Doug...." He got no further as the table dissolved into hysterical laughter.

We need to go back to events of the previous evening to explain the mystery. "Room-mate" had arrived in good time, had unpacked and tidied everything neatly away (he was probably an SE). He'd noticed at check-in that he was due to share with an unknown stranger (a salesman called Doug), but there was no sign of him. Could be my lucky day, thought room-mate, I might get this room all to myself. Alas, not so. Later that evening, as room-mate was about to go out for a few beers with his chums to discuss the latest release of TCAM, there was a pounding on the door. "Come in," shouted room-mate, "It's unlocked." No effect, the pounding continued. Finally, room-mate opened the door. In front of him was something resembling a tourist from hell – arms stretched almost to the floor by a bulging bag in each hand, camera around the neck and his check-in information pack stuffed down his waistband. The newcomer wore a broad grin. "Hello," he/it said, "my name's Doug," and marched into the room, dropped his luggage with a crash, and disappeared out through the door whence he/it had just entered. Room-mate shrugged – OK, he'd drawn the short straw but it wasn't going to spoil his evening, and out he went also.

Room-mate reappeared about midnight after a good evening with his pals – they reckoned they'd got a fix on what was causing all those TCAM abends. He washed, put on pyjamas and went to bed with a clear conscience. No sign of Doug.

Some time later room-mate was awoken by a pounding – on the door?...in his head,?... was it that second half of lager?. No, it was defi-nitely the door. Room-mate dragged himself thereto, and opened it to find our hero, again grinning, no luggage this time, but decidedly unsteady on his pins. "Evening!" he/it exhaled, breath strong enough to down a wrestler, and stomped into the room. Room-mate returned to bed while Doug banged and crashed his alcoholic way through a little unpacking, even less washing, managed to put the light out, and got into bed – with room-mate! Room-mate froze That it should come to this – a salesman, an untidy yob, a drunkard – and one of those! "Get out," yelped the virginal SE.

Too late. Doug was out like a light and not to be awoken. Room-mate heaved a sigh (of relief?), and slipped quietly into the other bed (it was a twin-bedded room). All fell silent, or as silent as was ever likely, given the physical condition of our two delegates. Until, that is, some hours later when room-mate was again aroused by crashing and banging, and noises which indicated that the considerable liquid intake had percolated through Doug's anatomy. At least, thought room-mate, he's had the decency not to put the room lights on. True, and perhaps that explained why Doug, fresh from his ablutions, and unsure of his bearings, got back into bed – with room-mate! "Hey," but it was a waste of time. Whatever Doug had been drinking, it was a pretty good cure for insomnia. Room-mate departed back to the first bed.

He was awoken only once more – when Doug, having clearly failed to find the loo, in desperation had opened the sliding doors to the balcony and had decided to water the window boxes. "Funny," thought room-mate, rain wasn't forecast. Then he realised – but nothing more would surprise him, so other than determinedly taking up a position to repel boarders should Doug again invade his bedspace, he said nothing. This time Doug made no mistake. He was still there at reveille and while room-mate deliberately and noisily went about his own ablutions, Doug remained prostrate.

Room-mate duly went down to breakfast, met up with his pals, and regaled them with his experiences. As they were all about to leave for the start of the formal programme, a hand was placed on room-mate's shoulder, and a voice was heard to say, "Hi, my name's Doug...."

We have referred to the Gala evening and what an superb night it generally was. As if this was not enough entertainment for one evening.

"Early to bed...."

Monte Carlo in early April was a spectacular place.

The final event of a convention was the Gala Evening, held at the

Sporting Club. Each branch had developed its own ways of celebrating the final evening. One in particular held a reception preceding the official event, and a party following.

The management team each had single (note) rooms/suites leading onto the balcony overlooking the Mediterranean. The layout of these rooms fitted the standard pattern – an entrance lobby with one door to the bathroom, and another to the main living/bedroom.

After the official events of the evening, everybody returned to the branch suite and the party got into full swing. As the night wore on, the tired and emotional retired to their beds. Those of proven stamina steamed on. Dawn broke over the Mediterranean and with the sliding windows to the balcony open, the fresh balmy morning air stirred the hunger pains.

A call to room service, and in a few minutes the feast arrived. Two smartly uniformed hotel staff wheeled in a rectangular trolley through the narrow entrance lobby. The trolley sides were raised and it rapidly transformed into a circular table.

The repast was demolished in double quick time. At this point, a senior guest, clearly domesticated, took it upon himself to clear the debris and return the dominating table back through the lobby into the corridor, whence it came.

To his anguish and utter confusion the table steadfastly refused to fit into the lobby. Turned this way, turned that way, it would not go through the entrance lobby. The onlookers stifled their amusement. It was apparent the guest was no "technical giant".

With much huffing and puffing he turned away from the lobby and eyed the balcony. The table, its plates, knives and forks, were unceremoniously thrust through the open patio windows.

Job done.

The balcony, onto which other suites opened, ran the length of the hotel – for what design reason it is not understood – but it soon became apparent that this balcony had an in-built slope.

By now, the table had assumed a mind of its own, and, gathering pace, it trundled noisily past the other suites. The chase was on, but the table had a head start. Amazingly, another design feature of the hotel was that the surrounding balcony wall was exactly the same height as the table top.

Despite the chase, the table won the race, crashed into the wall, stopping instantly, its contents continuing on and down into the awaiting Mediterranean.

These branch celebrations proved to be a little more expensive than planned.

For all the status of attending the Club, there was an even greater prize awaiting, for the privileged few....

The Golden Circle

This was for the mega-super European-wide sales performers, typically salesmen who had achieved 200 per cent, 300 per cent or even more, of their sales quotas. The USA and the Far East respectively, held their own events.

For European IBM'ers the reward was a week in a top-flight hotel in warmer climes – West Palm Beach, Bermuda and the like. More than this, spouses (not mere "partners" though) were allowed, something that never happened on Hundred Per cent Clubs, or any other IBM group business event abroad come to that. One Golden Circle was a cruise in the Mediterranean, but this was cancelled when there was trouble with a certain Mr Gadaffi.

There were regulation business sessions, and some of the spouses made a (usually first day) attempt to be excited about growth, technology, revenues, profitability, SRP, NPII and a plethora of IBM acronyms. Guest speakers delighted audiences with their speciality topics – Carl Sagan, the well-known US astronomer was present at one event to expand on the universe.

If you were a salesman or sales manager who had attended three Golden Circles, you were really somebody; four, well, that was incredible. One did hear of a German salesman who had been to ten – super-duper orbital stuff.

At one time, if a salesman achieved ten Hundred Per cent Clubs, he became a life member of the HPC. If he achieved 15, he was selected to attend the Golden Circle that year.

As ever, budgets starting to influence these events. One of the authors reached ten Clubs and the HPC life membership was cancelled that year. Likewise he reached 15 Clubs, and the honorary Golden Circle selection was cancelled that year.

If only he had joined the company one year earlier...?

Nostalgia Ain't What It Used to Be

So what does one remember after nearly 30 years working for IBM?

Well, there are certainly reminders everywhere. IBM was very fond of creating a gift for every occasion. Given that it was, in its heyday, a very wealthy company, these gifts were high quality, and the house abounds with them! More of that later....

Then there were the people. IBM is always remembered as a very egalitarian company. It was, by the standards of most of British industry then, a classless culture. Perhaps because the criteria for initial selection were high, and the training rigorous, the end-product was of a kind. You could walk into an IBM branch office anywhere in the world and immediately be able to relate to your IBM colleagues. You all spoke a common business language. Indeed, it was only when you left the office that you truly became aware you were in a foreign country. Greater "internationalisation" has made this more commonplace today, but it was most unusual 25 years ago.

There also seemed to be a much higher proportion of working-class graduates in IBM, fewer representatives of a public school education than might have been expected. IBM genuinely offered a fastpath route from rags to comparative riches for those able and willing.

In addition, there was that almost paranoiac determination of IBM senior management to appear approachable and unconscious of status. It was not uncommon at all for the most junior employee to find himself sharing a table at lunch, in the single-status canteen, with a very senior IBM executive. Some such executives seemed to regard this as a pretty good way of keeping in touch with the troops. It was a bit unnerving, at Armonk, the Corporate HQ in the early 70's, to find the then CEO, Vincent Learson, heading towards one's lunch table. He was a tall saturnine man, with the habit of wearing a dark coat thrown over his shoulders. This gave him the general appearance of Batman, particularly since there would usually be one of his several executive assistants scampering along behind, like Robin.

Those executive assistants – they were a strange lot. Most senior IBM executives, whether at Corporate HQ or in the countries, owned one. And just to keep the pecking order straight, the IBM CEO was able to have several! These were obviously "la crème de la crème", but all were special. They had clearly been singled out, and were marked as "senior management potential". They would have been doing some job, important and visible enough to have brought them into the limelight – maybe as a branch manager, or as a senior salesman for a major customer account, or, occasionally, in a key position in manufacturing or development. They had to be ferociously ambitious, and prepared to forsake all, or nearly all, for the greater glory of IBM. As executive assistants they collected a mixture of tasks, including acting as coffee-boy for their Lords and Masters. No doubt this was deemed important to instil a proper level of humility – a bit like the Roman system whereby a slave walked in front of a successful general, chanting the words, "Remember you are mortal". Most attained senior management status. Some rose to the dizzy heights whence a proportion, denied the "top job", left IBM, slighted that their ambition could not be further satisfied. They often, subsequently, resurfaced on the boards of IBM's competitors.

There were moments when IBM's mania for equal status might serve to hoist it by its own petard. One occasion springs to mind at the then HQ of the IBM World Trade Corporation, on UN Plaza, New York....

The then Chairman of the Board of IBM WTC, Gill Jones, was eating his lunch, in the single-status canteen, with one or two quite junior colleagues, when a young man and what appeared to be his girlfriend, entered. Clearly they were not IBM employees, rather they resembled scarecrows. Since it was neither April 1st (not that the US recognises the mystic significance of April 1st anyway), nor Halloween, nor any other meaningful date, all assumed they were early converts to what became known as the hippie generation. It was after all 1970 and they must have walked in, off the street.

What to do with them? Throw them out? You could just imagine the next day's headlines in the *Village Gazette*, certain to be syndicated world-wide. Politely ask them to leave? That was obviously the thing to do. Nobody was going to volunteer to do it though.

It was clearly a job for executive management! Gill Jones was up to the task – he thought. He stepped up to the young man and his accomplice, by this time in the queue for (IBM subsidised) food. "Excuse me, but this is a private canteen, not open to the general public. Would you mind leaving?" The hippie appeared not to hear, perhaps because he'd now reached the servery and was not to be denied. Again, the request, and again no response.

A different approach was required. "What is your name, young man?" "What's that to you, Mack?" At least a dialogue had begun, but not quite what Mr. Jones would have wanted.

By this time the whole canteen was agog, and the episode has assumed the proportions of a Western melodrama – young man rides into town and challenges the marshall! Will the marshall fill him full of lead, or back down? You know, "A man's gotta do what a man's gotta do..." Well, all credit, in a way, to Gill Jones. He might have said, like John Wayne, "Look, sonny, I've seen a lotta young men like you bite the dust, and I don't want to have to.... etc." But Gill Jones was hardly more than half the size of John Wayne, so all he said was, "OK, you can finish your lunch. But I will ask our security staff (where had they been all this time everyone was wondering?) then to escort you from the building."

Honour was satisfied. No blood had been shed. Hopefully, no headlines had been provoked. God knows what happened to the security staff, or the hippies, but it must have been a while before Gill Jones again ventured into a single-status canteen!

But, back to the "commemorative awards". What do we have? Well, there's all the memorabilia that came with product announcements. To be on the announcement team for any new product would guarantee some reward for services rendered – a classy paperweight, a scale model of the newly-announced product (yes, what do you do with a dinky sized version of a 3090 CPU?), an elegant leather folder, and so on. The trouble with these awards was that since they were IBM product-related they would all be "logo'ed" with the letters "IBM" as a minimum, and probably something further, like "...3850 Mass Storage System Announcement dd/mm/yy." That would effectively destroy any chances you might have harboured for using said award as an emergency Christmas present for a forgotten aunt.

Then there were the many and varied sales recognition awards, beginning of course with the accumulated 100 Per cent Club gifts, and the even more esteemed, and rarely achieved, Golden Circle awards. They all tell a story.

There's that posh pewter tankard – lucky to have that. It was a gift at the 1968 100 Per cent Club, held (to the irritation of the UK attendees) in London. The Club administrators were unwise enough to visit all hotel rooms before the IBM people checked in, placing these valuable tankards on the beds to await the arrival of the IBM occupants. What the Club administrators hadn't realised was that they were being closely followed by representatives of the local criminal fraternity removing said tankards! Luckily for some, the thieves ceased their malpractice when their sacks were full.

The unwritten rule for a Club gift used to be that it should not cost more than $25.00. Mind you, in the 1960's, that was a worthwhile sum of money, and could purchase, apart from the above-mentioned tankard, such desirables as an extremely smart document case or a fetching silver money-clip. Thereby hangs a tale. The American influence must have been brought to bear here. They must have assumed that the Brits yearned to carry around wads of notes just like they did with their dollar bills. A money clip with a couple of pound notes hanging limply in it always looked a bit pathetic!

Something must have changed through the 70's and 80's. Apart from inflation breaking the nominal $25.00 barrier, the other apparent rule – that the gift required to be reasonably portable – was also transgressed. Returning 100 Per cent Club attendees were to be seen humping empty in-flight suit holders, as well as the customary duty-free paraphernalia. Further, the prospect of several hundred IBM'ers tottering through UK Customs necklaced with such gift luggage caused IBM to produce a kosher form of words which were to be chanted should there be any challenge from the excise officers. The experience must have been salutary because IBM soon returned to gifts, both more easily carried and more readily concealed.

IBM would always fall over backwards not to be seen to be abusing, or even challenging, any personal taxation requirements. There was an occasion in the 1970's, during the days of Wilsonian prices and incomes legislation, when IBM became very concerned at its vulnerability to staff loss, since pay increases were pegged. Schemes were investigated to find other ways of rewarding people, in particular sales staff. Most were rejected as illegal, unaffordable, or just plain improper. About the only one that was adopted was to provide field sales staff with a smart briefcase, free and gratis. This was for the entirely valid purpose of conveying all the heavyweight material essential to doing one's job in IBM sales. Whether because of the time and effort required to get this past the Inland Revenue censor, or because IBM SE's all at once demanded equivalence (they were turned down!), this was perhaps the only occasion IBM dared to venture into this particular minefield.

And, finally, let us not forget the "in" words and phrases. Most of them were Americanisms picked up by the IBM locals in much the same way that children in the last war close to the D-Day embarkation points, picked up the slang of the GI's. While no visiting IBM US executive was accosted with the query, "Got any gum, chum?", plenty were made to feel at home with a transported language. What were some of these Americanisms?

In the early 70's everything suddenly became "leveraged" (pronounced to rhyme with "beverage"). If you insisted on pronouncing the word in the traditional way (to rhyme with "fever-age") then, if not actually anti-American, you were listed as clearly lacking ambition.

Then the moment came when every spoken sentence was subdivided into endless clauses with the words "...if you will." There was a theory that British diffidence, manifested by regular "ers, ums and aahs" was a clear sign of wimpishness and uncertainty. Much better to have a forthright American, "If you will".

There was one phrase that seems now to have become general currency, but which first appeared in IBM around the late 80's. People were so determined to use it that it almost came to fisticuffs. "Let me tell you where I'm coming from," said the first. "No, let *me* tell *you* where *I'm* coming from," insisted the second. "No, No," bellowed the third, " let *me*..." etc. It was amusing to watch, but as the meetings dragged on into the early evening the temptation was to say, "Let *me* tell *you* where I'm going – *home!*"

And here's an illustration of the obsession we found our American cousins had with politeness and never being left holding the baby....

Overheard in an elevator (lift) sometime in 1971 at IBM World Trade Headquarters, 821 UN Plaza, New York: two American executives are concluding a conversation:

First American serves: "Now you be reeeal sure and have a nice day."

Second American plays a regular cross-court return: "Waaall, thank you so much".

First American slips in a cunning backhand lob: "You're surely most welcome".

Second American is ready with a forehand, down the line: "Sure thing".

First American plays a desperate forehand lob... a winner: "You bet".

Twenty-five years later, of course, the second American could have delivered a triumphant overhead smash with... "Missing you already."

You must understand that this particular version of the culture never quite established itself in Europe.

11. Management Summary

(All convincing IBM proposals and reports had one.... naturally, at the front of the docmument)

"It was the 8th August 1960, 8.50 am, as he entered the IBM offices. Little did he know that his time with this company would last more than 31 years...."

So what happened during that time?

Our book has looked back from a personal perspective.

We have described the excitement of the Sixties and Seventies as IBM grew so dramatically. Those years saw huge changes in the IBM company: a "job for life" became a dynamic career path, perhaps; new advanced products were announced regularly to accelerate IBM's penetration of the computer market; revenues grew year on year at a pace to be envied, and IBM/Customer relationships flourished in what many IBM'ers would describe as the halcyon years.

We have presented the inner workings of IBM, with its commitment to recruiting the highest calibre people, its unique personnel management policies, and the focus on top-quality training throughout an employee's career. We have examined the ways IBM drove the business forward, and the motivations and rewards inherent in its approach to generating "success". We have also looked at the company's business ethics, its "business practices" policies (who will ever forget the "Thought Police"?), and its determination to see fair play by use of the employees' Business Conduct Guidelines.

We have celebrated the people, since our over-riding memories of IBM are the people with whom we worked – managers, systems engineers, administration, customer engineers. They all played their part. We particularly examined the salesman since IBM was a great selling company. We have illustrated the human side of the business with anecdotes that reflect being "at the coal-face" and "where the rubber hits the road". We hope that you have enjoyed the characters and personalities who have starred in our tales.

At the same time, we have been critical where we felt it just, as IBM became, in our view, over-bureaucratic, unaware in some instances of the changing market place, or insensitive to customers' needs.

We lived through the period when the IBM corporation saw its 60 per cent share of the world computing business eroded to less than 20 per cent – and we were a part of its "down-sizing" from 400,000 people to nearer 220,000.

So, what else is worth saying?

"There are no problems in the computer industry that would not be solved by the disappearance of IBM...."

Well, IBM went through an extraordinarily difficult time in the 1980's. However, it hasn't disappeared. When IBM was riding pretty high, there was no shortage of "tyre-kickers" who predicted its demise. It was once a vast corporation earning the best profits around. As everybody knows, it has been through the hard times described above, and those wise "told you so" men who predicted this, no doubt have received all the credit they deserve.

In 1995, the IBM Corporation's revenues exceeded US$70 billion, with profits of over US$4 billion! This is no chickenfeed company on its knees! IBM is clearly touching the parts of the IT industry that others would dearly like to reach.

Yet....

Is it fitter? Certainly it is leaner. IBM used to have a reputation for huge investment in Research and Development, Product leadership, a world-wide presence and customer focus. Over recent years, it has reduced its spend in R&D, reflecting the need to be more selectively focused on its marketplace engagement..

Is it providing what the marketplace wants? Judging by its recent financial results, it is providing what some of the marketplace wants.

Yet, there remain doubts about certain areas of its business.

How is its revenue increasing? Take hardware.....

If you take the acceptance of PC's in the retail marketplace as a measure, and trawl around the public shows, it is rare to find a heavy IBM presence. Within this arena, its PC products, excellent though they may be, have the reputation of being relatively high-priced.

The mainframe market has recently experienced a resurgence, due, to some extent, to its positioning as a "corporate server", but like the PC market it is very competitive. In both markets there are boxes out there that are perceived to be as effective and reliable as IBM's offerings – and cheaper.

Similarly, IBM's "UNIX" workstation products are corporately well-accepted, but by definition, face intense competition by specialist companies.

It is ironic, perhaps, that IBM's *proprietary* mid-range computers – the AS/400 for example – are still very popular and very much in demand.

One area where it does still have a unique position is mainframe systems software. Nobody else (yet) supplies a complete "hardware compatible" operating system. For a customer to embark on such a change would also be much more complex than a box replacement.

We must assume therefore that whilst IBM is holding onto sufficient of its traditional revenue sources – the mainframes, the intermediate systems, the key systems and communications software – it has also moved its business extensively towards "services". It is now deeply into outsourcing, consultancy, open systems, long-term contracts, and even risk-sharing. By these means, and by building its image as a supplier of these broader IT services, it is achieving new and growing revenues.

However...

In Chapter 5, the story "How we all became a bit wiser" ended on a successful note (for IBM). That story illustrated the importance IBM once attached to account management. Whatever happened within an IBM account (the "customer"), IBM held the account manager to be responsible. For the account manager this was both a plus and a minus. He had a great deal of power to ring the alarm bells when things were going wrong, but he was the immediate focus of attention (and possible blame) when things came off the rails.

If the IBM of today were to surrender that grip on the control of its accounts, then it would risk becoming just one more member of the pack. Even the dreaded "lost-business review" of yesteryear becomes ever more irrelevant if everybody can pass the buck. If a company with £1 billion annual revenues had no IBM account manager – that is, no single point of accountability for all IBM's business in the account – then that would surely cause T. J. Watson to turn in his grave.

The traditional account manger was the key to long-standing relationships. He was the one person who would take time to understand the customer's business, people and politics, and then glue all the IBM components together to deliver what the customer required. We used to call it "added value" – a way of justifying a higher-priced solution. Today you might use the phrase "relationship manager".

If IBM is facing the marketplace purely through individual business units it may have difficulty capturing and preserving the necessary customer confidence to bridge higher IBM prices. Further, if the only strategy for maintaining revenues from its corporate accounts is through large-scale, time-boundaried projects, then perhaps a partnership trick is being missed.

It will be interesting to see how IBM sustains its marketplace image. The IBM name still commands a high-profile respect in the marketplace. However, if Products and People are increasingly replaced by Services and Contractors, might this image ultimately become similar to that of a franchisor – where the name's the (only) thing?

Whatever happens, we look forward to the corporation continuing to deliver excellent results. The loyal shareholders will welcome that.

In the preface to this book we said, "We hope as you turn the last page that you feel as we do; we were privileged to have had the opportunity of being employed by IBM, working with our colleagues there, and most of all, meeting and supporting its customers".

We reiterate that statement.

To all our readers.....

We, Bob, Tony and Frank, had immense enjoyment and satisfaction writing this book. Even more important – we trust you have enjoyed reading it.

Registered names and trademarks

Amdahl: Amdahl Corporation
AT&T Bell: AT&T Bell Laboratories Corporation
Bull
Burroughs Corporation
Computervision
DEC: Digital Equipment Corporation
EDS: Electronic Data Systems
EE: English Electric Co Ltd
Hewlett Packard
IBM: International Business Machines Corporation
ICL: International Computers Ltd
ICT: International Computers & Tabulators Ltd
Microsoft: Microsoft Corporation
NCR: National Cash Register
Siemens

Microsoft Corporation: Windows

IBM: AS/400
                           Application System/400
                           PS/2
                           RISC System/6000
                           System/360
                           System/370
                           PROFS
                           OS/2

AT&T Bell Laboratories: UNIX

CopyCat Company: CopyCat

Glossary

1401	IBM 1401 Commercial computer announced early 60's.
8100	IBM Distributed processor, announced late 70's.
A&C	Appraisal & Counselling, part of IBM's employee assessment programme.
Amdahl	Company formed by ex-IBM employee Gene Amdahl. Products, mainly "Software Compatible" mainframes.
Application System/400	General purpose IBM computer.
AS/400	see Application System/400.
CADCAM	Computer Aided Design / Computer Aided Manufacturing.
CATIA	Computer Aided Three-dimensional Interactive Application.
COPICS	IBM predominantly-mainframe manufacturing industry package – Communications Oriented Production Information Control System.
CRM	Customer Relationship Management, an IBM programme concerning customer satisfaction.
DAT box	Dynamic Address Translation box (circa 1972), providing virtual storage capability for the IBM 370/155 and /165 mainframes.
DB/DC	Data Base / Data Communications.
DCA	Document Content Architecture, a "standard" for text structures.
DEC	Digital Equipment Corporation.
DIA	Document Interchange Architecture, a "standard" for intelligent exchange of documents between systems.
Disk	Computer peripheral which stores data magnetically on a coated surface, for random retrieval.
DPCX	Distributed Processing Control Executive. An operating system for the IBM 8100 computer range.
DPEI	Data Processing Executive Institute; an annual IBM technical symposium
DPPX	Distributed Processing Program Executive. An operating system for the IBM 8100 computer range.
EEC	European Economic Community.
GBG	General Business Group, an IBM marketing division.

Glossary

GEORGE	ICT/ ICL Operating system.
GNP	Gross National Product.
GSD	General Systems Division, an IBM marketing division.
HPC	Hundred Percent Club, an annual convention for successful IBM field staff.
IBM	International Business Machines Corporation.
ICL	International Computers Ltd.
ICT	International Computers & Tabulators Ltd.
IMS	IBM DB/DC software; Information Management System.
LOI	Letter of Intent, a document preceding a firm order.
LU6.2	Logical Unit 6.2 – a communications protocol.
MAAPICS/MAPICS	IBM S/3 & /3X computer manufacturing industry package – Manufacturing Production and Inventory Control System.
MAPS	Major Account Planning System.
MBA	Master in Business Administration, an academic business "degree".
MES	Miscellaneous Equipment Specification, features to attach to IBM machines.
MFT	IBM mainframe operating system – Multiprogramming with a Fixed number of Tasks.
Microsoft	Microsoft Corporation.
MRP	Manufacturing Resource Planning, or Materials Requirements Planning.
MVS	Multiple Virtual Storage, an operating system for large IBM mainframes.
NC	Numerical Control, of machine tools.
NOSS	National Office Support System; IBM's internal E-mail system.
NPV	Net Present Value.
OP	Office Products (division of IBM).
Open Systems	Hardware independent software, primarily for workstations.
OS/2	Operating system software for the IBM personal computer PS/2.
OS/VS1 OS/VS2	Operating system software for IBM System/370 mainframes.
Overlay/Prime	Designations of IBM salesmen.
PCM	Plug Compatible Manufacturer, typically of peripheral hardware for IBM mainframes.
PROFS	Professional Office System; see NOSS.
PS/2	IBM second generation personal computer.

RISC System/6000	Reduced Instruction Set Computer; IBM workstation.
ROI	Return on Investment.
S/1 or Series/1	Small IBM computer with extensive interfacing capability to external devices.
S/34 S/36 S/38	IBM "minis".
Sales Plan	The IBM plan defining field territories and commission payment methods, revised annually.
SCV	Software Compatible Vendor; typically a company making and selling the "equivalent" to an IBM mainframe.
SE	see Systems Engineer.
SIA	Selected International Account.
SNA	Systems Network Architecture.
SPL	Selected Product Line; preferred products out of the whole IBM range.
System/360	IBM universal mainframe introduced in 1964.
System/370	Successor to the System/360, retaining the same architecture as the /360.
System/3090	Successor to the System/370
System/7	IBM manufacturing industry shop floor computer.
Systems Engineer	A technical field person.
TBS	Terminal Business System; an on-line IBM computing service for bureaux customers.
TCAM	Telecommunications Access Method.
TLC	Tender Loving Care, a colloquial description of helping a customer.
TMO	Territory Management Objective; a commissionable element of the Sales Plan
TOC	Territory Objective Compensation; very similar to TMO.
TPC	Territory Performance Compensation; very similar to TMO.
UNIX	AT&T Bell hardware-independent operating system architecture, primarily for workstations.
VDU	Visual Display Unit.
Virtual System	or Virtual Storage; providing "main" memory exceeding the real memory through a technique known as "paging".
VM	Virtual Memory or Machine.
VME/DME	ICL Operating systems.
Windows	Microsoft's Personal Computer operating system.